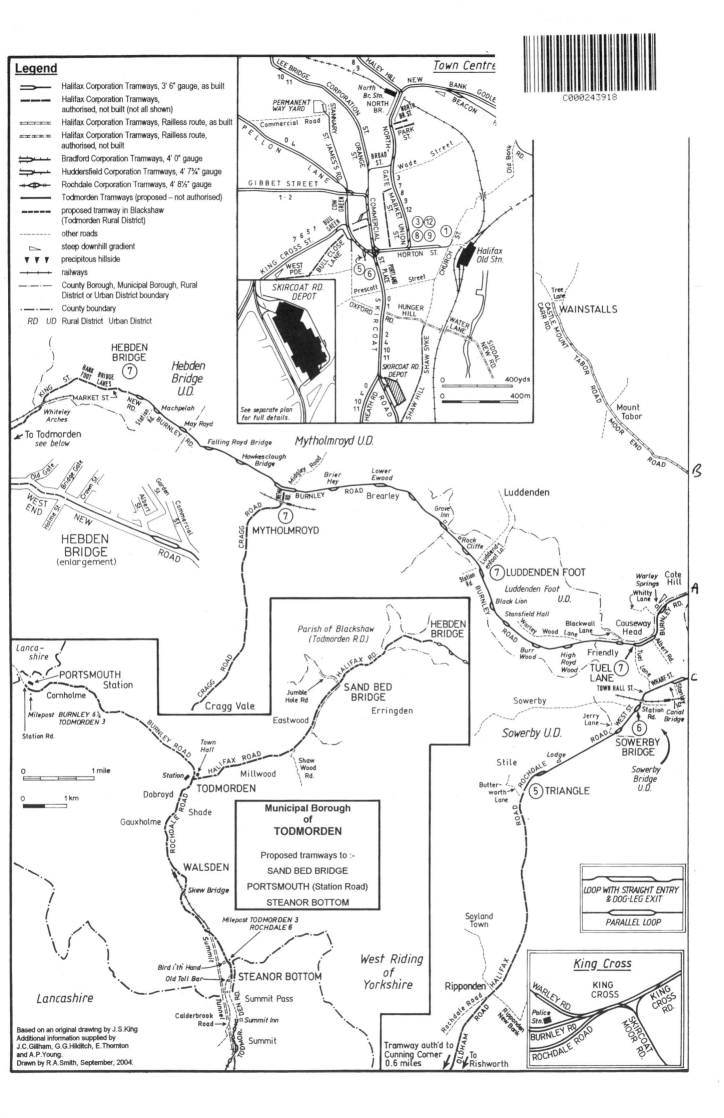

HALIFAX
CORPORATION
TRAMWAYS

By
E. THORNTON
J.S. KING

Published by Light Rail Transit Association
9 Hinderwell Road, Scarborough, YO12 4BD

www.lrta.org

ISBN :　0 948106 31 X

designed by Just My Type Gloucester GL4 4AE
printed by Delmar Press Ltd, Nantwich, Cheshire CW5 5LS

(Previous page) "De Luxe" car 118 halts opposite Hargreaves' hairdresser's shop in Keighley Road, Bank Top, Ovenden, before completing its journey to Mason's Green, 1938.
(Photo: W.A. Camwell.
courtesy National Tramway Museum, Crich)

HALIFAX CORPORATION TRAMWAYS

Foreword

by

Mr. G.G. Hilditch, O.B.E., Ch. Engr., F.I. Mech E., F.I.L.T., F.C.I.T., M.I.R.T.E., General Manager and Engineer, Halifax Passenger Transport, 1963 -1974

I regret to say that I was never able to travel on a Halifax tramcar, but I did actually see them on a few occasions. These happy chances arose from the fact that my father had joined the army in 1915 in Halifax, actually at the former Highroad Well tram shed that was then being used as an extension to the nearby Barracks. Later, as a small boy, I would go with him and my mother to visit friends he had made in the Army who were natives of the town. After the last war I came to visit Halifax much more often, thanks to my girl friend (later my wife) living locally, and being interested in transport this gave me the opportunity to investigate the numerous relics of the system that were still to be seen.

It was not, though, until I became the head of the Engineering department of Halifax Passenger Transport in 1955 that I was able to discover what a fascinating history the system had had, but there my researches were made very difficult by the absence of almost all of the whole of the Department's former tramway records.

Mr. King therefore has to be congratulated on providing such a detailed history of the tramways, and where appropriate of the men involved in the original planning and thereafter of bringing it into use, and keeping the service running.

As the story makes all too plain, theirs was a most difficult task, and it is right and proper that due acknowledgment be paid to these pioneering and daily efforts.

It is incredible to think in this year of 2004 that if someone living in Pellon, Northowram or King Cross wished to do some shopping in the town they had prior to the start of the tramways to walk both ways. The trams provided mobility and cheap travel for so many of the local inhabitants who prior to June 1898 had been deprived of such convenient facilities. One must wonder too at the stamina of those early drivers who up to the start of the 'twenties had to stand on the front platform of their car for hours at a time totally exposed to whatever the weather threw at them. This is a story that is well worth the telling, and I commend it to every reader.

Geoffrey Hilditch

POST OFFICE

Authors' Preface

Halifax is famous for Phyllis Bentley, Wilfred Pickles, Eric Portman, Mackintoshes' Toffee, the Halifax Building Society, the Piece Hall, its spectacular Town Hall designed by Sir Charles Barry, Square Chapel, the 282-foot high Wainhouse Tower, its large and ancient Parish Church and the soaring glory of All Souls', the bustling Borough Market, People's Park given by Sir Francis Crossley of carpet-weaving fame, Savile Park presented by Lord Savile – and much more.

This history of the Halifax tramways is based on a manuscript written thirty years ago by my colleague Mr. Eric Thornton, the well-known tramcar modeller and draughtsman, formerly of Bradford but now of Castle Cary, Somerset, who knew the trams well. As a 'Bradford lad' I should perhaps apologise for chronicling the trams of a neighbouring Borough, and can only plead that my earliest-recorded ancestors lived in the area (Heptonstall) centuries ago, and that as a member of Bradford's Passenger Transport Committee I had the pleasure of collaborating with Mr. Hilditch in the setting up of the long-overdue jointly-operated municipal bus service between Halifax and Bradford in 1971.

I acknowledge with gratitude the help, encouragement and advice I have received from Coun. Geoffrey Wainwright (Calderdale Metropolitan Borough Council), Messrs. Roy Brook, D.J. Smithies, and G. Lumb of Huddersfield, Mr. C.C. Hall, A.M. Inst. T., the late Mr. J.A. Pitts (Bradford), Mr. T. Cannon (Greetland), Mr. J. Kerry (Sowerby), Mr. Meek (Halifax), Mr. M. Skinner (Mytholmroyd). Mr. P. Bush (Stump Cross), Mrs. Stansfield (Pellon), Mrs. V. Marshall (Highroad Well), Mr. T. Hartley (Stourbridge, Worcs.), Mr. Bernard Fielding (Crosby, Lancs.), Mr. Denis Butler (Warrington), Mr. Harry Moore (Liverpool), Mr. G. M. Baxter, (Meltham), the late Arthur Brooke (Elland), the L.R.T.A., the National Tramway Museum (Mr. G. Wilton), Calderdale Libraries at Halifax and Todmorden, West Yorkshire Archives at Halifax and Bradford, "Tramway & Railway World", "Tramway Review", the "Brighouse Echo", the "Halifax Courier" (formerly the splendidly-named "Halifax Evening Courier and Sowerby Bridge, Elland, Brighouse, Hebden Bridge and Todmorden Reporter"), and to Mr. Hilditch for his kind Foreword. May I heartily recommend to readers Mr. Hilditch's recent Oakwood Press publications, "Steel Wheels and Rubber Tyres", vols. 1 and 2.

J.S. King
Heaton,
Bradford
on behalf of Mr. E. Thornton

(opposite) A tranquil, late Victorian scene: car 10 on a journey from Old Station to King Cross rests in Commercial Street before departing by way of Silver Street. In the foreground (bottom left) the track curve from George Square can be glimpsed, while beyond the Post Office trees and open land are visible.

(Courtesy Roy Brook

ABOUT THE AUTHOR

by Geoffrey Claydon

John Stanley King was born in Bradford in 1932 and has had a life-long association with the city and in particular with Heaton, where he resides and in respect of which he became Lord of the Manor in 1963. He has also long been a strong supporter of public transport, especially tramways and trolleybus operation, allowing himself the illicit pleasure of driving several trams through the streets of Bradford before the closure of that system in 1950! Subsequently, with the late John Pitts and Chaceley Humpidge, he was instrumental in rescuing and restoring Bradford tramcar 104, which operated on a section of track at Thornbury Works in the late 1950s (so providing an inspiration for those seeking to establish a national working tramway museum). Car 104 is currently a valued exhibit in the Bradford Industrial Museum.

Elected a city councillor in 1970, Stanley immediately became a member of the Bradford Transport Committee, an appointment which lasted until the establishment of the West Yorkshire Metropolitan County Council in 1974 On the abolition of the latter body in 1985, he became Leader of the Opposition on the new West Yorkshire Passenger Transport Authority, eventually succeeding as its Chairman in 2004. He was Lord Mayor of Bradford 2000 to 2001 and during his year of office he paid a formal visit to the National Tramway Museum, at Crich. where he had great pleasure in driving Bradford 251 (in its current guise as Sheffield 330)! He is currently engaged in spearheading the campaign for Leeds Supertram. This combination of civic and tramway roles has lead to his being identified as a kindred spirit of the legendary Alderman Foodbotham, the redoubtable Chairman of the Bradford City Tramways and Fine Arts Committee, immortalised by Peter Simple in his Way of the World column in the Daily Telegraph.

Stanley has been responsible for several authoritative works on transport subjects:
Keighley Corporation Transport (published in 1964), Transport of Delight (1972), Bradford Corporation Trolleybuses (1994), Bradford Corporation Motorbuses (1995) and Bradford Corporation Tramways(1998). Now, at the invitation of the Light Rail Transport Association, he has turned his attention to another WestYorkshire tramway system. also notable for its hills and narrow gauge, and long awaiting a definitive history: Halifax.

VIEWS OF HALIFAX

"Well, I'll go to Halifax!" – a traditional expression of surprise commonly used in the West Riding, though not in the town itself!

"Ah wished 'im in Halifax!" – a familiar Yorkshire grumble.

"From Hull, Hell and Halifax, good Lord deliver us!" – a prayer fervently offered up by "Beggars, thieves and other disorderly persons" desirous of escaping the attentions of Halifax's famous Gibbet, whose "mechanical method of disposing of malefactors" aroused terror far and wide.

"We quitted Halifax not without some astonishment at its situation, being so surrounded by hills, and those so high, as (except the entrance by the West) makes the coming in and going out of it exceeding troublesome, and indeed for Carriages hardly practicable, and particularly the hill which they go up to come out of the town eastward ……. which the country folk call Halifax Bank, is so steep, so rugged and sometimes so slippery that to a town of so much business as this is, 'tis exceeding troublesome and dangerous".

Daniel Defoe, c. 1724

"HALIFAX, West Riding, a parish, township and market town 8 miles N.W. from Huddersfield, 42 S.W. from York, 197 from London, inhabitants 12,628. Almshouses for twelve poor widows and a bluecoat hospital for twenty poor children were founded here by Nathaniel Waterhouse in 1642. Halifax is seated on the western declivity of a deep valley about a mile and a half to the north of the river Calder; the streets are narrow and rather crooked, but the houses in general are well built. In 1453 there were but 13 houses in the town; in the course of 120 years they had increased to the number of 520 owing to the introduction of the woollen manufacture, which has ever since proceeded with a rapid pace. The inhabitants have erected a spacious edifice called the Piece Hall in form of an oblong square, which contains 315 distinct rooms for the reception and sale of the various manufactures. The parish is the largest in the county, comprising an area of 124 square miles and containing 23 townships. Entire population 93,050."

Yorkshire Gazeteer, 1828.

"The atmosphere of Halifax was all of wool or worsted or cloth or something similar, that scented the whole town ……… the never–ceasing whirr and rattle of machinery, the clack of clogs at morn and night as the millhands went to their work, of the great canopy of dun-coloured smoke that seemed to hang night and day above the grey old town, from Beacon Hill to Skircoat Moor."

Mr. J.S. Fletcher, the popular Halifax writer.

"Halifax is a town of grit and courage and endeavour, and it is a town of the right size."

Mr. Arthur Farrar, quoted in the Halifax Courier, 1930.

CHAPTER I
LONG DEBATE

Ever since the dawn of time Beacon Hill has presided over the town of Halifax. Once thickly mantled with trees and teeming with wildlife, it endured, blackened and ravaged, almost two centuries of industrial smoke and commercial activity before a modest replanting scheme began to soften some of its exposed ruggedness once more.

For centuries its principal function was to provide a prominent site for a beacon fire whose flames periodically warned of perils and dangers threatened by Spanish armadas and French fleets, though nowadays its conflagrations herald civic anniversaries, royal jubilees and other joyful occasions. But if hills have thoughts and preferences, surely Beacon Hill's favourite period of history must have been the forty years during which it surveyed the busy activities of Halifax Corporation tramcars as they passed to and fro in the town below, and daringly ascended the lower slopes of the Hill itself.

Plans for tramways in Halifax were discussed for many years before they achieved reality, the chief obstacle being the extremely difficult terrain of the area, ranging from 1,139 feet at Queensbury to 189 feet at Brighouse, with many a steep ascent and descent in between.

The town itself, prosperously occupied in wool textiles since the Middle Ages, had grown up at the steeply–shelving foot of the Ovenden valley, whose hurrying waters swelled the Hebble Brook before emptying themselves into the River Calder near Salterhebble. Westwards a string of industrial townships – Luddenden Foot, Mytholmroyd and Hebden Bridge – occupied the bottom of the deep, winding Calder Valley as far as Todmorden, where Yorkshire civilisation ended in the folds of the high Pennines.

Not many years after Daniel Defoe had undertaken his hazardous, snowbound journey over the moorland tracks from Rochdale, viewing with approval the signs of a vigorous cottage industry in each of the valley settlements through which he passed, swift mailcoaches had begun to link Halifax with the wider world of trade and commerce, and the Rochdale Canal had boldly threaded its way between the dark, forbidding hills to transport Halifax goods not only westwards to Lancashire markets but also to the West Riding's important Aire and Calder Navigation. The best known of all the local road conveyances was the "Cotton Coach", which enabled manufacturers to rattle over the hills to Manchester, transact their business and return in the same day, although the fast speeds and indifferent highways rendered travel perilous at times – in January, 1833, the "Hark Forward" coach overturned when its axle snapped, hurling its passengers into the waiting mud.

The opening of George Stephenson's east-west Manchester to Normanton railway aroused great displeasure in Halifax, Huddersfield and Bradford, all of which found themselves bypassed, thus inflaming inter-county rivalry, particular criticism being directed in Halifax against rapidly–growing Manchester, which they coolly dismissed as "an upstart town..... which by repeated acts of conglomeration had got together a great heap of brick buildings". Even the opening of a single-track connection from the main line to a station at the foot of Hunger Hill, Halifax, failed to please local travellers, who, on arrival at Sowerby Bridge, were obliged to comply with the station porter's colloquial command to 'Swap here for Halifax'!

Not until 1854 was the borough properly served with a line which burrowed under the flank of Beacon Hill to reach Hipperholme and Bradford. Later still, other trains began to struggle up the taxing gradients of Holmfield, and to tunnel beneath Queensbury in pursuit of an alternative route into Bradford as well as to Keighley, with a high-level branch to Pellon and King Cross, although the cost of building and operating these arduous routes was high, and their accessibility limited. In the early days of the local railways, the quality of travel left something to be desired, especially in the primitive, seatless third-class carriages where a Halifax gentlemen once found himself cooped up with "two respectable well-dressed females, several mechanics and two pigs!"

Horse-drawn cabs first appeared on the streets of Halifax on January 21st 1849, supplemented by hansom cabs in May, 1858, but their fares were far beyond the reach of ordinary folk. In 1893 the minimum fare was 1/- (one shilling); a gentle jog-trot to Stump Cross cost 1s 6d and a safari to Hebden Bridge the stupendous sum of 8/- at a time when a man might earn little more than £1 (20s) for a week's work.

Tidings of a successful horse-bus venture in Bradford, which was able to pay a 71/2% dividend in its first half-year led to the formation of the Halifax Omnibus and Cab Co., Ltd., at a meeting at the "Old Cock" Inn on February 11th, 1865, with Lt–Col. Akroyd, J.P., and John Crossley, M.P., as trustees and twelve local gentlemen as directors. A share issue of £1,000 in £2 shares was agreed on May 8th, and on the morning of Wednesday, May 10th, "the running of one omnibus" began on a route between King Cross and Boothtown at a fare of 3d inside the bus and 2d on top, with a fare-stage at the Northgate Hotel in the town centre. However, the steep gradients which prevailed on every side made horse traction arduous and expensive.

The introduction of horse and steam-hauled tramways in Yorkshire and Lancashire, made possible by the Tramways Act, 1870, aroused some interest in the Borough. On September 30th, 1882, Charles Phillips & Co., solicitors, London, unveiled plans for steam tramways from North Bridge to King Cross, Commercial Street to Free School Lane and Skircoat Green, and Horton Street to Bull Green, but as Commercial Street was still under construction and Skircoat Road not even begun, no action was taken.

Simultaneously, a Halifax & District Tramways Co. (solicitors Holroyde & Smith) advocated San Francisco type cable-hauled trams, and a deputation from the Hallidie Cable Co. attended a meeting of the Halifax Library and

Philosophical Society, when they informed an interested audience that in comparison with horse trams (cruel to animals), steam (noisy and dangerous), electricity (impracticable) and compressed air (not worth discussing), cable cars could ascend and descend Halifax's hills in complete safety.

However, unwilling or unable to raise the large amount of capital which the scheme would entail – about £10,000 per mile of track – the company representatives solemnly stated their belief that tramways in public streets should be constructed and owned by the local authority and leased to the tramway operating company. Not surprisingly, the cost of the scheme, which envisaged routes to Highroad Well, Pellon, Ovenden, Boothtown, Stump Cross, Salterhebble and Sowerby Bridge, was as unpalatable to the Corporation as it was to the company, and the Board of Trade refused to accept the scheme in its entirety, pointing out that a good deal of road-widening would be necessary.

Messrs. Hallidies' lack of faith in electricity as a motive power was not shared by Mr. Michael Holroyd Smith of Halifax who in April, 1883, notified the Corporation that he was in the process of perfecting "electrical appliances" for tramways, in pursuance of which he was constructing an experimental electric tramway in the extensive grounds of "Moorside", the property of one of the wealthy Crossley brothers, carpet manufacturers and generous public benefactors. A few years earlier, Holroyd Smith had installed a telephone system in Crossleys' mill at Dean Clough as well as electric lighting in "Moorside" generated by a small gas engine and a "Gramme" dynamo.

The little tramway was proudly unveiled on July 19th 1883, when visitors to the Salterhebble & District Rose Show were treated to circular rides around L.J. Crossley's kitchen garden. Although the rose-growers were pleased and impressed, the Corporation felt themselves under an obligation to pursue their negotiation with Hallidies, whereupon Holroyd Smith sought more promising prospects at the other side of the Pennines. On July 14th, 1884, he demonstrated a full-size standard gauge electric tramcar on a 100 yard-long track in a field near Chester Road, Cornbrook, Manchester. The power was supplied by a $2^1/2$ h.p. 920 r.p.m. engine coupled to a 150 volt Siemens generator with an output rating of 40 amperes, all the equipment being housed nearby at the works of Smith, Baker & Co., of which Mr. Smith was a director. The happy outcome of this demonstration was the successful inauguration of Britain's first electric street tramway in Blackpool a year later, under Mr. Smith's direction.

Still ambitious to see his birthplace in the forefront of modern transport development, he again approached the Corporation in 1891 with plans for electric tramways from the Old Station to North Bridge, Highroad Well, Skircoat Green and Savile Park, the plans and estimates having been drawn up for him by Messrs. Ulten and Grow, engineers and surveyors, of Waterhouse Street, Halifax.

The Borough fathers remained unimpressed, and realising that "a prophet is not without honour save in his own country", Holroyd Smith betook himself to Bradford, some 8 miles away, where the Corporation, anxious to be rid of the noise, smoke and track wear caused by the heavy steam tram engines as they laboured up their steep gradients, allowed him

In 1883 the Salterhebble and District Rose Show, held in Mr. L. J. Crossley's garden at 'Moorside', was celebrated not only for the excellence of its blooms but also for Mr Michael Holroyd Smith's experimental electric tramway. The small four-wheel car was powered by an electric motor beneath the seat, and its inventor is seen (top) driving the car and (bottom) bare-headed behind it.

[Courtesy Halifax Courier, Ltd.]

to electrify a section of line climbing at 1 in $13^1/4$ out of the town centre. Launched in March, 1892, the experiment was entirely successful, although the cost of electricity was (at that period) too high to permit immediate conversion from steam. Nevertheless, more enterprising than their own public representatives, a group of Halifax businessmen met on September 7th at the Midland Hotel, Bradford, when 28 of those present rode upon Holroyd Smith's tram which had been brought out of store for their benefit.

Subsequently, in May, 1893, Mr. Smith's revised plans for electric tramways in Halifax were submitted to the Corporation's Board of Works Committee by Mr. J.B. Holroyde, solicitor, but once again the Corporation's reluctance to provide the necessary installations at its own expense caused the scheme to founder.

Determined to force the pace, Alderman Michael Booth, J.P., on being elected Mayor on November 20th 1894, publicly proposed that the Bradford and Shelf Tramways Co. should be invited to extend their steam operations into Halifax by way of Northowram, Stump Cross, Godley Cutting and New Bank. Unfortunately, as their leases were due to expire within 7 years, the company directors did not feel justified in undertaking any new commitments, although they commented to Ald. Booth that,

"If they had to begin again, they would not think of going in for steam, but would adopt either the cable system or electricity. There is so much wear and tear on the rails by the steam engines that the life of a tramway is nothing like as long as one in which electricity is the motive power."

More proposals emerged in August, 1895, when a Scottish syndicate offered to build an Edinburgh-style cable system, subject to a 25-year lease from the Corporation. More progressively, Messrs Easton and Anderson of Erith (Mr. Holroyd Smith's associates) proposed yet another electric scheme. Lastly, on November 16th Messrs. Land and Foster, solicitors acting for Mr. Alfred Parrish, one of the promoters of the Halifax and District scheme, submitted proposals for electric tramways almost as extensive as their original cable scheme. The promoters aimed to raise £200,000 capital in £10 shares and to use the overhead wire system with double-deck cars 14'6" in length. They had used Mr. Holroyd Smith's patents on several occasions and expected to use them on their Halifax lines, as he had acted as their engineer on various projects in London, Pressing home their argument, they added that both they and the Halifax ratepayers would object to any attempt by the Corporation to operate tramways outside its boundaries, even if Parliament were prepared to permit it.

The tramways topic attracted much interest at the municipal elections, especially when Mr. J.T. Spencer suggested that trams could be powered hydro-electrically by water flowing through the town's mains. Evidently his ideas appealed to the electorate, as he was immediately elected to the Borough Council and quickly elevated to the rank of Alderman!

Cable haulage continued to find favour with one of the existing members of the Council who quoted comparative costs of tramway operation in Birmingham:-

Cable	7d per car mile
Horse	11d " " "
Steam	1s 2d " " "
Electric	1s 7d " " "

but it seems unlikely that these comparisons took into account all aspects of tramway operation, and in any event the quoted cost of electrical working related to unsuccessful experiments with storage batteries only. Fortunately, the assertions provoked a letter to the "Halifax Guardian" which was to have a profound effect on the tramway question:-

"Sir - Having been a resident of Halifax for over 30 years, I am naturally interested in my native town. I am pleased that there is a movement on foot to lay down tramways, which will be a great advantage to the public and will materially increase the rateable value of the town. Having had over 11 years' practical experience of electric traction, I feel myself competent to say with some degree of authority that Halifax cannot do better than adopt the overhead electric system. The accumulator system in use at Birmingham is a very expensive method of propulsion, but with the overhead system the cost both for equipment and working is less than any other system. There seems to be an opinion in Halifax with its steep gradients that tramways would not be practicable, but I know of no system more suitable for the steep gradients of the Halifax district than the electric. We have gradients here I think equal to any on the suggested routes, and the cars mount them without the slightest difficulty.
Yours truly,
F. Spencer, M. Inst. E.E.
436, Oxford Terrace, Pleck, Walsall, Staffs.
Dec. 4, 1895"

Mr. (Fred) Spencer was in fact the manager of the pioneer South Staffordshire Company which had been operating electric trams since 1892, and had gained his earliest experience with Mr. Holroyd Smith as his electrical engineer at Blackpool.

The question of ownership was settled a few weeks later. The surrounding urban districts, when approached by the 'Guardian', declared themselves in favour of municipalisation; the Mayor of Blackpool (somewhat improperly but very effectively) asserted that "all Corporations and Local Authorities should construct and work all tramways within their boundaries", while his Finance Committee Chairman even more daringly advised Halifax not to permit a private company to have entrée to their streets, adding that Blackpool had recently imposed so many conditions that no company had troubled to apply!

Following an inconclusive Council meeting on January 14th 1896, the Mayor summoned a meeting of ratepayers at the Mechanics' Hall eight days later. The meeting was tumultuous and controversial; even the authority of the Mayor himself (Coun. G.H. Smith) was challenged, as he was Mr. Holroyd Smith's brother! Indeed, an impudent supporter of the nascent I.L.P. exhorted him to "Hod thi din and sit thi dahn" (i.e., Stop your noise and sit yourself down)! More important, however, was the public's "vigorous and unqualified declaration", in favour of Corporation ownership and operation as soon as Parliament would grant permission. Unwilling to brook any further delay, the editor of the 'Guardian' promptly wrote to the Lord President of the Privy Council on January 28th and received a reply only three days later which revealed that the Board of Trade were actively considering the issue. Newly elected Ald. J.T. Spencer therefore moved at the Association of Municipal

Corporations A.G.M. on March 13th that "in the opinion of this Association it is desirable that the power to work and use tramways be conferred on all local authorities who now own or may in the future lay down or acquire tramways within their districts."

As the principle of municipal tramway operation had already been established by default in Huddersfield, Leeds and Glasgow, the Association's resolution encountered little opposition, and on August 12th Standing Order No 171 agreed by Parliament obligingly removed the offending section from the 1870 Tramways Act.

It was therefore both fitting and ironic that, having been racked with indecision for so many years, Halifax Corporation had made amends by assisting their fellow municipalities to confer such a great benefit on the travelling public. The benefit was to be widely shared and long lasting.

Losing no time, the Town Clerk drew up an application to Parliament to enable the Corporation to construct and work tramways within the Borough by means of animal, steam, gas, electric, cable or any other motive power. Confirmed by the Council on January 5th 1897, and subsequently by a town's meeting, it was despatched to Westminster for approval.

Alderman Michael Booth,

Alderman Michael Booth, J.P., the "Father of the Halifax Tramways"

["Tramway and Railway World",
courtesy National Tramway Museum]

CHAPTER 2

MUNICIPAL ENTERPRISE

In December 1896, the Tramways Committee delegated to some of its members the task of settling the question of motive power. The members subsequently published the result of visits to British, Continental and American electric tramways made by the Corporations of Glasgow, Leeds, Sheffield and Bolton, all of whom had returned convinced that electricity supplied through an overhead wire was the ideal source of energy for tramcars.

In Hamburg, they reported, "an extensively developed system of Overhead (Wire) Electric Traction can be seen in full operation in narrow and busy streets, and the cars are under the most perfect control". Other trams in Genoa had been seen ascending gradients of 1 in 9, whilst in Remscheid $5^1/_2$ ton trams, each powered by two 20 h.p. motors, were negotiating sharp curves on steep gradients, not least an 80-yard length of line on a gruelling 1 in $9^1/_2$ gradient.

The conclusion was that "the difficulty of Halifax's gradients is no bar to the system.......the steepest part of Gibbet Street is 1 in 12, this being the steepest section of the lines now proposed. In addition, there are special reasons why electricity is to be preferred, viz.,

1) We have already built Municipal Electricity Works which are capable of supplying all the power required.

2) The production of power as well as lighting from the same works will considerably cheapen both.

3) The cable haulage system is more economical than electricity only when the service of cars is very frequent, at least every 3 minutes.

4) The present electric light mains (i.e. ducts) have a spare tube which would be available for tramway purposes along five–sixths of the routes, thus saving considerable public expenditure."

As argued above, the provision of a regular 'day load' for the Corporation's power station was an important economic factor, but since both trams and the lighting mains would be drawing power simultaneously during the winter months, the Borough Electrical Engineer advised the installation of large banks of accumulators to supplement and steady the output. Following approval on April 5th, 1897, detailed specifications and estimates were compiled for the laying of the tram tracks, erection of tram poles, overhead wires and a depot, provision of rolling-stock and plant, and the provision of underground feeder cables linking the tramway with the power station 600 yards away.

Curious to see electric tramways in actual operation, the Tramways Committee visited Bristol, Birmingham and Coventry, and also Walsall, where they were interested to meet Mr. Fred Spencer, the manager of the South Staffordshire tramways. A cordial and fruitful contact was thus established.

Royal Assent to the Halifax Corporation Bill was given on July 5th, 1897, bringing to an end the long years of indecision. Halifax was now ready to join its neighbours in adopting the most reliable, robust and evocative form of urban transport ever devised – the Electric Tramcar.

A depot site was purchased at Mile Cross in Gibbet Street, and the Committee decided to construct the tram tracks by direct labour, having been offered the services of Huddersfield Corporation's permanent–way foreman, Mr. George Patefield, together with track–laying equipment not needed on its home territory for the time being. Tenders for the supply of materials were accepted as follows:-

Leeds Steelworks	- 630 tons of rails	@ £8-10s-0d per ton
	- 30 tons of fishplates	@ £8-10s-0d per ton
E. Heaton & Son	- boiler	@ £ 415
J. Proctor, Burnley	-mechanical stoker and fittings	@ £101-4s-0d
Askham Bros. and Wilson, Sheffield –		
	- 29 sets of Marshall's patent sprung points	@ £19 per set
	- 2 sets of special curved points	@ £15-2s-6d per set
J. Spencer, Wednesbury –		
100 poles and brackets for carrying overhead wires		£1090-10s-0d
G.F. Milnes & Co., Birkenhead –		
10 tramcar bodies …………..		£1850-0s-0d
The Electric Construction Co., Wolverhampton –		
Electrical equipment for 10 trams ……		£4171-10s-0d
Supply and installation of trolley wire, insulators, copper rail bonds etc...		£984-17s-0d
Supply and installation of two generators at the power station................		£1800-0s-0d
Callenders Cable and Construction Co. –		
Supply of underground cables and feeders		£1237-5s-0d
Chloride Electrical Storage Syndicate –		
Supply and installation of two banks of accumulators and two years' free maintenance		£3070-0s-0d

The above specifications were based on a proposed 10 minutes service frequency from the Old Station to Highroad Well and King Cross respectively. The electrical energy needed to start a loaded car on the 1 in 14 gradient of Horton Street (Old Station) was calculated as 4,380 units @ 2d per unit (£37) with a 10 minute frequency.

A track gauge of 3'6" was adopted, apparently without debate; the decision was probably based on the success of that particular gauge in Birmingham, Coventry and Walsall as well as the extreme narrowness of some of the streets to be negotiated. However, as the trams themselves were to be up to 6'6" wide, thus overhanging the tracks by 1'6" on each side, the benefits of the narrow gauge were perhaps more apparent than real. Not being able to foretell the future any more accurately than present–day transport planners, the Borough Engineer and councillors no doubt did what seemed best for the town.

When considering what type of rolling-stock might best suit Halifax's needs, the Tramways Committee firmly rejected anything resembling the "clumsy" trams seen at Bradford and Leeds. Their ideal vehicle was an open-top double-deck car seating not more than twenty or thirty passengers, of neat appearance and a pleasure to behold. To be fair, the "clumsy vehicles" referred to were the old 58–seat bogie double-deck steam-tram trailers widely used not only in Bradford and Leeds but also in Huddersfield, Dewsbury and many places further afield.

Tramway construction work was soon in progress, with materials of all kinds being brought into the town by canal and railway; setts were piling up in the staiths; hardwood paving blocks had been despatched by Millars, Karri and Jarrah Forests Ltd; a deputation had been to Wednesbury to inspect the poles being manufactured at J. Spencer's works; a rail–bender had been ordered from James Thackrah and Sons, and a wire–stretcher from R.W. Blackwell, and tenders had been sought for a tower–wagon for overhead wire construction and maintenance. The wires themselves were to be 0 gauge (0.324" diameter).

Enthusiasm was spreading quickly – and not only within the Borough. The little Skircoat Parish Council, with the approval of the Halifax Rural District Council, volunteered the use of its highways for tramway purposes in anticipation of early incorporation into the Borough, while the more distant Stainland–with– Old Lindley Urban District Council alluringly advised that as the long tentacles of Huddersfield's tramways were stretching out to moorland Outlane not many miles distant, "It would be greatly in the interests of Halifax to get hold of their district, as there was no doubt that owing to the inconvenience of Stainland railway station, a great deal of people might travel to Huddersfield rather than Halifax."

Prior to the delivery of the Spencer poles which were to support the overhead wires, the Tramways Committee cautiously tested public reaction by erecting a sample pole near the Post Office in Commercial Street. Purchased from James Russell for £12, it was of the type used in Leeds, but being semi-tapered, it was less adaptable than the conventional 3-stage tubular variety, and the Spencer poles were duly installed on the intended routes at 40 yard (120 feet) intervals except at corners and junctions. The exact position of each pole at the edge of the causeway (often termed "pavement" in other parts of England) was determined by the Chairman and a few of his colleagues, and when Mr. Abraham Greenwood objected to the pole which they had caused to be erected outside his shop at 111, Gibbet Street, the Borough Electrical Engineer generously offered to remove it – at Mr. Greenwood's expense! Not surprisingly the offer was declined. The contract for the painting of the poles was awarded to Thomas Harrison of Crown Street, who laboured for many a week (at a fee of 4s 6d per pole) with long ladders and cans of red-oxide coloured paint, this being the preferred colour for gas lamps as well as tram poles.

The new post of Tramways Manager was formally awarded on January 20th, 1898, to Mr. Frederick Spencer, whose Halifax antecedents and advocacy of electricity had already created a favourable impression. Shortly after his arrival, he was despatched to Bristol to observe the electric trams which had been operating there since 1895, and on his return he advertised for staff – six drivers (Class 1 @ 5s per 9 hour day, Class 2 @ 4s 9d and Class 3 @ 4s 6d), six conductors @ 3s per day, two clerks, two cleaners, an inspector, a storekeeper, a night foreman and a labourer. In the event, twelve drivers were appointed, of whom W. Evans

F. Spencer,

Mr. Frederick Spencer,
Halifax's first Tramways Manager.
["The Railway World",
courtesy National Tramway Museum, Crich]

and W. Bamber had been employees of Mr. Spencer's South Staffordshire tramways and whose task as "Class 1" drivers was to train their Halifax colleagues in the mysteries of tram driving. All eleven conductors were respectable Halifax men. The fitter (labourer) was to receive a wage of $7\frac{3}{4}$d ("sevenpence-threefarthings") per hour, and the successful applicant for the post of storekeeper and engineering assistant at 15s (shillings) per week was Mr. Spencer's younger son, Charles Henry Spencer. Smart navy-blue frock coat uniforms and hats for the "platform staff", (i.e. drivers and conductors) were bought from Moore, Taggart and Co., Glasgow and Hibbert and Co., London, respectively.

Track-laying commenced on August 30th, 1897, when the stone setts in Horton Street were removed to allow Mr. Patefield and his 'gang' to lay a concrete foundation whose depth varied from 6 inches on the straight sections to 9 inches where points were to be laid; in width it extended 2 feet either side of where the rails were to be laid, as the Tramways Department were to be responsible for the provision and upkeep of the paving not only between the tracks but also 1 ft 6 inches outside them, a legal liability which was to prove a heavy burden on tramway finances.

As soon as the first lengths of rail were in position, on September 27th, Ald. Booth and his deputy, Coun. Whiteley, ceremonially screwed home the first tie-bars which were to

Making a start — tracklaying commenced in September, 1897, in Horton Street and (above) at Ward's End, where the curve into Commercial Street was laid by workmen equipped with mallets, wedges, crowbars, shovels, gauges, spanners, rail cramps and a wheelbarrow. The two bowler-hatted spectators were being kept at bay by a rope, and a red oil-lit lamp (centre left) protected the area by night.
[Courtesy Halifax Courier, Ltd.]

maintain the correct track gauge. Evidently Coun. Whiteley was no handyman, as "his spanner kept slipping and threatening to throw him on his beam ends," but when his task was accomplished, Ald. Booth delivered an impromptu speech from the top of a pile of fishplates.

In Ward's End at the top of Horton Street, double track soon surrounded the statue of the late Prince Albert, no doubt with the posthumous approval of that progressive gentleman, after which it advanced along Commercial Street where wooden paving blocks were used in the pursuit of "peace and quiet."

Not everyone welcomed the tramways wholeheartedly. The Lancashire & Yorkshire and Great Northern railways refused to entertain tramlines on the Old Station forecourt, and the Halifax Drapers and Hosiers Association respectfully drew the Corporation's attention to the loss and inconvenience being suffered by their members through some of the streets being impassable "for many days or even weeks" while construction work was in progress. At Pellon Lane the Baptists objected to the proposed laying of a double track outside their chapel, as it would leave insufficient room for carriages, while, even more seriously, their neighbours at the "Bradford Hotel" feared that the tram service might interfere with deliveries of beer. In a more visionary vein Mr. E. Zietz of Hamburg wrote to notify the Corporation of the recent invention of motor cars, but the news did not deflect the Tramways Committee from their plans.

The electricity supply for the tramways was to be brought from the Corporation Electricity Works in Wade Street via mains laid in Victoria Street East, Winding Road, Wade Street, Crossley Street and Waterhouse Street to a Tramways Dept. underground control room in George Square where the current was to be metered and earth leakages checked. From the control room underground feeder cables were to radiate to the two tramways in King Cross Lane and Gibbet Street.

Looking forward to delivery of the eagerly-awaited tramcars, the Committee resolved that they should have electric headlamps and should be painted according to the supplier's "Sample no.4," i.e., in Prussian blue and ivory, a smart combination of colours also favoured by Bradford, Leeds and Sheffield. Several miles of gleaming hard-drawn copper wire purchased from Frederick Smith of Salford were strung up along the now–completed tramways; a departmental telephone system was installed by J. Sunderland and Co.; John Hitchen of Hall Street erected a travelling crane in the tram depot, and tramcar stopping–places (known in Victorian and Edwardian Halifax as "Tramway Stations") were provided at generously frequent intervals.

Gibbet Street, steep, narrow and densely-populated, was barely wide enough for a tramway.
["The Railway World",
courtesy the National Tramway Museum Crich]

The laying of the tramways had not been achieved without the demolition of some property, including the old "White Hart Inn" at Bull Green. When Mr. Stafford of King Cross Lane agreed to demolish his shop for road–widening purposes, the Corporation laid tram tracks to within an inch or two of the existing kerb, but Mr. Stafford then changed tack and demanded £20 per yard for the land he had agreed to surrender. Conscious that the Board of Trade would not sanction a situation whereby the trams would overhang the pavement by as much as 1ft 6 inches, the Corporation had to negotiate a new settlement.

Problems with the rolling-stock were encountered too. Although the ten tramcar bodies under construction at Milnes' works in Birkenhead had already been inspected by the Committee in January, 1898, an engineering strike – an event not usually associated with the closing years of Victoria's golden reign – delayed delivery of the mechanical and electrical equipment, i.e., the four-wheel motor trucks on which the bodies were to be mounted, the motors, resistances and controllers and the power station generating plant. The depot at Mile Cross was complete and ready to house up to eighteen trams on six parallel tracks or "roads", of which two were to serve as the repair and overhaul shops. Inevitably the intended inauguration of the tramways in March, had to be deferred despite repeated pleas for the Electric Construction Company to complete their part of the great enterprise.

This photograph almost certainly depicts the first tram to be completed and displayed in the forecourt of Mile Cross Depot in May, 1898 – Car no. 3, not yet fitted with slipper-brake equipment. Details of the pioneer Dickenson trolley-mast and springs can be clearly seen, but apart from the destination board, the tram bears no identification marks. The five gentlemen are unidentified also, except that the bowler-hatted man standing on the forecourt (left) is obviously Mr Fred. Spencer, the tramways manager, while the gentleman leaning on the rear dashplate is probably Mr White, the E.C.C. representative.

["The Railway World",
courtesy the National Tramway Museum, Crich]

Mile Cross Depot under construction. The yard has not yet been paved, and poles and wires are still to be erected, but at least six trams have been delivered, including nos. 2 and 3 (right).

["The Railway World",
courtesy National Tramway Museum, Crich]

The "Halifax Courier" kept its readers well informed about "the wonderful objects" which were destined to "put the jolting old buses in the shade."

"The preparatory work for the electric trams which will revolutionise traffic is steadily progressing, and some of its features have caused no little astonishment to those who have never seen an electric tram before. When the wires were fixed, some wondered what their purpose was, and how they were to be used.....'Where does the electricity come from?' asked one. 'Oh, don't you know?' came the facetious reply. 'It's brought over in boxes from America!'

As soon as the first three tramcar bodies arrived during the second week of May, they were mounted on their trucks and prepared for service. First to be completed was tramcar no. 3, and on the morning of May 17th the hastily convened Tramways Committee made its way up to Mile Cross, where to the delight of the public the gleaming new vehicle was "pushed out into the road and connected to the overhead wire" – in other words, a member of the depot staff raised the trolley boom by means of a trolley rope and placed the grooved trolley wheel on the underside of the overhead wire, which had been energised by temporary plant loaned by the Electric Construction Co. pending the installation of the two permanent (strike–bound) generators. So pleased were the onlookers and so anxious to be associated with the historic event that a few of them scratched their names on the gleaming paintwork, to the exasperation of Ald. Booth and Mr. Spencer.

With great anticipation the Tramways Committee (six aldermen and eight councillors) joined Mr. Spencer and his colleagues Mr. Escott (Borough Engineer) and Mr. Wilmshurst (Borough Electrical Engineer) on board the tram at 11 a.m. At a given signal Mr. White of the E.C.C. moved the brass controller handle with his left hand, and to the beholders' amazement and fascination the car moved off at a smart pace down Gibbet Street. Little power was needed, and as the vehicle gathered speed down the gradient Mr. White shut off the current, and firmly grasping the vertically-mounted handbrake with his right hand he brought the tram to a halt a few hundred yards downhill. Then, as soon as the trolley had been reversed, he strode to the opposite end of the tram and drove it to the Highroad Well terminus at the "Horse and Jockey Inn".

For almost an hour no. 3 and its illustrious cargo travelled to and fro, the inspection–hatches in the saloon floor having been removed so that viewers could observe the motors, gearing and brake-rigging in action. Then, thoroughly satisfied, the party adjourned to the "Granby Hotel" for a celebratory luncheon. Unnoticed by his colleagues, Councillor Simpson chose not to join them immediately; instead, fired by the altogether understandable ambition of being a tram driver, he took the controls, and with "his ruddy face aglow with pride, he drove the horseless vehicle up the hill as far as the 'Golden Lion'". As the stifling constraints of "Health and Safety" regulations lay far ahead in the future, he soon became the "hero of the hour" to his fellow committee-men and the envy of tramway connoisseurs to this day!

The Corporation had advised drivers of "Carriages, 'Buses, Cabs and other Vehicles" to exercise great care in passing the "Electrical-driven Tram Cars" until the horses became accustomed to them – a wise precaution, as some of the horses displayed signs of unrest, shying and prancing as the tram passed by. One rider deliberately rode his mount forward and held its nose within a few inches of the tram – a wise precaution which quickly allayed the animal's fear.

The morning's trials demonstrated that the tramcar brakes would prove to be inadequate for steep inclines, especially when the cars were fully loaded. Discussions with the makers quickly produced a supplementary Milnes "Slipper" track brake comprising four hardwood blocks mounted between the wheels and forced down on to the surface of the rail by means of a handwheel mounted on the driver's platform next to the handbrake.

Resplendent in their smart Prussian Blue and ivory paintwork embellished with gold leaf lining on the blue areas and blue and red on the ivory, the ten tramcars represented the latest products of the tramways industry, despite being relatively small vehicles whose dimensions were dictated by the narrow track gauge and the many sharp curves. Their Milnes bodies were of the four windows per side variety with longitudinal (inward-facing) wooden seats for 22 in the lower saloon and 24 on reversible 2 and 1(i.e., double and single) seats on the upper deck. Typical of electric trams in the spartan late–Victorian era, they had open top decks and stairs as well as open platforms at each end of the car for the driver and conductor.

The car bodies were mounted on four-wheel (i.e., two axle) American-built Peckham type 8A cantilever trucks with a short wheelbase of only 5'6", and 30" diameter chilled-iron flanged wheels made by the New York Wheel Company. Their motive power comprised two E.C.C. 25 h.p. 4–pole d.c. motors, each of which was connected to one of the axles by spur gears. Power was fed into the motors by hand-operated Thomson-Houston type K10 series–parallel controllers with an emergency braking feature which was in effect a short-circuiting device. Normal service braking was applied manually by the driver via a pedestal– mounted "wind-on" handbrake which forced a soft-iron shoe on to the wheel tyres. Contrary to specification the headlamps were initially feeble oil-fuelled units which were soon replaced by more powerful electric headlamps.

In view of the narrowness of the upper-deck gangway, current collection was of the Dickenson type with a trolley mast mounted at one side of the upper deck and a swivel-type trolley head containing the trolley wheel. Lifeguards comprising a wire mesh tray were attached to each end of the truck frame, and for a short time drawbar couplers were provided, presumably in case trailer operation was adopted, which fortunately it was not.

The various delays referred to above had persuaded the Corporation to delay the official opening of the tramways until the Golden Jubilee of the incorporation of Halifax as a Borough, thus allowing the newly-appointed drivers and conductors to become thoroughly acquainted with their splendid new steeds and the intricacies of the routes.

The "old order" did not give way to the new without a strong rearguard struggle. Messrs. G. C. Bowman declared their willingness to withdraw the King Cross horse-buses provided that the Corporation would adequately compensate them, but when the local authority declined to entertain the idea, the buses contrived to suffer a few scrapes with the new trams in the hope of compensation. The attempt failed, and the business was sold by auction, when the horses realised up to £32-11-0d each, a "garden seat bus" £75, a home built "char-a-banc" £50 and a "Clarence" carriage £80.

The future was close at hand now: in the last days of May one or two trams were driven down to Commercial Street in the heart of the town, where they "caused a great sensation" – the first of many.

Commercial Street awaits its trams, June, 1898.
["The Railway World", courtesy of the National Tramway Museum, Crich]

CHAPTER 3
CORPORATION TRAMWAYS

On Thursday, June 9th, 1898, the burgesses of Halifax proudly celebrated fifty years of continuous municipal progress and industrial growth. Awarded borough status in the troubled year of the People's Charter and European revolutions, the old town had steadily evolved into one of the foremost manufacturing centres in Yorkshire, and the ceremonial opening of the new electric tramway undertaking formed the centrepiece of the Golden Jubilee celebrations.

George Square and Commercial Street were thronged with eager crowds when the three special cars rumbled down Gibbet Street and halted near the Post Office, where they were boarded by the Mayor and Corporation. Microphones not having yet been invented, the Mayor's macebearer was obliged to call for "Order!" and "Silence, please!" before the amused throngs would quieten down, after which Ald. Booth briefly reviewed the growth of the town and the development of its public services, notably the newest – the electric tramways. Coun. Whiteley took pride in the powerful motors which were going to propel the tramcars up Halifax's challenging hills, as well as the brakes which, in his view, were sufficient to halt a tramcar on gradients twice as steep as those in Halifax

It would seem that the Mayor was not well versed in new technology, as when he drove the leading car, no 3, around the corner into Crown Street it halted and refused to move.

Ward's End, June 1898, with tracks and wires curving out of Commercial Street (left) into Horton Street.

Eventually it was restarted but travelled sluggishly (perhaps the track was tight to gauge) as far as Bull Green, where it regained its proper vigour and sailed up King Cross Street in fine style, leaving a horse bus far behind. The return journey via George Street and Silver Street and the 1 in 12 ascent of Gibbet Street were accomplished with ease, Ald. Brook commenting contentedly that, "It's a deal nicer than riding in a bus!"

As the permanent generating plant was still not available, it was not possible to open the public service immediately, to the great disappointment of the would-be passengers. However, the plant – two d.c. 4-pole E.C.C. generators driven by a compound horizontal condensing steam engine supplied by Pollit and Wigzell of Sowerby Bridge – was in place by June 18th, allowing the official Board of Trade inspection to take place at last, eleven days later.

Thus, on Wednesday, June 29th, 1898, Sir Francis Marindin, R.E., K.C.M.G., minutely examined the electrical installations and Major Cardew, R.E., the permanent way, their only untoward comment being that at Ward's End where the overhead wires were suspended from three poles placed centrally between the tracks, the trams would pass dangerously close to the poles, for which reason the Horton Street track had to lie fallow while the offending rails were moved outwards. The other two lines were pronounced to be entirely satisfactory.

The Golden Jubilee of Halifax Corporation on June 9th, 1898, was splendidly marked by the opening of the tramways, and vast crowds in Commercial Street and (right) George Square greeted the official convoy of three decorated trams. On the top deck of the nearest tram the Mayor of Halifax (standing, centre of picture, in ceremonial robes) is addressing the public, accompanied by his macebearer (standing, wearing, a cocked hat). The seated gentleman above the OL in "Old Station" may be Alderman Booth. Headgear of every description – top hats, billycocks, straw boaters, cloth caps and helmets – was favoured by the majority, as Victorians rarely braved the midsummer sun without protection.

[Courtesy Halifax Courier, Ltd.]

Surprisingly, a few of the Tramways Committee began to query the wisdom of opening the tramways immediately, as they "feared some untoward accident on the gradients when cars were packed with passengers", and would have preferred to wait until the Halifax Fair Week was over. No such doubts troubled the imperturbable Town Clerk, who impressed on them the ideal opportunity being presented to them by the enthusiasm of the public, with the result that the public service began in the evening.

> "There was a tremendous rush to board the novel conveyances", the press reported. "After seeing the loaded cars running one after the other without the slightest hitch, the Committee began to laugh at the fears they had entertained."

Three cars provided the initial service to Highroad Well and two to King Cross. On that evening 4,000 happy Halifax folk paid a penny each to travel on their wonderful new acquisitions; next day 7,200 followed their example, and in the first month the weekly takings totalled £238, more than twice the estimated break-even point.

At first the trams ran almost at random as a means of ascertaining what the regular demand was going to be. Unexpectedly, the chief problem lay not in persuading people to ride on the cars but in inducing them to alight; it was not uncommon for passengers to keep their seats when a car reached a terminus, and some made as many as a dozen consecutive return journeys. Others not already on board fought to join in the new form of pleasure; women and children were jostled aside and genuine travellers left behind. The age of joy-riding had dawned.

By the time that a regular pattern of operation had been decided upon, the initial excitement had died away, and a formal timetable was brought into operation on Monday, July 25th, when the first tram left Highroad Well at 5 a.m. and King Cross at 5.15, returning from town at 5.15 and 5.30 respectively. Presumably the first King Cross car had left the depot at about 4.30 a.m. and "travelled light" through the town centre. The Highroad Well service frequency was half-

This view of no.3 passing the Albert Statue at the top of Horton Street was no doubt taken at the opening of the Old Station line in July, 1898.
[Courtesy Halifax Courier, Ltd.]

hourly until 7.30 a.m. and every 10 minutes thereafter until 11p.m., the King Cross trams following a similar pattern before and after 8 a.m. Sunday services did not commence until 2 p.m. Economic benefits soon followed: land values doubled at the outer termini, and within a short time over 200 houses had been built and occupied.

The track alterations at Ward's End having been completed, the two routes were extended down Horton Street to Old Station on July 26th, when it was found that the journey times from that point to King Cross and Highroad Well were 14 and 17 minutes respectively. Until other road

Another view of tram no.3, probably marking the opening of the public service from Highroad Well to Old Station. The driver and the two conductors wore smart uniforms, "Foreign Legion" - style caps, stiff collars, ties and well – polished boots. The driver was holding the power controller handle with his left hand and the hand-brake with his right, beneath which was the horizontal wheel for the "slipper" brake. The drawbar under the fender was used in the early days of the tramways for hauling disabled trams back to Mile Cross Street.

[Courtesy Halifax Courier, Ltd.]

users became accustomed to the undeviating movements of the trams, several unwarily-driven greengrocers' carts were overturned and waggonettes damaged, fortunately without serious personal injury.

An unexpected complication arose when Messrs. R.W. Blackwell of London, tramway contractors, notified the

Gibbet Street in the early days, with car no.9 travelling uphill near St. John's Hospital. The overhead wires were rigidly attached to the bracket arm of the elegant Spencer tram poles, and the steeply cambered highway was paved with local stone setts.
[Courtesy Halifax Courier, Ltd.]

November and placed in service in December, at a cost of £800. Their design was identical with that of the first batch of trams, but as the E.C.C. equipment on cars 1-10 had proved unreliable from the outset – as many as three cars out of the ten could be out of action at any time – two of the additional trams incorporated British Thomson-Houston (BTH) equipment and the other two Westinghouse units. Several further batches, all equipped by Westinghouse, were ordered in successive months and numbered 15 to 58.

Within a month of the opening of the tramways it was realised that wet weather considerably diminished the takings, as passengers were reluctant to sit on the drenched seats on the open upper deck, and were prohibited from standing. Accordingly the Committee accepted a tender from Messrs. A.H. White of Halifax for "sixteen combination covers for tramcar roof seats" at £4 each, but these, the first of a hopeful series of patent "dry" seats, failed to justify the claims made for them.

Following completion of the track widening at Wards End, George Patefield and his gang were asked as a matter of urgency to lay a siding in George Square to accommodate E.C.C.–equipped cars which had developed faults, prior to their being repaired or towed back to the depot, a process which rarely failed to attract a press comment. The pace of work then quickened dramatically. On September 19th the tracklayers revisited Wards End to begin work on the Salterhebble line; on November 17th others commenced excavating Haley Hill and a third gang turned its attention to Skircoat Road on December 1st.

Those who rode on the trial journey to Salterhebble on January 16th, 1899, enjoyed the distinction of being driven by that enthusiastic layman Coun. Simpson, the recently-elected Mayor of Halifax, who had daringly and unofficially gained the necessary skills at Highroad Well six months previously. Despite pouring rain his performance must have satisfied the Board of Trade inspectors, as they unhesitatingly approved the new line as far as its terminus at the "Falcon Inn" at the top of Salterhebble Hill. Although

By the time that the Salterhebble route opened in January, 1899, it had been realised that rigid suspension of the trolley wires from the bracket arms was causing metal fatigue, a problem which was cured by the introduction of flexible "bowstring" bracket suspension as seen in this view of the original terminus at the top of Salterhebble Hill. Tram no.11 was one of the four cars (11 — 14) placed in service in December, 1898.
[Courtesy the late R.B. Parr]

Corporation that they were sole licensees of the Dickenson patent side-mounted trolley used on Halifax's trams, and that as the patent related not only to the trolley itself but also to "its radial relation to the overhead wire" (i.e., its ability to swivel and follow the varying paths of the wire), they wished to know the length of tramway now being operated. The matter was promptly referred to the Electrical Construction Co. for whom Blackwells had acted as sub-contractor, and no more was heard of the claim.

Large, artistically-painted destination indicator boards were provided for the trams by Mr. J.S. Swale of Halifax at a cost of 10s. per car, and from 1902 they were illuminated by a single electric bulb following a trial with car 38 on March 4th.

Meanwhile the Corporation's second Tramway Bill had already received the Royal Assent, authorising the Borough Engineer to construct lines to Boothtown, Pellon, Illingworth, Skircoat Green, Stump Cross and the borough boundary in Stainland Road, Salterhebble, with a connecting line between King Cross and Mile Cross by way of Spring Hall Lane and Warley Road (West End).

As the initial fleet of ten tramcars was obviously going to be inadequate for the increasing demand, four extra cars (nos. 11-14) were ordered on July 30th, 1898, delivered in the parallel tramway to Skircoat Green was not quite complete when Major Marindin inspected both routes four days later, he nevertheless felt able to approve it subject to a formal certificate from the Town Clerk when it was ready for use in mid-February, by which time the Salterhebble trams were doing "enormous business".

Unfortunately it was not possible to open the Skircoat Green line for public service because the Electricity Works were by this time loaded to capacity, and such was the nation-wide demand for new generating plant that neither British nor American manufacturers could supply new equipment in less than 31 weeks. By early March the hours of daylight had lengthened sufficiently to allow one of the existing generators to be transferred from lighting purposes to traction uses, allowing the new tramway to open on the afternoon of Tuesday, March 14th, 1899. A half-hourly service was commenced from Old Station to the terminus one furlong south of Skircoat Moor Road. Eleven tramcars were now needed to maintain all the scheduled services.

Time to stand and stare: boys and men watch the photographer as he records tramcar 9 setting out from the Post Office for Skircoat Green. New, neat arc-lamps suspended from the tram pole bracket arms have superseded the original enormous lanterns.
[J.A. Pitts collection,
courtesy West Yorkshire Archives Bradford]

Winter had arrived early that year; heavy snowfalls on November 23rd, 1898, had halted the tram services until teams of snow-shovellers had cleared the blocked tracks. Determined not to be outwitted by the elements on future occasions, the Tramways Department purchased a snowplough from Mr. H. Wadsworth, presumably in a form suitable for attachment to the fender of a tramcar.

The severity of the winter had also hampered the construction of the Boothtown tramway; work had begun in November, but it was not until March 29th, 1899, that Sir Francis Marindin was able to give his approval for the route to open immediately, with two trams providing a half-hourly frequency. There were conditions, of course. As Haley Hill and its continuation, Boothtown Road, incorporated

gradients up to 1 in 12.89, compulsory stops for inward-bound cars had to be observed at each end of Haley Hill, and a maximum 6 m.p.h. speed restriction was decreed for the descent from the outer terminus, with a cautious 2 m.p.h. crawl around the sharp curve which led on to North Bridge. The efficiency of the slipper brakes and the prudent practice of renewing the wooden brake blocks every day attracted favourable comment, although the tramcar lifeguards were considered disappointing. Not for the first time the Board of Trade reminded the Corporation that each tram should possess a speed indicator, but when pressed to inform the Corporation of the names of suppliers and users of such equipment, they were obliged to admit that they did not know of any! The matter was therefore not pursued.

Passenger approval for the new service was immediate. "It's t' best thing 'at ivver came ta Boothtahn!" they declared, and Ald. Booth was "the hero of the hour".

The town terminus of the Boothtown line was in Union Street near its junction with Horton Street, into which a track connection was later constructed for access to Skircoat Road depot. As in all densely-populated parts of the town, the stopping places were closely spaced – Borough Market, Crown Street, Crossley Street, Winding Road, Cross Hills (at the south end of the bridge), Charlestown Road (at the north end), the "Coach and Horses", Akroyd Park, Chester Road, Iona Street, Rawson Street and of course the terminus near the end of Claremount Road. This seemingly over-generous provision was appreciated by the public, who were happy to ride short distances of only two or three stops, a practice still observed a century later, even though present–day bus fares are somewhat higher than the original penny fare!

The Boothtown trams were the first to traverse North Bridge, an impressive Victorian stone and iron structure which spanned the Hebble Brook and the Great Northern

Boothtown Road, looking towards the distant "Punchbowl Inn" and the towering hills.
[Courtesy Trevor Hartley]

20

Railway's Ovenden branch. As the Borough Electrical Engineer was anxious to avoid lateral stresses to the structure, he suspended the tram wires from rigid horizontal tubular gantries bolted at each end to tram poles which in turn were braced by ornamental supports clamped to the bridge. To his relief, the result was considered aesthetically pleasing to late-Victorian eyes. Poles for the new routes were purchased from Macartney, McElroy and Co, of 53, Victoria Street, London, and were painted by Mr. J. Lambert of 11, Lawson Street, Wheatley, at a cost of 4s 6d each.

The narrowness of some of the thoroughfares posed a problem: if a single track were to be laid in the middle of the road, there might be insufficient space for carts or carriages to squeeze past the trams, for which reason the single line in Portland Place (Salterhebble section) was laid on the eastern side of the carriageway. When double track was installed in Gibbet Street in later years, it occupied almost the entire width of the road.

Everyday matters presented fewer problems. A batch of fareboxes offered for sale by Blackpool Corporation was bought for £26, and change-bags, conductors' cash bags and guards' lamps were purchased from Messrs. J. Glossop, D.W. Orr and F. Whiteley respectively. Civic hospitality was extended to delegations from Batley, Rochdale, Newcastle, Derby, Brighton and Burton-on-Trent who wished to experience the delights of up-to-date public transport.

The Pennine rains which swelled the local brooks and sometimes caused the nearby River Calder to flood the valley bottom so vigorously that corpses were washed out of their graves, descended also on the heads of passengers awaiting tramcars in the town centre, and in March, 1899, Mr. J.T. Riley agreed to allow the Tramways Department "to erect a Veranda over the Causeway in Commercial Street between the Old Cock Yard and Cheapside as a Shelter for passengers". Mr. Riley soon had reason to regret his neighbourly impulse, as the causeway was regularly blocked by crowds who threw caution to the winds whenever a tramcar approached, thus compelling the Tramways Committee to insist that, "with a view to preventing crowding and disorder, tram conductors be authorised and instructed to carry out the Queue System amongst passengers waiting for cars." The order proved unenforceable: Yorkshire folk did not queue.

Other public facilities similarly failed to please. When passengers complained that tramcars were not departing punctually from the town centre, the Tramways Department explained that neither the Post Office nor the Town Hall clock displayed the correct time. In reply, the postal authorities claimed that their clock was being subjected to vibration from passing vehicles, presumably the trams, whereupon the tram conductors were instructed to comply with the Town Hall clock, right or wrong!

In preparation for the authorised tramways at "the top of the town," to Savile Park, Pellon and Illingworth, the Borough Engineer's staff were hard at work. The Savile Park line was designed as a link between the Skircoat Green and King Cross routes by way of Free School Lane, Savile Park and Skircoat Moor Road, but matters were delayed by the inability of the tracklayers and paviors to keep pace with the increasing demands on their services. In consequence, piles of rails accumulated at the sides of the roads, to the great inconvenience of pedestrians. Although the tram poles had been in place for five months, it was a mere three days before the scheduled Board of Trade inspection on June 6th, 1899, that the overhead linesmen were able to erect the wires. The sense of urgency had an unfortunate sequel: the horse-drawn tower-waggon overturned and catapulted three of the linesmen to the ground, fortunately without ill effects. Happily, Sir Francis Marindin was pleased with their handiwork, and a quarter-hourly tram service commenced at 3.30 p.m. on the same day. It was soon realised that for the E.C.C. equipped trams the 15 minutes journey time on the

Tramcar 79 has just arrived at King Cross by way of Savile Park, and the conductor on the top deck is in the act of swinging the trolley pole to the opposite end of the tram and placing it on the overhead wire for the return journey. The double set of wires just above the trolley head serves the Burnley Road line.

[Courtesy the late R. B. Parr]

Savile Park route (Post Office to College Terrace) was insufficient; the frequent halts at stopping places and the need to change the track points at Wards End, Heath Junction and Free School Lane bottom detained them so long that by the time that the trolley had been reversed at the terminus it was already time to begin the return journey.

It would appear that the division of responsibility between the Tramways Manager (provision of services and maintenance of the rolling-stock), Borough Engineer (construction and upkeep of the permanent way) and Borough Electrical Engineer (supply of current and erection and supervision of the overhead equipment) sometimes resulted in a lack of co-ordination and foresight. The tram depot at Mile Cross had been designed for eighteen tramcars with room for expansion, but was situated at the top of steep, narrow Gibbet Street – a source of great inconvenience when defective trams had to be pushed or towed up the taxing gradient. Hardly had Mr. Spencer found time to settle into his new home alongside the depot when the Corporation resolved to seek a more suitable location.

In September, 1898, a central site was acquired half a mile from the town centre, in Skircoat Road, near the junction of the Salterhebbble, Skircoat Green and Savile Park routes. Contracts were let in May, 1899, for a depot and workshop capable of housing 44 trams initially and up to 100 if required at a later date, and of course a new "Tramway House" for Mr. Spencer. Sections of single track in the vicinity were quickly doubled to accommodate the large volume of trams which would soon be leaving and returning to the new premises at various times of day or night, and by November 16th the depot was able to house 20 trams. When it was complete, the Mile Cross shed was offered for sale, but as no purchaser could be found, the tracks and wires remained in place.

The first exploratory journeys on the Illingworth and Pellon lines were made by Ald. Booth and the Manager on July 28th, 1899. Three days later the Committee enjoyed a similar outing, to Pellon in the morning, and after lunch to Illingworth (Post Office) when the Mayor confidently took the controls once again and within 18 minutes triumphantly drew up at the new terminus, 2½ miles from the departure point in Waterhouse Street. Both were challenging routes. On the Illingworth line, Ovenden Road was barely 17 feet wide in places, and Lee Bridge Road little better at 18'6"; in addition, there were tortuous curves and gradients rising to 1 in 13.4. The Pellon line formed a continuous ascent

Ovenden Road about 1904, with a tram returning to Halifax.

[Courtesy National Tramway Museum]

culminating in a 1 in 13.9 climb, and in view of highway widths as little as 14'10", most of the track (single with three loops) had to be laid at the side of the road. Not surprisingly, Sir Francis Marindin called for high standards of driving when he carried out his inspection on August 5th.

Subject to cautious speed restrictions, both routes opened immediately, with a 15 minutes frequency to Pellon and a half hourly service to Illingworth. Whilst the fare on the mile-long Pellon section was a modest penny, the much longer Illingworth journey was fixed at 2d with a penny stage at Athol Mount, Ovenden; however, following fierce protests and a 1,040 name petition, the stage was moved outwards to Nursery Lane. The dispute did not detract from the popularity of the service; indeed, the frequency had to be increased, and a lady was heard to claim (with some exaggeration, one hopes) that a friend had seen "ovver fower hundred get off one tram!"

The annual Ovenden Show imposed such a strain on the tramway facilities that one of the Skircoat Green trams had to be diverted from its normal route, to the wrath and indignation of Coun. Thomas Hey, who represented the Skircoat Ward. Jumping on board one of the remaining Skircoat trams he tore down an advertisement for the Show, for which presumptuous action he was seized by the collar and ejected from the tram. Fortunately, for the civic worthy, he was recognised by the hastily summoned constabulary, who laughed loudly at his discomfiture and returned to their duties. The arrival of eleven further trams in September eased the rolling-stock shortage for a while.

Tramcar no.15, new in September, 1899, was one of the first to display the Borough coat of arms in a roundel on the side panel. The trolley mast springs were of an improved type, and drawbars were no longer fitted. Contrary to popular belief, Victorian ladies sometimes rode on the upper deck, as in this view taken in Pellon Lane.

[Courtesy Roy Brook]

On the formidable ascending gradients now being encountered by the trams, it was important for drivers to remain in full control at all times. They soon acquired the technique of not fully releasing the handbrake until they had moved the controller handle to the first power notch, thereby avoiding runbacks, loss of adhesion or wheel-spin. On descending journeys they used the track ("slipper") brake to control the rate of descent, applying the hand/wheel brake to halt the car at the "tramway stations". Emergency stops necessitated a quick backward movement of the controller handle (causing the motors to act as rheostats) coupled with an application of the sand pedal to prevent a forward skid along the smooth rails.

The approach to facing points or sharp curves called for a maximum speed of about 6 m.p.h. (officially 4 m.p.h. or even 2 m.p.h) as a means of avoiding discomfort for the passengers and possible derailment of the tram, and complex junctions such as Wards End had to be negotiated sensibly to ensure that the trolley did not jump from the overhead wire and cause damage or delay. Drivers soon learned to beware all such pitfalls, as each one had to be reported to higher authority or even, in serious cases, to the Board of Trade itself. Most of the loops, i.e., passing-places, were of the "straight run in" variety, which inevitably entailed a sharp "dog-leg" turn for cars leaving the loop and re-entering the single line, an arrangement which naturally prevented the loops from being parallel with the highways in which they were laid.

The tram tracks and their associated foundations and paving were collectively known as "the permanent way", and the Corporation hoped that they would justify their title, as the expense of laying them had been great, and the loans raised from Government sources had to be repaid with interest over a fixed term of years, all of which had a direct bearing on the profitability of the tramways.

At the height of the tramway construction programme, in 1901, no fewer than five gangs of labourers were employed by the Borough Engineer, each being known by the name of its foreman, i.e., Clifton's, Bower's, Billington's, White's and Slack's, and "slackness" was nowhere to be seen. Indeed, the rate of progress which they consistently achieved with sledgehammer, pick, shovel, spanner and muscle would have been a revelation to 21st century construction companies hemmed in with restrictive legislation and complex computerisation. Only atrocious weather or capricious councillors could deter the gangs from their labours.

Most of the early tram rails were bought from the Leeds Steel Co., and "special work" (points and crossings) from Askham Brothers and Wilson or Edgar Allen, Ltd., all being rigidly bolted to each other with steel fishplates. Within a

few years the pounding of the tram wheels over rail joints tended to loosen them, and in 1901 Cooper & Smith patent anchor joints were tried.

In the early years, when the track and the rolling-stock were new and speeds low, they generated little noise, so that until the public became accustomed to them, several accidents occurred, such as the death of the three year old son of a soldier stationed at Pellon Barracks, who ran out into the path of an oncoming tramcar and was killed. Major Druitt advised that some better form of lifeguard was needed than the wire-mesh tray attached to the pilot board at each end of the tramcar trucks, and ultimately the Corporation adopted the Tidswell Patent Tram Guard manufactured by its patentee in Bradford and fitted to the Bradford trams. The

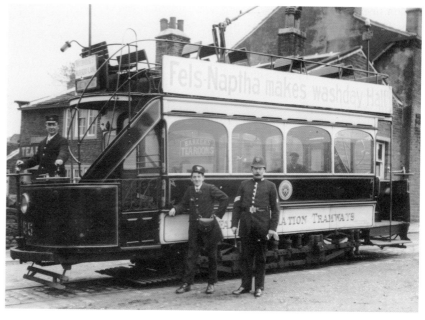

The Tidswell patent lifeguard equipment, adopted in 1901, saved many lives. Whenever the two-bar "gate" beneath the fender encountered an obstruction, it swung backwards and caused the wooden slat "tray" to drop and thus scoop up the person or object. Car no.55, seen here at Causeway Foot terminus, probably acquired its lifeguard during its first major overhaul about 1902. Also seen are the tall upright stanchion whose electric lamp cast light on the upper deck; a second lamp which illuminated the destination board ("Waterhouse Street, Nursery Lane and Causeway Foot"), the borough coat of arms (incorporating the head of John the Baptist) on the side panel, the proud municipal title, "Halifax Corporation Tramways" compared with the more modest name of "Fredk. Spencer, Tramways Manger" on the rocker panel, and on the upper deck side panel the more challengeable claim that "Fels Naptha makes washday half"! Standing next to the borough constable is cheerful young conductor Andrew Nash, who later served with the Colne and Huddersfield tramways.

[Courtesy Roy Brook]

mechanism was actuated by a two-bar wooden "gate" suspended beneath the tramcar fender; when it struck an object, it swung backwards and dropped a slatted wooden lifeguard tray which safely scooped up the object. In this way, on May 4th, 1901, a young girl who ran across the path of Halifax tram no. 7 escaped with a few cuts and bruises because she had wisely chosen a Tidswell-equipped tram.

Concerned at the possibility of trams running backwards on steep gradients if drivers released the handbrake too quickly when moving off from a stop, the Manager and Vice Chairman collaborated in a "Spencer and Whiteley patent scotch brake" embodying wedges located behind the wheels. So long as the car was moving forwards, the mechanism was inactive, but should the car move backwards, the scotch was designed to drop on to the rails and lock the wheels.

At all stages of tramway construction and maintenance, care had to be taken to ensure continuity of electrical circuits and avoidance of current leaks. The overhead wires were therefore carefully insulated from the roadside standards, and rail joints were copper-bonded in order to conduct the return current back to the power station via the rails and the underground feeder cables and not by means of water mains or (more explosively) gas pipes. Overhead telephone wires crossing over the tram wires had to be protected by earthed guard wires, and a failure to fulfil this legal obligation caused considerable damage on July 10th, 1899, when a broken telephone wire fell on to the tramway overhead equipment, and the ensuing 550-volt short-circuit caused a blaze which spectacularly "destroyed the means of intercommunication" at Halifax Telephone Exchange!

Matters such as working conditions and ratepayers' requests were reviewed from time to time. In November, 1901, eighteen drivers were awarded wage rises of 3d per day and four conductors $1/2$d (a halfpenny) per hour; all except Driver Kelly (no. 159) bore solid Northern names such as Brearley, Butterworth, Dawson, Frankland, Greenwood and Holroyd. And when a courteously-phrased "Petition was submitted from Owners and Ratepayers residing in the vicinity of Heath Park Avenue, asking for a Station to be appointed at the terminus of the footpath from Well Head Fields", the Committee naturally felt unable to reject it.

Sad to say, the hard work and dedication of the staff did not always receive due respect. In September, 1902, Frank Skelton of appropriately-named Slippy Lane, Mixenden, was prosecuted "for using offensive language in a Tram Car"; subsequently four boys were reprimanded for having thrown a length of string with wood attached to each end over the trolley wires in Orange Street, and, more shockingly, Coun. Clay had to be "requested to explain to the Committee why he had torn down a notice displayed in one of the Pellon cars in connection with the Salterhebble Rose Show"! Obviously Coun. Hey's earlier contretemps had not gone unnoticed.

The practice of running all the King Cross and Highroad Well cars down to the Old Station at the foot of Horton Street had failed to please the public, as the irregular pattern of railway arrivals and departures made proper connections impossible. In August, 1899, therefore, the trams began to use the Post Office in Commercial Street as their terminus, with a separate shuttle service to and from the Station, but as the new arrangement entailed not only a change of car but also an additional halfpenny fare, special transfer tickets were issued to enable passengers to change cars at no extra

cost at Union Street (Boothtown route), Hall End (Pellon and Illingworth) and Fountain Street (all other routes).

The transfer system gave two rides per ticket, and allowed passengers to transfer to and from the Station cars within a limited period, but purchasers often presented the tickets long after their expiry date. The tickets were therefore replaced by 2,000 brass discs or "checks", a system which needed at least 500 of the checks to circulate every day, but, for unexplained reasons, passengers began to hoard them so avidly that before long 1,872 of the 'checks' had vanished entirely, to the amusement of the Committee, who reinstated tickets in a different form.

At Wards End the Albert Statue did not enjoy its status as a "Tramway Station" for long; having already sacrificed its ornamental railings to create extra space for passing trams, it was removed altogether in the Spring of 1900 to the junction of Heath Road and Skircoat Road, a bold move of which the old Queen, then in the last year of her life, would certainly not have approved. Similarly, the fountain at King Cross had been uprooted and compelled to flow in a different channel.

In the interests of ensuring that their tramways were being built and operated in accordance with the best available practices, the Corporation allowed the Borough Electrical Engineer and the Tramways Committee vice-chairman, Coun. J.H. Whiteley, to inspect tramways in Canada and the United States. Their voyage took place in December, 1899, when they visited New York, Brooklyn, Philadelphia, Washington, Pittsburgh, Cincinatti, Chicago, Buffalo, Niagara, Toronto, Montreal, Quebec, Schenectady, Boston, Albany and Providence. On their return they were able to recommend practical improvements such as:-

1) flexible suspension of the trolley wire from the rigid bracket arms as a means of reducing arcing and metal fatigue;

2) longer (60 foot) rails with a wider groove to lessen flange wear and improve adhesion;

3) more powerful motors to allow the trams to climb gradients more confidently and cope with the effects of voltage drop;

4) single-deck trams with open sides for quick loading and unloading;

5) imposition of a minimum waiting time in the town centre as a means of reducing congestion – hence, more cross-town services which would eliminate reversals;

6) on the longer routes, electricity sub-stations fed from Halifax via a.c. high-tension cables which would also be able to supply industrial power and lighting to the outer districts as well as (by means of rotary converters) d.c. traction current for the trams.

All these practical recommendations were ultimately adopted, and the onlyone which aroused controversy was a scheme for tramcar lifts, examples of which they had sampled in Cincinnati and Pittsburgh, and which, in their view, would be needed in Halifax for steep gradients such as Beacon Hill Road and Salterhebble Hill. As their colleagues could not accept the principle or the likely cost, the proposal was deferred indefinitely.

CHAPTER 5

OVER THE HILLS AND FAR AWAY

Having successfully launched tramways within the Borough, the Corporation were now at liberty to consider the insistent demands for extensions into the surrounding districts

As early as October, 1897, Warley Urban District Council (U.D.C.) had requested two extensions of Halifax's as yet unbuilt tramways, firstly, from King Cross to the top of Tuel Lane on the Burnley Road, and secondly, from the boundary at Highroad Well to the little village of Warley Town. In a more visionary vein, Greetland U.D.C. recommended a longer line via Salterhebble to West Vale and Jagger Bridge, thereby reviving the interest of their neighbours, Stainland-with-Old Lindley U.D.C. A further extension of the Burnley Road scheme into Luddenden Foot U.D was then called for, and Ald. Booth's home township of Northowram waxed so enthusiastic for tramways and the other fruits of modern civilisation that it voted for incorporation into Halifax, a worthy ambition which it achieved on the same day as Warley, in November 1900.

Initially, Sowerby Bridge U.D.C were less enthusiastic. Reluctant to see Halifax-owned tram tracks embedded in their highways, they dallied with the notion of constructing and operating their own tramways, but when warned by the press of the unhappy fate of a microscopic horse tramway at Shipley near Bradford, they changed their mind and clamoured for early inclusion in Halifax's proposals, a reaction which, correspondents said, was to be expected from "a council where unanimity is hardly ever a strong point"!

Faced with such heavy demands on their services, Halifax refused to include in any of its Parliamentary Bills any tramway which could not be constructed within the statutory 5 years time limit, but even so, some projects had to be repeated in more than one Bill, while others never materialised at all. The press warned against unrealistic requests, forecasting that there might be "applications to continue round to Buckstones and Nont Sarah's or even Hardcastle Crags", all of which were rural retreats far from human habitation.

Fortunately, Halifax Corporation enjoyed friendly relations with most of their neighbours, a happy state of affairs by no means universal in the West Riding, and were therefore favourably disposed towards tramway expansion, although the West Vale project had to be deferred because of the difficulty in finding a safe route from the existing Salterhebble tram terminus into the valley below.

The first moves were made in May, 1899, when the Tramways Committee agreed to lay the Burnley Road line as far as the existing boundary, and to extend it to Tuel Lane as soon as parliamentary powers could be procured. Further west, Luddenden Foot renewed their blandishments; Mytholmroyd began to take an interest, and even distant Hebden Bridge U.D.C cautiously agreed to discuss the question after a little prompting from Halifax, who considered that the scheme would be incomplete without them.

The outcome was the Halifax Corporation Act, 1900, which empowered the Council to lay tramways to Stainland (with a branch from Exley to serve Elland, Elland Wood Bottom and Brighouse), Siddal, Hebden Bridge, Bolton Brow Top, Southowram and Causeway Foot (with a branch from Lee Bank Top via Wheatley Lane to Ramsden Street, Wheatley), as well as a few connecting lines within the borough, including Parkinson Lane where 300 yards of concrete foundation had already been laid (it was never used) and Stump Cross.

Much patient discussion and negotiation had been needed, and the Tramways Committee had sallied forth on many occasions in a horse-drawn waggonette to view the intended routes; predictably, these excursions were usually misinterpreted by Halifax residents who were heard to say "Hello – off they go again on another picnic at the ratepayers' expense!"

Hebden Bridge U.D.C., not having initiated the tramway proposals for their area, felt free to lay down conditions, insisting on their right to purchase their section of line after the lapse of 21 years, but when Halifax stoutly declined to entertain any such limitations, the U.D.C. agreed to the laying of a Halifax– owned line through their district to its farthest boundary at Whiteley Arches, Calderside, where the Lancashire and Yorkshire railway crossed over the Todmorden road.

Next, Brighouse Corporation pointed out that the proposed route into their borough by way of Elland Wood Bottom was not only circuitous but also sparsely populated, and suggested an alternative and much more profitable line via Stump Cross, Hipperholme and Hove Edge and thence via Laverock Lane, Garden Road and Bonegate Road, to which Halifax agreed.

However, serious doubts were raised as to the ability of the trams to struggle over the formidable hill between Halifax and Stump Cross. True, the hill's gradients had been mightily improved since Daniel Defoe had condemned it as "exceeding troublesome and dangerous" – the turnpike commissioners had carved out a deep cutting known as New Bank and Godley Road on the Halifax flank of the precipice and Godley Lane on the Shibden slope, — but even so, New Bank incorporated a formidable 1 in 9.8 gradient which many considered too steep for trams. Reassuringly, Mr. Spencer and the Borough Engineer declared it to be perfectly safe, the only doubt being whether the existing 25 h.p. motors would be adequate for the purpose, for which reason the matter was deferred until an equally precipitous extension of the Boothtown route had been tried.

Construction work then began, firstly within the Borough and the areas about to be added to it. The Illingworth route was extended around the sharply-curved ascent of Wrigley Hill and on to the enclosed moorlands, heading northwards, thereby enabling a tram service as far as Ratten Clough to open on August 30th, 1900, and reaching its final destination at the Causeway Foot Inn on September 21st. This was a bold venture, as few habitations were to be seen, and the only substantial source of income that could be expected would stem from holidaymakers seeking fresh air at Ogden Moor and its scenic reservoirs, but as Ald. Booth viewed the latter as "the seaside of Halifax" or "our local Lake District", the economics of the line were not in doubt.

Nevertheless, the initial half-hour frequency before midday and quarter-hourly thereafter was sustainable only in summer, and with the advent of winter it was reduced to a basic service of one car every 40 minutes with a 20 minutes shortworking frequency as far as Illingworth (Raw Lane) and a 10 minutes service to densely-populated Lee Bank Top. Even this proved to be too generous, and from November, 1900, no cars ran beyond Bradshaw except on Sundays (afternoon and early evening). Eventually the Causeway Foot service settled down into a regular pattern, with a 15 minutes service in summer and three daily cars in winter, although the track as far as Ratten Clough was in more regular use by works trams serving the Bradshaw Stone Depot, a quarry site approached via a spur across the fields, where stone was quarried and dressed into setts.

When the Tuel Lane route opened in December, 1900, it was served by trams such as no. 55, seen here at King Cross in original condition, without lifeguard gate, municipal title or coat of arms. Note the large arc lamp suspended from the tram standard (right) as well as the gas lamp surmounting the fountain.

[Courtesy Roy Brook]

Wrigley Hill, Illingworth, with a Halifax–bound tramcar (no. 50?) approaching Illingworth Corner, a sharp curve on a falling gradient.

[Courtesy National Tramway Museum]

This experience instilled a slightly more cautious outlook into the Tramways Committee's policies. Having allowed poles to be erected along the previously agreed branch to Wheatley, the Committee realised that the income from the line would probably be as little as £1-18-11d per day, and the scheme was formally abandoned in August, 1904.

No such caution was needed on the long Burnley Road section along the populous Calder Valley, where the tram service was extended from King Cross to Cote Hill on August 30th, 1900, and to the newly-extended Borough boundary at Tuel Lane on December 18th. Gratifyingly, the initial half-hourly frequency proved inadequate, and a 10-minutes service from Old Station commenced at 2-5 p.m. on December 22nd.

Proudly surveying the rapid enlargement of his empire, Ald. Booth jocularly warned the Chairman of London County Council that he would be well advised to visit Halifax at an early date, because at the current rate of tramway expansion it would be only four or five years before Halifax reached London!

Throughout the winter the "navvies" continued to toil towards Luddenden Foot, much thought being given to the quality of the new paving. As the Tees Brick Co. scoria blocks used between King Cross and Tuel Lane had been condemned as slippery by local residents, granite setts were used thereafter. Messrs. Longbotham and Son, of Luddenden Foot, warned that if the tracklaying works continued to impede their horse-drawn omnibuses, they would discontinue the service and claim compensation, whereupon Halifax Corporation prudently arranged for the West Riding Constabulary to control traffic outside the Borough until the work was complete.

In the meanwhile, another tramway scheme was being formulated in the manufacturing village of Queensbury, a few miles north of Halifax, where Queensbury U.D.C. and its neighbours in Clayton had obtained a Parliamentary Act enabling them to extend the 4 foot gauge Bradford electric tramways through their districts to the then Queensbury/Northowram boundary at Stocks Gate, Catherine Slack. Halifax were cordially invited to extend their Boothtown route to meet the new line, but this they refused to do, as the gauge difference would have entailed a change of car at Stocks Gate, and it was not sensible to construct a route extension which would depend on someone else's tram service for its profitability.

With some reluctance, Queensbury agreed to transfer its powers to Halifax and Bradford Corporations, on the sensible proviso that the two systems should meet in the centre of the village, but disagreements rumbled on. Bradford's trams, having climbed 4½ weary miles out of their city centre, sought a terminus on level ground outside

Queensbury Parish Church, whilst Halifax, determined not be barred from the centre of affairs, insisted on the right to overlap the Bradford tracks as far as the "Granby Inn", about 50 yards north of the church, or even further, to the "Stag's Head", opposite Messrs John Foster's famous Black Dyke Mills, which would have necessitated a quarter of a mile of mixed-gauge track and delays to both operators. Ultimately common sense prevailed: Halifax's tramway was to terminate at Foster Street, between the church and the "Granby", at an altitude of 1,139 feet above sea level, whilst the Bradford tracks were to overlap by a few feet at an oblique angle and a slightly lower altitude – a mere 1,137 feet!

Having actually inspected the terrain on foot, the Halifax Borough Engineer felt obliged to warn his Queensbury counterpart that awkward, winding Priestley Hill would have to be expensively straightened, widened and regraded before it could be negotiated by trams, but faced with protests from Queensbury, he agreed to forego the straightening of the S-bend, whereupon the track extension from Boothtown was put in hand.

As originally laid, the Boothtown track had terminated at the pre-1900 borough boundary at the "Punch Bowl", obviously in anticipation of the Queensbury connection, but no service car had ever run further than about 200 feet north of Claremount Road, and puzzled residents were informed that the disused rails existed solely for "experimental purposes". The new extension consisted of a single line with a few loops, temporarily terminating at the new Halifax/Queensbury boundary at Stocks Gate, a particularly exposed and mountainous location.

Indeed, the Stocks Gate line must have ranked among the most awe-inspiring tramways in Britain. Although the Boothtown trams had already ascended a few hundred feet by the time that they reached Claremount Road, a much stiffer challenge faced them when they ventured on to the new extension. There the real climb began, culminating in a 1 in 9.7 struggle up to the point where the road became a mere ledge on a mountainous hillside which towered above the trams on one side, and on the other fell precipitously down to Ovenden and Holmfield far below. Not until the road turned inland as it neared Stocks Gate could tramcar passengers feel confident of reaching their destination. No wonder that when the Board of Trade officials inspected the line, they promptly imposed a 4 mph speed limit between Boothtown and the "Punch Bowl" and 6 mph beyond. Stopping-places were provided at the "Punch Bowl" and at Howcans, Collier Topping, Crow Point and Pleasant View, but there were few passengers to board or alight at those exposed heights.

A half-hourly service was inaugurated on December 22nd 1900, with a 15-minute service after midday, and within a month the trams were able to continue to a new railhead at the "Cavendish Inn", near the top of Priestley Hill. Finally, on Thursday, April 25th, 1901, the whole of the Queensbury tramway was ready for its ceremonial opening, to the delight of the villagers who were at last released from their hilltop isolation.

Riding in a convoy of three tramcars, the Halifax contingent met their Queensbury counterparts at the boundary, where the controls of the leading car were handed over to Col. H.A. Foster, chairman of Queensbury U.D.C. and also of Black Dyke Mills, who had skilfully conducted the negotiations between the three local authorities. Flags were flying from houses along the route, and the residents of Catherine Slack and Ambler Thorn lined the roadside. Finally arriving at Queensbury, the gleaming trams were loudly cheered by a crowd estimated at more than 4,000 people, who warmly applauded Ald. Booth's invitation to use the trams to visit Halifax, especially as the long-talked of service from Bradford had not yet materialised. After further speeches and the singing of the National Anthem, the ceremony drew to a close, only to be repeated in an appropriately different guise when the first Bradford tram arrived on August 2nd.

To be fair to both parties, the Halifax line was a quickly-laid single track with only five passing-places ("loops"), whereas the equally long Bradford extension was double track throughout. And, in addition, there may have been a little friendly family rivalry, as the Bradford tramways manager, Mr. Christopher John Spencer, was the eldest son of Halifax's own manager, Mr. Fred Spencer!

The regular passenger service from Halifax commenced at 5 p.m. on the day of the official opening, thereby enabling two venerable Queensbury residents to revisit the scenes of their youth. George Bairstow (91) and Elijah Cockcroft (82) took the tram into Halifax and strolled around the busy Borough Market.

Uncertain as to whether the adoption of the 3'6" gauge on the Halifax section of the line within Queensbury (in place of the originally specified 4 foot dimension) had been properly sanctioned by Parliament, the Board of Trade inspector approved it nevertheless, but cautiously imposed a maximum speed restriction of 8 mph., with a 4 mph limit at four locations, including the awkward descent of Priestley Hill and the long curve at Ford.

Subsequent speed relaxations allowed a half-hourly service to be provided beyond Boothtown, although until Queensbury folk acquired the habit of using the trams on a regular basis, this proved to be over-generous, and was superseded by an hourly service until 2.30 pm, followed by a half-hourly frequency until the departure of the last car at 10 pm from Halifax (10.30 pm on Saturdays).

The town terminus was in Union Street, where families frequently foregathered to experience the spectacular "trip" up the long gradient with the tramcar floor tilted skywards, followed by the undulating panoramas of Ambler Thorn, Windy Bank and Shibden Head, with the square bulk of Queensbury church tower continually disappearing and reappearing in the distance. The press shared the popular enthusiasm, comparing former years, when few people ventured by railway to Queensbury because its station was "in a dreary wilderness", with the modern, progressive era. "There is hardly a finer ride than the one to Queensbury", they proclaimed. "We shall be surprised if the village is not mildly besieged by trippers this year!"

The prediction was soon fulfilled, although not all the "trippers" received a hearty welcome, as the press duly recorded:-

> "On August 8th (1901) a gentleman on the top deck of a Queensbury tram was carrying a box containing about a dozen snakes. The novelty of a tramway journey obviously excited the reptiles' curiosity, and two of them slid stealthily onto the floor. They were soon missed, and when their owner reclaimed one about a yard long and put it in his pocket, much consternation was aroused, especially as he admitted that one was still missing. Much agitation and tucking up of dresses ensued. The snake was not recovered."

Meanwhile, back in Halifax, the authorised connecting link between Mile Cross and King Cross, by way of Spring Hall Lane and Warley Road, had been completed and inspected on August 29th 1900, but not opened for traffic until January 12th 1901, because of a lack of rolling stock. Twenty-six additional trams had been ordered a year previously, but as manufacturers were overwhelmed with orders from all parts of the country, it was November before the first was delivered; however, by mid–December a total of 33 trams was available for service, with 12 more nearing completion.

The Warley Road line was worked as a circular route in both directions, to and from Cow Green via Pellon, Mile Cross and King Cross on a half hourly basis, with intermediate cars to Pellon (Barracks) only. Disappointingly, the circular service proved so erratic and ill-patronised that it had to cease on January 21st, when the original service to Pellon was resumed. The Warley Road section lay fallow until June, when an experimental service was commenced from the Post Office to Warley Road (Hopwood Lane) via King Cross, but this too had to be withdrawn on June 30th.

Greater success was achieved by a variation of the Old Station to Highroad Well service, where, on reaching Mile Cross, cars worked alternately to Highroad Well terminus and to Parkinson Lane top, West End, via a new curve from Gibbet Street into Spring Hall Lane. Adjustments were made to the Pellon service also; the outer terminus was moved from the Barracks to the Cricket Ground entrance in Spring Hall Lane, being then re-extended to the Barracks before being cut back to Albert Road in July, 1908 and re-established at the Barracks at a later date. From 1901 the town terminus was at the Grand Junction Hotel, near the bottom of Pellon Lane, instead of in Cow Green as previously.

The continued search for perfect paving ultimately led to standardisation with granite setts bought from the Threlkeld Quarries near Penrith, suitably grouted with tar from the Corporation Gasworks. These and similar materials were stored at the Stannary Permanent Way Yard to which a 2 furlong single line had been laid in St James' Road from Cow Green. The tracks had already been in use a year before they were inspected in September, 1902, by B.O.T. officials who solemnly imposed an 8 m.p.h. speed limit, even though no passenger cars were to travel over them. Tram rails were also stored for a while in a yard at North Dean, leased from the Halifax Co-op., although material for the long Burnley Road route was delivered by the railways direct to a temporary local store.

A four-wheel permanent way truck was ordered from Mr John Hird of Iona Street, Boothtown, and delivered in August, 1900. A repeat order soon followed, and by April,

1901, both cars were in use on routes under construction, having been motorised and designed to carry the equivalent of 6 horse-cart loads of material or a gang of workmen. One of them had its brief hour of glory in June when, with carpeted floor and sides covered in red baize, it transported 65 Sunday scholars " packed like herrings in a barrel" on an outing to Causeway Foot, but as the episode was deemed "unseemly", it was not repeated. An unmotorised trailer truck completed the works fleet, and all three were available for salting and gritting the tramways in winter. Determined to prevent snowfalls from disrupting the services, the Department bought 41 snowploughs at £1 each from Mr Hird for attachment to passenger trams when needed.

Then, in anticipation of better weather, a water cart was acquired from Mr Joshua Ellis of Shaw Syke for the purpose of "slecking th' dust", i.e. moistening the dry, dusty limestone surfaces of highways which were not fully paved. Wet weather brought its own problems in the form of water which ran down the rail grooves, and track drains had to be provided at regular intervals to divert the flow into street drains, or, by permission of landowners, into adjacent fields. In this way, for example, Fred Barker of Catherine Slack and Messrs. Riley of Ewood Hall were paid two shillings per drainpipe per annum for the privilege of allowing the discharge of water into their fields at Boothtown and Brearley respectively, with catchpits to trap salt and silt.

Having bestowed so much care and forethought upon their tramways, the Corporation little expected that their best endeavours would sometimes be jeopardised by age-old household habits. In June, 1900, Halifax housewives had to be warned against throwing used soapy water ("slops") on to the streets and tramlines, as the discarded lubricant was causing the trams to lose their grip on the tracks.

The success of the Boothtown tramway had reassured the Corporation that their trams could ascend and descend steep gradients with ease, and in the spring of 1900 they began laying tracks up New Bank, over the summit and then downhill between the 60 foot towering stone sides of Godley Cutting and the trees of historic Shibden Park, coming to rest at Stump Cross where the waters from Shibden Valley hurried down to Sunny Vale and the River Calder at Brookfoot. The "terminal station" was located at tram pole no. 43, Staups Lane.

Intent on guaranteeing the line's safety, the Committee decided against providing any tram stops on the ascent of New Bank between North Bridge and Prospect Place. The Board of Trade approved this cautious approach, and recommended maximum speeds of 4 mph on the descent of New Bank and 6 mph on the Godley Lane descent, with compulsory halts for downward cars at Prospect Place and the bottom of Haley Hill where the tracks from Boothtown joined in. The efficiency of tramcar brakes was demonstrated during the trial run on June 5th, 1900, when the tram was brought to a standstill within 56 feet. The opening of the public service was delayed by the construction of an overbridge spanning the Cutting, and regular workings did not begin until June 27th. During the ensuing holiday season, all the tram services were in great demand for family excursions; on July 21st an extra car provided a shuttle service between North Bridge and Shibden Park entrance, and on the occasion of an Exhibition and Carnival on August 11th, three special cars ran from the

Post Office to a point near the Halifax Cricket and Football field (Thrum Hall) at a penny fare.

The inclusion of Northowram into the Borough enabled the Tramways Department to extend the New Bank tramway a further 150 yards to the old Stump Cross Inn near the junction of the roads to Hipperholme and Shelf; trams began to use the new terminus on January 28th, 1901, at a quarter-hourly frequency.

Six days earlier, Queen Victoria had passed away peacefully at the end of a long and eventful reign, and as a mark of respect on the day of her funeral, Saturday, February 2nd, the tram services did not begin until 9 a.m. With the advent of a new and glittering reign, the pace of life quickened. Already, the rails for the extension from Stump Cross to Northowram and Shelf were being deposited on site, and by mid-April the tracks were ready for use as far as the "Stocks' Arms" near the Northowram/Shelf boundary, to the delight and curiosity of Halifax folk, who, according to the press, "never visit that spot owing to its inaccessibility, unless they are forced to do so!"

Seven miles westward, other "navvies" had also completed tracklaying operations as far as Luddenden Foot Congregational Chapel, and Major Druitt carried out his formal inspection on the warm spring morning of April 25th, 1901. With a shrewd eye for business, the Tramways Department immediately opened the line for public service, and after lunch drove out triumphantly in a specially-prepared tramcar, halting at Tuel Lane where the controls were courteously handed over to the chairman of Luddenden Foot U.D.C. (Coun. Greenwood). Charmed by the novel experience, the "Halifax Guardian" reporter who was riding on the car wrote lyrically that, "the scenery en route was so delightful and the air so pure and dry as to almost convince one that we were in the middle of summer". Local children displayed similar enthusiasm; having been allowed a day's holiday, they happily cheered the tram on its way.

On its return journey, the official car met other trams making their way out along the valley, each one fully laden with holidaymakers escaping from the town to enjoy the pleasant, ever-changing panorama of high hills, distant upland habitations, densely overhanging trees, small stone-built towns, mills large and small, imposing chapels and council offices, the winding Calder, the placid canal and impatient railway trains - smoke as well as the song of birds and the country air.

To the discomfiture of the official party, the trolley mischievously sprang from the overhead wire as their tram trundled through Cow Green, striking a bracket arm and bending itself beyond further use. Complete with bunting and potted plants, the car had to be propelled by a Skircoat Green car along to the depot, where a spare vehicle was hastily decked out to allow the civic party to resume their interrupted journey. Off they went, up and down the switchback line to Stump Cross where Alderman Wallace, lately chairman of the now defunct Northowram U.D.C., was invited to take over the controls, which he obligingly did, "making a splendid run" up the long, curving hill and arriving in fine style at the "Stocks Arms", Northowram, where the waiting crowds were treated to congratulatory speeches. A half-hourly service from Union Street began at 3 p.m.

The officials revisited the area on Monday, July 1st, this time to open the final section of the line, from Northowram to Shelf, following an inspection by Major Druitt in the morning. When the Committee's special trams arrived at the "Stocks Arms" in the evening they were joined by enthusiastic villagers as well as the newly-formed Northowram Subscription Band. The latter were assigned to the upper deck of one of the trams, from which vantage point they played lively music as the car rolled majestically over the elevated plateau – the 'shelf' which gave the village its name – leaving the more agile members of the public to clamber "in high glee" on to every available foothold.

Safely arrived at the new terminus outside the gates of Shelf Hall Park, they doubtless espied the hourly Bradford & Shelf company steam tram which had been serving the village since 1886 and which, if Ald. Booth's plans had been heeded, would have provided the first tram service into Halifax eight years previously. Well pleased that the gleaming new electric vehicle on which he was now riding was in every way superior to the hissing, steamy vision whose ungainliness his colleagues had criticised when choosing their own original tramcars, Ald. Booth declared that riding on the top deck of a Halifax tram was better and cheaper than a bottle of medicine. Then, assuring the villagers that the day's events marked the beginning of prosperity in Shelf, "he joined his colleagues in a substantial tea at the 'Shoulder of Mutton'". The public service began the same evening.

In an attempt to minimise the inconvenience caused by the gauge difference at Shelf terminus, the Halifax track construction gangs had laid their rails as close as possible to the end of the Bradford track – too close for comfort, perhaps, and in August five yards (15 feet) of rail were removed to prevent physical contact between the old and new modes of transport. A different form of contact was achieved two years later when electric trams superseded the steam cars, as the new Bradford overhead wires were anchored end-on to the Halifax wires although electrically insulated from them.

At the opposite side of the valley carved out by the Shibden Beck and reached by a long, arduous ascent across the flank of Beacon Hill lay the village of Southowram, famed for the high quality of the sandstone hewn from its vast quarries. Although anxious to enjoy the benefits of a tram service, the local council had been observing with keen interest the attempts of neighbouring Elland UDC to wrest concessions from Halifax Tramways Committee, but when these came to naught, Southowram UDC concluded that nothing was to be gained by delay, and reached agreement with Halifax for a tramway which would terminate at Towngate in the village centre.

Considerable roadworks were necessary, however, and although in April, 1900, the Tramways Department agreed to lay tramway foundations at Bank Top, they deferred the installation of the rails until the highway improvements were complete. Not until the Shelf tramway was finished did the track gangs set to work at the bottom of Beacon Hill Road (i.e., the junction with New Bank), but by August, 1901, Macartney, McElroy tram poles and overhead wires were in place. In the meanwhile, having viewed the extreme narrowness of the lanes in the village itself, the Tramways Committee had decided to terminate the route at Bank Top, within the portion of Southowram previously absorbed into the Borough, the precise location being opposite the "Cock and Bottle" and the schoolroom, 15 yards north-west of the end of Higgin Lane and 1 mile 1 furlong 12 chains from New Bank junction.

"The opening of the tramway to Southowram yesterday was hailed with more enthusiasm than has been evinced in any other district", claimed the press on September 20th. "No one can be surprised at this. Hitherto the journey has been a formidable undertaking. Tell any friend you had business to transact on the hill top, and he would gaze at you pitifully. Now all that has changed. The journey can now be performed in a most comfortable condition – in fact, in fine weather a visit to Southowram will be a positive pleasure, for an unrivalled view of the borough can be obtained from the tram route."

The formal opening ceremony was performed by Southowram ward councillor Wadsworth, who entertained the Tramways Committee and the U.D.C. members to tea in honour of the event and of his birthday, in return for which he was allowed to drive the first tram – a fine birthday present indeed. On his safe arrival at Bank Top the local subscription band hailed him with the genial strains of "A Fine Old English Gentleman", as well as "Auld Lang Syne" in anticipation of his forthcoming victory at the November elections. Three waiting trams were then filled with schoolchildren who enjoyed a free ride through the generosity of their elders, after which a half-hourly service

Bystanders, passenger and conductor seem happy to be photographed with car 42 as it rests at Southowram terminus ("Cock and Bottle" Hotel) before making the steady, winding descent to the town terminus in Broad Street, c. 1905.

[J.A. Pitts collection, courtesy West Yorkshire Archives, Bradford]

was begun from a town terminus at Broad Street, at a penny fare. Official "tram stations" were marked out at various places on the steep incline, but they saw little use, as there were few habitations between New Bank and Bank Top.

When inspecting the new installations the Board of Trade representative warned the Corporation that tramcars serving the route must be equipped with the Spencer/Whiteley patent anti-runback trailing wheel-scotches, even though only twenty cars out of a fleet of seventy were thus fitted. The matter was considered so important that a year later a Board of Trade inspector revisited Halifax in order to observe the brake in action, but having done so, he expressed disappointment that the device was not as efficient as had been claimed, and no further trams were so equipped.

The absence of human habitation on the higher reaches of Beacon Hill Road gave rise to a new phenomenon best observed at night from the platforms of the Old Station far below – the famous "tramcar in the sky", an illusion created by the brightly-lit Southowram tramcar as it climbed steadily against a background of almost unbroken blackness. Some years later a discerning comment by the Dean of Manchester that "a lighted tramcar is a very beautiful thing", drew a response from the Halifax press that the Dean "cannot know the full beauty of such a sight unless he visits Halifax. Then, if he lifts up his eyes unto the hills he will behold wondrous sights… the most beautiful nocturnal spectacle in the area – a tramcar radiant with light gliding along invisible and seemingly impossible heights".

A somewhat more visionary south-country visitor who once arrived after nightfall excitedly told his Halifax host that he had just espied the planet Venus glowing with unusual brightness in the heavens. Glancing casually in the direction indicated, his host replied deflatingly, "Nay, lad, it's nobbut th' gas lamps i' Beacon Hill Road!"

CHAPTER 6

VALLEY VENTURES AND COURTING COUPLES

Pressing onwards along the Calder Valley, the trams reached Brearley on July 2nd, 1901, and the small but busy woollen-manufacturing town of Mytholmroyd on September 7th, but the planned extension of the line as far as Hebden Bridge and Whiteley Arches came to a standstill when it was found that Halifax had not supplied Hebden Bridge U.D.C. with detailed plans of the tramway to be laid in their main street, and the U.D.C. had not troubled to ask for any.

It had been agreed that as soon as the track gangs had completed their labours at Queensbury, they would transfer their plant, implements and skills to the Mytholmroyd extension, and on that assumption, other necessary preparations had begun. The through fare was to be 6d., with 1d stages at King Cross, Tuel Lane, Luddenden Foot (Board School), Brearley, Mytholmroyd (Board School), Hebden Bridge and Whiteley Arches. The Tramways Committee had accepted that the existing method of fare collection by means of the farebox would be unsuitable for such a lengthy route, as the system depended upon every passenger dropping a penny into the box every time the tram passed a fare stage, and to repeat this procedure up to six times per journey would have been resented by the passengers. Also, the vast quantity of pennies already being accumulated every day was proving problematical, as the banks were refusing to handle them. The Bell Punch system with tickets representing different fare values was therefore adopted for the route. Also, the erection of the tramway poles was to be accelerated by the purchase of a small petrol-engined "lurry" in place of the leisurely horse-drawn carts used hitherto.

It was, in fact, the arrival of the "lurry" and the erection of the first few poles in their area that had alerted Hebden Bridge U.D.C. to the possibility that an important local custom was under threat. The section of Burnley Road which lay within their area was mostly rural, with few habitations. Consequently, only one causeway had been laid, on the north side of the highway, and in fine weather the causeway was constantly used by young 'courting couples' as well as their elders for the purpose of "promenading" i.e, strolling and socialising. The intrusion of tram poles on to a path no more than 6 feet wide would clearly hamper this hallowed practice, and something had to be done to protect couples with 'stars in their eyes' from seeing stars of a different kind.

Hebden Bridge therefore requested that the poles be placed on the opposite side of the road, alongside the wooden telegraph posts which carried the trunk telephone wires along the valley, and which, in the absence of a causeway, stood in the carriageway adjacent to the wall. However, having already agreed the siting of the poles with the West Riding County Council who were the actual highway authority, Halifax were reluctant to make any changes, especially as they had already been castigated by the Board of Trade for having placed a few poles in Mytholmroyd's carriageways. As neither side would give way, construction work had to cease, although at the urgent request of the local Tradesmen's Association, the Tramways Dept. attached overhead wires to the poles already planted, thereby allowing a tram service to open to a point a few yards beyond Fallingroyd Bridge, three-quarters of a mile short of Hebden Bridge, on December 2nd 1901, with a half hourly frequency from Cow Green until 7-10 pm, and thereafter from Old Station.

Invited to act as arbitrator, Major Druitt ruled in favour of Halifax. Work therefore resumed in mid-February 1902, and on March 13th the first trial tramcar rumbled along to the new terminus at the end of Crown Street, Hebden Bridge, followed next day by a tram bearing Coun. Hey who marked out the new stopping-places and ordered the trimming of overhanging trees.

The rural nature of much of the Hebden Bridge route is well portrayed by this view of Mayroyd, between Fallingroyd Bridge and Station Road, about 1910. The causeway (pavement) on the right is occupied by Halifax's tram poles as well as Hebden Bridge's gaslamps, to the inconvenience of "promenaders" and courting couples, while the telegraph posts have to content themselves with the grass verge and the hedgerow.
[Copyright: the Alice Longstaff Gallery Collection, Hebden Bridge]

Unfortunately, the longed-for facility could not be fully operated at first, because there was insufficient electricity. A year earlier, aware that Hebden Bridge was almost 8 miles from the Halifax generating station, Halifax had bought a plot of land on the Garden Square estate with the intention of building an electricity sub-station fed from Halifax via a 3-phase 5,500 volt a.c. supply. Work had began in April, 1901, but had halted while the highways dispute was being resolved; even then, Hebden Bridge stubbornly insisted that as (in their view) Halifax had not acquired a right to construct the substation within their district, the Corporation ought to supply them with domestic electricity at a reduced rate! Anxious to make progress, Halifax humbly sought specific permission (which was probably implicit in their Tramways Acts) to connect the sub-station with the tramway by means of a cable to be laid beneath Old Gate, to which the U.D.C. did not consent until March 26th.

In the meanwhile, Major Druitt had already inspected the line, travelling in a special car which left Halifax at midday on Thursday, March 20th, and granting unconditional approval. Ominously, no member of Hebden Bridge U.D.C. accepted an invitation to be present, but nevertheless the public service was inaugurated on the following morning with the 8-15 departure from Cow Green. Until the cable was connected up on May 3rd, the severe voltage drop prevented more than one tram from venturing beyond Mytholmroyd at any given time, but thereafter a full 550 volt d.c. supply was available for a regular service along the whole route ,with extra cars to Tuel Lane and Luddenden Foot as well as an early-morning car from Luddenden Foot to Tuel Lane for the benefit of workers employed at nearby Sowerby Bridge.

There were minor teething-troubles and excitements, of course, particularly in the Mytholmroyd area, where fire station alarm bells began to ring spasmodically for no apparent reason, the fault being traced to passing trams whose trolleys were pushing the trolley wire upwards to make contact with the telephone wires. On one occasion the local council's surveyor witnessed an instance of damage caused to a Council building by a fast moving horse-drawn cart. Being an enterprising man, he commandeered a passing tramcar for a thrilling chase as far as Brearley, where the miscreant was overtaken and apprehended. Equally unfortunate was a flock of sheep bought at Manchester and being led homewards after nightfall by their purchaser, Mr Helliwell of Mytholmroyd. In the absence of street lamps or "tail" lights, the sheep were struck by an approaching tram, killing two and injuring two others. More prosaically, densely-overhanging trees at Fallingroyd Bridge had to be trimmed, as their branches were brushing against the heads of upper-deck passengers.

The new tramway also provided opportunities for activities of other kinds, one of which aroused the wrath and indignation of Halifax Corporation. An anonymous contributor to the 'Halifax Comet' had mischievously observed that,

> "Somebody wants to know what the tram inspector saw, who travelled by train down Hebden Bridge way and then boarded a tramcar which had been drawn up at a quiet part of the road with the lights switched off. If early departures from country terminals, refusal to stop on signals and shouts from intending passengers, and furious driving to permit spare time en route are not now accounted for in the case of certain men, what will the public think of the state of discipline in a concern where the men are audacious enough to stop the trams along main roads for disorderly purposes?"

Outraged civic pride demanded a public apology, which although eventually given was not formally accepted until seven months later, in the full panoply of a Council meeting.

But what had the tram inspector seen, and what form of disorderliness had allegedly occurred? Was it amorous, or a case of sheer necessity? If the latter, it no doubt lent urgency to the Tramways Committee's earlier decision to provide or arrange for strategically-placed urinals for use by drivers and conductors during their 9-hour working day. After negotiation, these invaluable facilities were located at Luddenden Foot (Dugdale's grocery shop),Mytholmroyd (blacksmith's forge, Bridge End), Highroad Well (Mr. Baines'), Pellon (Mile Cross tram depot), Causeway Foot (Mr. Priestley's), Queensbury (Mr Longbottom's, Foster Street), Stump Cross ('The Driver' tavern – presumably the conductors were admitted also!), Northowram (Mr Ed. Brearley, The Square), Shelf Hall Lodge and in the George Street office cellars.

Thereafter, tramway schedules returned to their customary clockwork precision, except when Sunday School processions and other public celebrations hindered their progress. Lesser beings made their mark also. On August 12th, 1904, the Hebden Bridge service was seriously disrupted by a traction engine making its ponderous way home to Blackburn, while

Far from home — tramcar 73 rests at Hebden Bridge terminus prior to the hour-long return journey to Cow Green. The tram track (bottom of picture) terminated at the junction of New Road (foreground) and Holme Street. The imposing building in Crown Street (left) was owned by the Manchester and Liverpool District Banking Co., Ltd. The neatly-dressed ladies (blouses, long skirts, elegant hats and a shawl) are enjoying the summer weather, but the gentlemen, in serge suits, waistcoats and hats, are impervious to the heat.

[Courtesy Roy Brook]

32

on January 24th, 1908, no fewer than 165 cows ambling through Halifax town centre spread disruption far and wide. Nature also intervened occasionally. A severe drought in September, 1901, depleted the Corporation's water supplies so drastically that the washing of trams and other vehicles had to be prohibited, and electricity supplies were in jeopardy until autumn rains returned.

Other causes of delay were the long stretches of single line on the out-of-town routes, on which meticulous timekeeping was needed if unwelcome waits at passing-loops were to be avoided. Sometimes the dilemma was overcome by the laying of extra loops such as in Burnley Road (Warley Wood Lane) or Beacon Hill Road (Old Bank), but a much cheaper and more flexible remedy had been developed by Mr Spencer's other son on the Bradford tramways, in the form of automatic light signals actuated by tramcar trolleys when entering and leaving loops. Following an inspection of the new devices by Ald Booth and Mr. Fred Spencer, a trial set of semaphore signals was installed on the Causeway Foot route between Lee Bridge and Bank Top, with such an encouraging improvement in timekeeping that a dozen similar sets were erected in the congested Northgate area of the town centre.

By this time, hardly any of the original tramcar motors supplied by the Electric Construction Co. were still in use. As early as April, 1900, two of them had been returned to their makers, and in August, 1901, it was noted that out of a total of 169 motors owned by the Tramways Dept., 3 ECC motors were now being used in the Works; 14 had been written off, and only 2 were considered of any value. They were replaced by reliable Westinghouse units.

In August, 1901, the Department took delivery of 12 additional trams from the Brush company. Slightly more modern than the earlier Milnes cars, with neat, oblong side windows surmounted by etched-glass quarter-light ventilators, and flat panelled ceilings in the saloon in place of the tongued-and-grooved arched ceilings used in the older cars, they nevertheless retained the obsolescent upper-deck "short canopy" design which limited the overall seating capacity to a modest total of 46. This time the trucks were of the Brush "A" pattern, with Westinghouse controllers and General Electric GE58 motors of 35 h.p. capacity, giving them an advantage on the gradients they were due to encounter. Numbered 59 to 70, they were joined by twelve identical cars, 71 to 82, a year later.

Meanwhile, in the furthest reaches of the Calder Valley the local authorities were hoping for a further extension of the already long Hebden Bridge tramway. In 1899 the tiny Blackshaw Parish Council had invited Halifax to lay a line through their area from the authorised terminus at Whiteley Arches to the Todmorden borough boundary at Sandbed Bridge, a distance of 1,530 yards or seven-eighths of a mile, and Halifax had included the proposal in their 1902 Parliamentary Bill. Blackshaw's parent body, the Todmorden Rural District Council, warmly supported the plan, although in view of the recent events in Hebden Bridge they insisted on

supervision of highway matters and the siting of the tram poles.

These discussions aroused the interest of the Borough of Todmorden, which until its incorporation in 1896 had been equivocally described as "lying half in and half out of the best county in England", as the former Yorkshire/Lancashire county boundary had passed beneath the Town Hall! Plans for municipal tramways from the town centre to Sandbed Bridge (Halifax Road), Station Road (Portsmouth) and the borough boundary near Steanorbottom (Rochdale Road) were unveiled in November, 1901, when, urged on by the West Riding County Council, the borough fathers asked Halifax not to lay any track on Sandbed Bridge "until such time as the Todmorden Tramways are ready for coupling up to the Halifax lines".

Halifax's attitude to these approaches was little more than lukewarm. As early as August, 1901, the Tramways Committee had decided to defer any extension beyond Crown Street, Hebden Bridge, as the town's main street was narrow, congested and unsuitable for trams. Consequently, they were unable to express a view (when asked) as to which of the Whiteley Arches the proposed tramway would pass through, and would not commit themselves to a firm date for the commencement of work. Indeed, on learning that their 1902 Parliamentary Bill would be opposed by the Lancashire and Yorkshire Railway if it included the extension through Blackshaw, they deleted the offending clause altogether.

Within a month, however, Hebden Bridge were enquiring impatiently when the existing Parliamentary powers for the 1,750 yards Whiteley Arches line were going to be exercised, and having received no firm undertaking, promptly complained to the Board of Trade. However, as Parliamentary Acts for tramways authorised promoters to construct them, but did not compel them to do so, no official sanctions were possible. Hebden Bridge Council reacted angrily. "If looks could kill," the press observed, "there would be many widows in Halifax!", so strong was the language used. Venting their frustration by different means, the U.D.C. criticised the existing tram poles, which, they claimed, caused long shadows to be cast across the highway when the gas street lamps were lit. Politely forebearing to question whether the gaslighting was in fact strong enough to give rise to any shadows, Halifax allowed the U.D.C. to mount the street lamps on the tram poles, provided that no holes were bored in them, a privilege also extended to Luddenden Foot, Shelf and Queensbury councils – and, more theoretically, to Blackshaw.

Halifax Corporation's tramway employees were a hardy, resilient breed who were never dismayed or deterred by minor day-to-day challenges. On August 25th, 1901, a brief but violent thunderstorm passed over the district, causing a bolt of lightning to strike a tramcar at Tuel Lane, fuse one of the motors and hurl Driver Langhorn into the road. Dusting himself down, the driver promptly re-mounted the tram and drove it back to Skircoat Road depot with the aid of the remaining motor, not troubling (as he might have done a century later) to seek counselling and compensation!

CHAPTER 7
LETTERS, LIFTS AND LOSSES

The expansion of the tramways created an opportunity for the transportation of non-bulky goods, and in June, 1902, the Tramways Department commenced delivery and collection of parcels. Three parcels offices were opened in the town centre, i.e. in George Street (Pellon, Highroad Well, Savile Park, Skircoat Green, Salterhebble and Hebden Bridge services), Waterhouse Street (Southowram and Causeway Foot services), and Union Street (for Queensbury and Shelf). In the outskirts, parcels agents were appointed from the ranks of local grocers, drapers, florists, paperhangers, confectioners, saddlers, cobblers, postmasters and boat repairers. Mr. James Killingworth of Bradford was appointed overall parcels agent with the responsibility of ensuring that parcels were collected from the offices and transported by tramcar and hand-cart to their destinations, but he encountered financial problems and terminated his contract in 1904.

Thereafter the parcels traffic was handled by the Tramways Department, with the assistance of smartly-uniformed parcels boys. Collection and delivery within half a mile of the central offices was free, and a penny for longer distances, with a fixed scale of charges for conveyance by tramcar:-

I to 3 Fare Stages		Over 3 Fare Stages
Up to12 lb –	1d	2d
12 to 28 lb –	2d	3d
28 to 56 lb –	3d	4d
56 to 112 lb –	4d	6d

Postmen and bags of mail destined for out-of-town post offices had been carried by tram since 1900 at a fee of ¹/₂d per fare stage, and from 1901 letters could be posted on the trams themselves every evening at advertised times. Small letterboxes of the type used in Huddersfield and attached to a hook on the tramcar dashplate, were purchased from Fred Whiteley of Victoria Street, Halifax, at 19s each. The boxes were in use for periods of half an hour on the Pellon, Highroad Well and Southowram routes, one hour on the longer Shelf, Queensbury, Bradshaw, Skircoat Green, King Cross, Savile Park and Salterhebble routes, and two hours on the Mytholmroyd route, the availability being regulated by the length of time taken by the tramcar to complete its return journey.

Milk cans were also carried on the trams from January, 1907, but the maximum distance allowed was three miles, presumably in case the jolting of the cars turned the milk into butter! Charges ranged from 1d (1 to 5 gallons) to 6d (20 to 32 gallons), and returned empties cost 1d each. All goods were placed on the driver's platform.

Man's best friend was not overlooked either: from April, 1908, dogs accompanied by their owners were allowed to travel for 1d per stage.

The rapid expansion of the tramways beyond the compact town network originally envisaged by the Corporation was now beginning to unsettle the Department's finances. Although operating costs had remained stable at about 12¹/₂d per car mile, the income per mile had dropped alarmingly from 16.2d in 1898 to 10.1d in mid-1901, the reason being that although the Highroad Well service was earning a very satisfactory 31.02d per mile, the "better-class" Skircoat Green line inhabited by "carriage folk" was attracting only 8d. Even more disturbingly, it was clear that the track would not last more than ten years, instead of the twenty-year period for which the loans had been raised. Similarly, the trams were so heavily loaded that their bodywork was unlikely to reach its estimated 15-year lifespan.

Ald. Booth therefore recommended that no further route extensions should be undertaken until greater efficiency had been achieved. In the belief that journey times and wear and tear on trams and trackwork could be reduced if some of the single-track and loop sections were replaced by double track, he persuaded the Corporation to promote a new Bill authorising the doubling of 23 sections of line. Surprisingly, in view of the financial situation, the Bill also authorised further tramways expansion:-

1) an extension of the Hebden Bridge tramway to the Todmorden borough boundary,

(2) a moorland route from Pellon to Wainstalls,

(3) further proposals for Sowerby Bridge, and

(4) connections with the railway goods yards at Shaw Syke, North Bridge and Pellon.

Sowerby Bridge U.D.C. enthusiastically renewed their demands, making light of the Corporation's fears for the safety of trams descending and re-ascending the steep gradients between King Cross and the valley below. Not to be rushed into an unwise decision, Halifax adamantly declined to allow their trams to negotiate the relentlessly steep and sharply-curving carriageway between Rochdale Road and the upper reaches of Bolton Brow, preferring to seek the use of a new highway across Major Edwards' parkland at Pye Nest.

Practical preparations began in May, 1902, by which time tramway finances had shown signs of recovery. A new type of anti-runback device was fitted to six trams (evidently from the 61 to 70 series) which were to be set aside for the Sowerby Bridge service. Then, in defiance of protests from the Halifax Ratepayers' Association, the line was thoroughly surveyed and its cost estimated at £11,550. Excavations began on May 24th (two months prior to the Royal Assent to the Bill), and the entire operation, including tracklaying, electrical installations and the construction of substantial embankments in Pye Nest Park, was completed within 110 days, with a trial run to the terminus at Wharf Street (Church Bank), Sowerby Bridge, on September 12th, and Major Druitt's formal inspection on the following day.

Alas, the inspection was no mere formality, as Major Druitt was disturbed by what he saw. While it was true to say that the tramway had been constructed in conformity with the plans submitted to Parliament, the plans had failed to convey a sufficiently vivid impression of the terrain being traversed. As the new highway, Pye Nest Road, had been built solely for tramway purposes, the distance between the kerb and the outer rail was no more than the statutory minimum of eighteen inches (1'6"), and there was no causeway.

In addition, as the road had had to be raised up to a height of 15 feet above ground level in some places, there was a steep embankment with an uninviting aerial view of the fields below. The inspector had no doubt that,

"....any derailment will almost certainly cause the car to go over the precipitous sides of the road, with very disastrous consequences to the occupants."

Without hesitation he forbade the use of the tramway until the road had been widened by six feet on each side, with earth banking, safety barriers at the tram stops and efficient electric lighting mounted on the centre poles between the tracks.

As the borough boundary intersected the new road halfway down its disturbing descent, the cost of the alterations had to be shared between the two local authorities, who unwisely invited Major Druitt back for his final approval before the works were fully completed. This he declined to give, although he allowed the use of the uphill track as a temporary single line, and a convoy of three tramcars performed the inaugural journey on the following day, October 17th, 1902, when suitable refreshments were provided by Coun. Hey, who had succeeded Ald. Booth as Tramways Chairman a year earlier.

Gratifyingly, when the downhill line was brought into use on November 15th, revenue from the Sowerby Bridge trams was soon found to be as high as 14.25d, rising later to 24d (2 shillings) without any abstraction of passengers from the parallel (but much higher-level) Burnley Road route.

Had the interested parties been content with their achievement, all would have been well; instead, Halifax allowed themselves to be persuaded to extend the line to the limits of Sowerby Bridge U.D. at Jerry Lane. Opened on the morning of May 21st, 1903, the extension was an embarrassing failure, with revenues of only 5.46d per car mile. From September 7th no cars ran beyond Station Road, Sowerby Bridge, on weekdays, and on December 3rd the line was closed down, Station Road being the terminus for all cars.

To reach the new terminus, the trams had to turn out of Wharf Street, cross the River Calder and squeeze under the Lancashire and Yorkshire company's low railway bridge before coming to rest on a wide section of road, where the crew could prepare themselves for the return journey. When inspecting this section of route, Major Druitt had insisted that an extra tram pole be planted in the centre of the river bridge, as he had not liked the way in which the overhead live wires had drooped perilously near to his shiny top hat when he rose from his top deck seat.

Better prospects beckoned some six miles eastward at Hipperholme, a pleasant upland area once renowned as "the

garden of Halifax Parish", but now more famous for its busy brick and tile works which lay just below the village on the Brighouse road. Nearby Sunny Vale Gardens, opened in 1880 with 17 acres of pleasure grounds and a lake, were patronised yearly by some 57,000 visitors eager for sedate Edwardian entertainment, refreshments and wholesome fresh air, provided, one assumes, that the wind was not blowing from the dusty east!

Triangle-bound car 62 seen outside Sowerby Bridge Town Hall before crossing County Bridge and squeezing under the railway arch. The tram pole in the foreground was planted at the insistence of Major Druitt.

[Courtesy Roy Brook]

Hipperholme U.D.C. shared with its industrial offspring, the Borough of Brighouse, a keen desire to be served by Halifax trams, and statisticians calculated that as the combined populations of the two districts were 60% higher than those in the Calder Valley area, the profitability would be correspondingly higher – a challengeable forecast, perhaps, as Brighouse folk looked to Huddersfield and Bradford as much as to Halifax. Aware that an extension from Stump Cross to Brighouse via Hipperholme and Hove Edge would cost as least £25,868 and would increase the already large sum paid every year by Halifax into their neighbours' rate funds, the Tramways Committee held back until September, 1902. Then. although they would have preferred to avoid any capital outlay until March, 1903, they nevertheless authorised the Borough Engineer to proceed, on the proviso that he could construct the line as far as Hipperholme within six weeks!

Evidently a sporting man, the Engineer rose to the challenge, and on November 7th 1902, only four weeks after the work began, Major Druitt was able to ride on the trial tramcar to the Hipperholme terminus in Brighouse Road, 53 yards south of the crossroads. The Mayor travelled by a special car from Broad Street and entertained the official party to high tea at the Country House Hotel, and for the rest of the day a tramcar provided free travel between Stump Cross and Hipperholme. The normal public service commenced on Monday, November 10th.

Brushing off determined resistance from the Lancashire and Yorkshire Railway, the trams soon established themselves in the area, and it was not long before Brighouse Corporation were pressing for an extension to Hove Edge, on the outer fringes on their borough.

Plans for tramways in Brighouse had been mooted in 1899, envisaging a circular service via Hipperholme, Lightcliffe and Bailiffe Bridge and drawing power from the Hall Street electricity station. Huddersfield Corporation were interested in providing a link via Rastrick; the British Electric Traction Co. had ambitions for a line from Cleckheaton to Huddersfield via Clifton, Brighouse and Rastrick: Bradford Corporation ardently desired to extend their Wyke tramway into Brighouse via Bailiffe Bridge, but Halifax traders urged their Tramways Committee to be the first in the field - and they were.

This time the work occupied six weeks, and such was the eagerness to ensure that all was ready for the scheduled Board of Trade inspection on June 29th, 1903, that Mr. Spencer took advantage of the long layover time at Hipperholme terminus to take the hourly tramcar for several runs to Hove Edge, blithely disregarding the possibility that the concrete foundations were not yet completely set.

Then, satisfied that the extended service did not require any additional vehicles, he declared the route ready for use, and on the following day (June 30th) the Tramways Committee and Hipperholme U.D.C rode out together to the boundary at Broad Oak, where the Brighouse councillors joined them for the short distance to Hove Edge terminus. At this point the Halifax representatives were persuaded to walk along the remainder of the proposed route into Brighouse town centre, where an enticing meal was provided at the George Hotel. As the return journey to Hove Edge would have necessitated a 1½ mile uphill toil, one assumes that the Halifax contingent retuned home by train!

The Board of Trade inspector had evidently enjoyed his visit to Hove Edge, as he permitted a generous 12mph speed limit in both directions, except at two level crossings in Brighouse Road where quarry tramways intersected the highway; here a 4mph restriction was imposed, as the crossing jolted the tramcars, which, in any event, had to be ready to halt if a mineral train was about to cross. A sub-station at Hipperholme fed by a high-tension cable from Halifax ensured an adequate power supply at all times.

Looking forward to the completion of the project and sensing that they were "pushing at an open door", Brighouse immediately began widening Well Green Lane and Laverock Lane, and pointed out that both Corporations would save a good deal of time and money if the tram tracks were laid at the same time. Indeed, Brighouse were willing to excavate the highways, pay for the road dross, the rolling thereof and the granite setts, leaving Halifax to lay the concrete foundations, the rails and the granite paving between the rails, The bait was swallowed; Yorkshiremen always like a good bargain. Tram poles were duly installed in August and the rails in September, so that the continuation via Bonegate Road and Bradford Road to the terminus at the George Hotel was complete by mid January 1904.

Although Brighouse had volunteered to lay a continuation of the Hipperholme high-tension cable to a further sub-station in their town, Mr Spencer suspected that there might already be sufficient power to allow a lightly-loaded tram to venture to Brighouse and back. The sight of workmen sweeping out the rail grooves on the morning of February 5th alerted the good folk of the town, who waited expectantly until nightfall, when at last a brilliantly-lit tram descended

Bonegate Road and made its way through the throngs to the "George". Such was the interest and excitement in the town that the Deputy Mayor of Brighouse was permitted to formally declare the line open, and while the dignitaries were feasting in the "George", the public enjoyed free journeys on the tram between the terminus and Waring Green.

Ald. Hey, the Tramways Chairman, stressed that as the tramway was a commercial and not a philanthropic venture, he hoped that the people of Brighouse would use it well. They did, but not necessarily as he envisaged, as when the public service began on Friday, February 26th – a few days before the sub-station was brought into use - the best-patronised section of the new route was between Hove Edge and Brighouse; clearly, not many locals intended to change their shopping or working habits. "Briggus folk" liked their town; indeed, in their leisure hours they foregathered in the centre in such numbers that the trams were unable to rest at the terminus, being obliged to take on passengers outside the Oddfellows' Hall.

Car 14 enters Hipperholme on a journey to Brighouse
[Courtesy Trevor Hartley]

On weekdays the first tram left Halifax at 4.45am and commenced the return journey at 5.30, while the last car set out at 10.45 pm and did not reach Halifax again until 12.15am. As the single track in Bonegate Road had to be laid entirely on the western side of the highway, all downward cars had to observe a 6mph speed limit followed by a cautious 4 mph crawl around the blind corner into Bradford Road. In February the terminus for cars reversing at Hove Edge was removed a short distance to the junction of Upper Green Lane and Spout House Lane. When a severe thunderstorm erupted on July 24th, lightning "was observed to be playing round the Hipperholme trams in an alarming fashion, and frequent fears for safety were expressed." Eventually a Brighouse-bound tram was struck and disabled (without injuries), the spectacle providing a providential escape for Mr J Davidson and family, whose house was badly damaged while they were outside.

Determined to maintain the momentum of progress, Brighouse pressed for an extension of the tramway along Commercial Street to the "Wellington" hostelry, but Halifax refused to venture any further into the crowded town centre. A Brighouse resident, Mr. T. Cheetham, sought and obtained permission to demonstrate to the Tramways Dept., "a Device for cutting off the Electric Current in case of the breaking of

Brighouse folk flocked to witness the commencement of their regular tram service on February 26th, 1904, and the smiles on the faces of the upper deck passengers indicate that the speech was a good one! The tram is standing at the "George," facing towards Huddersfield.

[Photographer unknown]

Within five years of the opening of the tramways it was realised that the original low-capacity trams were not an economic proposition, and the twelve cars (83-94) which entered service in 1903 incorporated balconies which provided extra seating as well as better protection for the driver and conductor. Car 85, in need of repainting, was photographed at the Infirmary.

[Courtesy Roy Brook]

the Wire", and the Department, interested but unwilling to take responsibility, allowed him "to fix his Device on the Brighouse section at his own cost, and he to remove it at the end of twelve months and take all risks in connection therewith". Presumably no Brighouse wire chose to break or fall during the trial year, as no more was heard of the device.

Twelve additional trams, nos. 83 to 94, entered service in July/August, 1903. Once again the bodies were built by Brush and mounted on Brush "A" trucks with Westinghouse motors and controllers, but this time balconies extending over the platforms increased the upper–deck seating to 28 and provided better protection for the driver and conductor. The new arrangement also provided space for a 180° staircase which proved much safer than the straighter form of stair used hitherto. Locally made Walkers' 'Patent Dry Seats' were fitted on the upper deck, but like other optimistic

attempts to provide dry seating in wet weather æ hinged wooden flaps, removable canvas covers etc æ they were of little use to passengers who were already soaked.

A more logical solution had been offered in 1902 by Milnes Voss of Birkenhead in the form of a "Kennington Patent Collapsible Car Cover" designed by a Mr. Campbell of Sunderland. This comprised a rigid framework mounted on the upper deck and supporting a full length plank on which the trolley was mounted. Wooden slatted rubber clad flexible roof sections and full-drop side windows were accommodated within the framework, allowing the top deck to be enclosed in bad weather and opened on warm days. Resembling a roll-top desk, the cover was fitted to tramcar 71 which made a successful public debut on February 3rd, 1903. Unfortunately, within four months an electrical fault in the trolley base ignited a fire which damaged the cover beyond repair, leaving the top-deck passengers exposed to the elements once more. Fortunately, Edwardian travellers were a sturdy breed who dressed sensibly and endured climatic extremes uncomplainingly.

In 1904 British municipalities were dismayed to learn of a House of Lords decision to grant a private company running powers over the Newcastle Corporation Tramways. As this obviously had wider implications, Halifax fully shared the dismay, remembering an earlier approach made in 1901 by a B.E.T. subsidiary, the Spen Valley and Morley Light Railway Co., who had vainly tried to interest Halifax in a 3'6" gauge line to those distant parts; now a London syndicate was offering to acquire all Halifax's unexercised operating powers outside the Borough. This revived the long-running wrangle with

Tramcar 72 at Brighouse terminus on a summer morning. Cloth-capped men and a boy with a sack converse casually in the carriageway while others read newspapers outside the "George".

[Courtesy Roy Brook]

Elland, who had requested Halifax to provide tramways on terms which the Corporation had been unable to accept.

As in many parts of the Halifax area, the principal problem was one of access. Elland lay three miles south of Halifax, at the opposite side of the Calder Valley, and the only practical access was via Greetland and Salterhebble Hill. Still wary of the dangers posed by the Hill, the Corporation chose to revive the 1899 proposal for the Salterhebble Lift, and purchased land from the Waterhouse Charities for use as the "top station".

Yorkshire caution then reasserted itself, and the Committee investigated the alternative possibility of an extension of the Skircoat Green tramway to Dudwell Lane and an inclined highway down the hillside. Dubious as to whether this would serve their purpose adequately, they sought advice from Sir Douglas Fox, an eminent civil engineer. On the basis of a stroll down Salterhebble Hill and an inspection of the terrain, Sir Douglas recommended the Lift, which, he said, could be situated near All Saints' Church in Dudwell Lane.

The Lift itself was to comprise two cradles each 48 feet long and 12 feet wide, running up and down a 10 foot gauge railway on a gradient of slightly more than 1 in 3. The cradles would be interconnected by steel cables attached to a stationary steam engine. With a quarter-hourly tram service and a toll of 3d for all other vehicles, the lift would cost £100 per week to operate, but with a slight increase in traffic could be made profitable.

Hearty scepticism in the Council Chamber led to a public meeting on January 13th, 1903, when the Mechanics' Hall was packed with critical and vociferous residents. Recommending acceptance of the lift, the Mayor compared the steepest local tramway gradients, i.e.,

Gibbet Street	– 1 in 12.32;
Priestley Hill	– 1 in 11.76;
Pye Nest	– 1 in 10.50;
New Bank	– 1 in 10;
Boothtown Road	– 1 in 9.70;
Salterhebble	– 1 in 9.69.

Unwisely, he went on to explain that the gradients of Boothtown Road and Salterhebble Hill differed by only 3/4 of an inch in 220 yards, a comparison so absurd that a gale of derisive laughter swept the room. Condemned as "an American fad," the lift scheme was voted out, whereupon the Corporation washed their hands of the entire West Vale and Elland scheme.

In Elland and Greetland the news was received with indignation, and Elland called on Halifax to hand over their powers to lay tramways in the U.D. in favour of a new B.E.T. scheme for an ambitious Dewsbury — Cooper Bridge — Brighouse — Elland Wood Bottom — West Vale scheme. Halifax refused, and spent the next twelve months in fending off B.E.T.'s approaches. Obviously, matters could not be delayed indefinitely, and the Corporation accepted that they would have to lay a conventional tramway down Salterhebble Hill to West Vale, Greetland, with a branch up Saddleworth Road and Long Wall to Elland. Elland's response was to demand extensive road widening at Halifax's expense, whereupon Halifax decided to terminate the line at West Vale. Determined not to be disadvantaged by Elland's obstinacy, Greetland U.D.C. decided to put Halifax's sincerity to the test, and, following the example set by Brighouse a few years earlier, they began to carry out improvements to Stainland Road, and invited Halifax to lay tram tracks at the same time.

Halifax duly obliged, but only to the limits of the excavations, i.e. from the Calder bridge to a few yards beyond the railway overbridge, where the U.D.C. had lowered the carriageway by 2' 4" beneath the crown of the arch in order to allow trams to pass underneath on a section of specially interlaced track. The rest of the line was laid in the Spring of 1905 down the much feared Salterhebble Hill, past the "Punch Bowl" Inn and on to the West Vale terminus at the bottom of Saddleworth Road.

Duly inspected and approved on August 2nd, 1905, the West Vale service was triumphantly inaugurated next day by a special tram (no. 59) from Waterhouse Street. "All Greetland and West Vale seemed to be gathered there," the

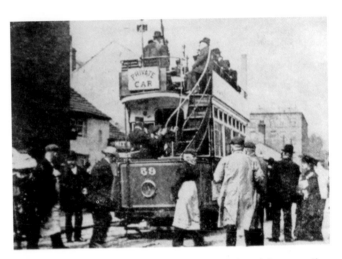

"All Greetland and West Vale" turned out to see the arrival of the first official tram, no. 59, at West Vale on August 3rd, 1905.

[Courtesy Roy Brook]

press reported. The great gamble had succeeded. No Halifax trams ever failed to meet the challenge of Salterhebble Hill; uncomplainingly they ascended and descended in defiance of fog, rain, ice, snow or gravity.

Other developments had also been taking place. As a means of forestalling the threat of B.E.T. incursions into the Brighouse area, Halifax had used its existing powers to build a branch line northwards from Brighouse along Bradford Road to Bailiffe Bridge, thereby simultaneously thwarting Bradford's ambitions for trams to Brighouse. Unusually for Halifax, the line was virtually level and double track throughout, although the poles were of the familiar John Spencer variety, and Major Druitt had no difficulty in approving all that he saw on Thursday, October 13th, 1904. Subject to the trimming of trees at the bottom of Bonegate Road, he authorised the highest speed limit – 14 mph – permitted so far.

As soon as paving works were completed five days later, a special tramcar, no. 76, bearing the Tramways Committee arrived in Brighouse to welcome on board their Brighouse colleagues, who, after the customary speeches, set out along the new line with the Deputy Mayor of Brighouse at the controls. At the borough boundary the Chairman of Hipperholme UDC took charge of the car for the remainder of the journey, after which the official party enjoyed a festive lunch at the "Martin's Nest" while the tram travelled back and forth, conveying delighted schoolchildren free of charge. The public service opened later in the day at a penny fare from Brighouse to the new terminus 5 yards short of the Hipperholme/Clifton parish boundary, in the shadow of T.F. Firth's imposing carpet factory which provided employment in the area.

The construction of the branch line necessitated a junction with the existing Halifax-Brighouse single track, and in view of the restricted clearance at the bottom of Bonegate Road, trams returning to Halifax from Brighouse had to negotiate a new facing crossover in Bradford Road, which transferred

Tramcar 86 arrives at Skircoat Green. Note for the patches of oil which have seeped on to the road surface from the axle-boxes of trams standing at the terminus.

[J.A. Pitts collection, courtesy West Yorkshire Archives, Bradford]

When tramcar 86 arrived at Bailiffe Bridge terminus on the trial run, October 13th, 1904, the paving was far from complete, but all was in order for the official opening five days later.

[Courtesy the late R.B. Parr]

them to the "wrong" track for a few yards before they swung left to head for Hipperholme and Halifax. Regular through journeys from Halifax to Bailiffe Bridge were not envisaged in the early years, and the branch operated as a shuttle service.

Determined to extend the benefits of modern transport to other parts of their borough, Brighouse encouraged Halifax to build a tramway to the isolated village of Rastrick, famous for its brass band, but despite long-drawn-out negotiations and promises, nothing materialised until 1923, when Huddersfield constructed a line through the area to Brighouse. East of Bailiffe Bridge, the little Clifton Parish Council caught a distant scent of tramway fever in December, 1904, inspiring them to request a line from Brighouse to Hartshead Moor, which Halifax rejected out of hand. Back in Halifax, an equally unlikely extension from Pellon to Wainstalls was surprisingly approved by the Committee but wisely rejected by the Council.

Sporting facilities were viewed more favourably. Ever since the introduction of the tramways, the Highroad Well trams had been periodically overwhelmed by the large

volumes of visitors to the Halifax Cricket and Football Club grounds at Thrum Hall, and as a means of relieving the pressure, a 187 yard double-track spur from Gibbet Street into Thrum Hall Lane was brought into use on December 21st, 1905. From 1910 special trams conveyed visiting teams direct from the Old Station to the ground at an agreed charge – an early version of "the team coach".

Up to this point the Jerry Lane extension of the Sowerby Bridge route had lain derelict since December, 1903, and when in mid-1904 the Sowerby and Ripponden U.D.C.s persuaded Halifax to extend the line further up the Ryburn Valley for the benefit of millworkers who had to walk long distances to and from their workplaces, the Tramways Committee accepted the proposal as a means of recouping their losses. As the viability of rural lines was diminished by the amount of rates payable by Halifax on their tramways outside the Borough – as much as £5,000 per annum – the two U.D.Cs volunteered to forego receipt of rates for five years. Naturally it was not long before the Lancashire & Yorkshire Railway Co. learned of this arrangement and vowed to oppose it by all possible means, as their railway to Ripponden was heavily rated, and the trams would filch their passengers.

Halifax decided nevertheless to proceed with the extension, but only as far as the limit of economic operations at Stile Triangle. Following the statutory inspection on February 5th, 1905, the Triangle route was ceremonially opened five days later, when a special car from Cow Green made its way to Jerry Lane. As it crossed the boundary into Sowerby U.D., the chairman of the council took the controls for the delightfully scenic run to the new terminus in Oldham Road, 183 yards east of Butterworth Lane. Even though the speeds permitted along the line were insufficient to cause genuine alarm, the Board of Trade were implored to reduce them to a mere 6 mph when large numbers of people were around, i.e., "when th' mills were loosing!" – but the drivers were merely asked to exercise caution.

A new threat to the integrity of Halifax's tramways arose in November, 1905, when the National Electric Construction Co. unveiled plans for a long 3'6" gauge line from Fartown

At the quaint rural terminus of the valley route to Triangle, the driver of car 61 is content to let his conductor pose at the controls.

[Courtesy Roy Brook]

(Huddersfield) via Elland to West Vale, with mixed-gauge track from Fartown to Huddersfield and running powers over the Halifax route from West Vale into Halifax. The Corporations vowed to oppose the scheme if it should ever reach Parliament, but the necessary capital could not be raised, and the threat receded, whereupon Halifax formally abandoned all its proposals for tramways to Elland, Rishworth, Stainland, Cragg Vale and Wainstalls.

The municipalities next became aware of the intention of the railway companies to seek Parliamentary powers for the operation of petrol buses, and realising that the railways would use such powers to wreak vengeance for the passengers lost to the tramways, Halifax and Manchester joined in strenuous opposition. As a precaution, Halifax officials inspected "Motor Omnibuses" at the London Automobile Show, and resolved to buy two Milnes-Daimler buses for £950 each. However, when the Town Clerk ruled that the Corporation had no powers to operate buses, the matter lapsed, as did the railway threat.

These agitations had a lasting effect upon Todmorden Corporation, who, realising now that they could not look for help from outside, discarded their tramway ambitions and in August, 1906, resolved to buy four petrol buses. The "Todmorden Motor Bus Service" duly opened on the first day of 1907, but within a few weeks began to encounter daunting mechanical problems. Leyland bus no.3 burst into flames and suffered severe damage, prompting the agitated Council to debate whether to persevere with the pioneering project. However, they did, and there was no further serious talk of trams at the head of the Calder Valley.

A tranquil scene at West Vale on a summer afternoon as well-dressed local residents climb on board car 53 for a journey to Halifax.

[Courtesy the late R.B. Parr]

(Above) Parasols shield lady passengers from the summer sun as car 68 halts at the Porter's Lodge on a return journey from Triangle c. 1906.

[J.A. Pitts collection, courtesy West Yorkshire Archives, Bradford]

(below) A late afternoon scene at Triangle terminus as car 67 prepares to return to Halifax, c. 1906.

[J.A. Pitts collection, courtesy West Yorkshire Archives, Bradford]

CHAPTER 8

DEMI-CARS AND COVERED TOPS

The perennial problem of the loss-making Horton Street line from Wards End to Old Station surfaced again in January, 1904, when the Mayor proposed that the King Cross and Highroad Well trams should revert to their original terminus at the Post Office, Commercial Street, with a shuttle service from that point to the station. Having visited Southport to inspect a "demi-car" in service there, the Committee decided to buy two similar cars for that purpose.

Ordered from the Brush Co. and delivered in early July, 1904 as nos. 95 and 96, the "demi-cars" were small, totally-enclosed single-deckers designed for one-man operation. Passengers boarded at the front, dropped their fares into a box and entered the saloon, being separated from the driver by a hinged rail which, when lifted, cut off the current and halted the car. Seats were provided for up to 26 passengers including two alongside the driving positions. On arrival at the end of the line the driver changed ends, raising the step at what had then became the rear, in order to ensure that everyone boarded and alighted at the front only.

The electrical equipment had been specially designed by the Raworth Co. for one-man operation, with regenerative motors which fed power back into the overhead line and acted as a brake when cars were descending a gradient, an arrangement which when used on the Devonport tramways had reputedly achieved a 30% reduction in current consumption.

On July 8th, Mr. Spencer and Mr. Raworth junior drove one of the cars from the depot to the Post Office and Salterhebble, and following intensive trials, nos. 95 and 96 entered service on the Skircoat Green route on August 1st, as a means of enabling all the drivers to experience their novel control and braking systems. Then, as soon as conventional slipper-brakes had been fitted for the descent of Horton Street, they inaugurated the Post Office–Old Station shuttle service on October 3rd. Simultaneously the Highroad Well and Salterhebble routes were linked as a cross-town service, and a new circular service was commenced to and from Commercial Street via King Cross and Savile Park, but as the single-line sections encountered en route frustrated all attempts to secure punctuality, the original Savile Park service was reinstated a month later, when the town terminus of the King Cross cars was removed to Silver Street.

For the first ten days of service the demi-cars performed faultlessly. Then on the morning of October 14th, car 95 with Driver John Rhodes at the helm got out of control while descending Horton Street and collided with car 96. Observing the rapid approach of no. 95, Driver Broadbent immediately halted his car, and as it was not designed to be driven in reverse, ran to the other end of the tram in an attempt to drive it downhill and thus lessen the force of the impact; his three passengers hastily "abandoned ship". The force of the impact rammed no. 96 round the curve into Church Street while no. 95 left the rails and upended a Corporation dray, trapping its driver underneath.

After the badly-damaged cars had been towed back to the depot and the service re-started with conventional trams, Lt.-Col. (ex Major) Druitt presided over the inevitable public inquiry. He found that the primary cause of the runaway was the tripping of a circuit-breaker at the power station, which had rendered the regenerative brake useless. Incredibly, although Driver Rhodes had driven the demi-cars over 184 miles, he claimed that he had never tried the emergency brake (a simple backwards movement of the controller handle), and did not know that the cars were fitted with slipper-brakes – statements which were angrily denied. Drivers Jonas and Wilson had been trained by Mr. Raworth junior in the special features of the patent control equipment so that they could instruct all the other drivers, a process supervised by Inspector Bamber. Driver Wilson stated bluntly, "Driver Rhodes was on my car for instruction. I cannot say as to what day, but I remember showing him the emergency brake on the Raworth controller", to which Mr. Spencer added scathingly, "It seems incredible to me that Rhodes could have driven these cars 184 miles and not have understood what the word, 'Emergency' meant on the controller lid!"

On the grounds that, contrary to regulations, the demi-cars were not fitted with anti-run back devices, their use was prohibited until the deficiency had been remedied. They returned to service on May 7th, 1905, initially on the Hebden Bridge route. When tried on the Bailiffe Bridge branch line, they achieved impressive savings over a ten day period:-

Double-deck tram		
2 drivers @ 5s 6d per day for 10 days		£5-10-0
2 conductors @ 3s 9d " " " " "		3-15-0
Current for 1,040 car miles @ 1d per unit per mile		6-10-0
		£15-15-0d
or 3.63d per car mile.		

Demi-car		
2 drivers @ 5s 6d per day for 10 days		£5-10-0
Current for 1,040 car miles @ .7d per unit per mile		5-11-0
		£11-1 -0d
or 2.32d per car mile.		

However, as the seating capacity of the demi-cars was only half that of the double-deckers, the savings were achievable only on lightly-trafficked routes

At the end of the Summer, the Committee agreed that, "suggestions for the running of the single-deck car on the Southowram route be referred to Coun. Broadley and the Manager", æ clearly, patronage on the Southowram line was low in the early years, and from August 22nd to September 19th, 1905, the service had been suspended altogether while the Highways Dept. improved the levels in Beacon Hill Road. Presumably the other demi-car was maintaining the Horton Street service single-handed.

Re-equipped with "new motors, brakes and controllers" sometime after April, 1906, (probably by Westinghouse), the two little cars resumed their Wards End–Old Station shuttle on July 1st, 1907, when they proved themselves to be "the easiest and safest cars in service". Then on October 21st one of them began to work the Southowram route single-handed except on Saturdays when a double-decker was required, leaving the other demi-car to "the Horton Street patrol".

A few months after the accidental destruction of the "roll-top" upper deck cover of car no.71 in June, 1903, the Department tried a different method of protecting passengers from some of the elements. This was "Mozley's Patent Wind Guard", designed by the Burnley tramways manager and used also on the Sunderland District Tramways at a later date. The "guard" comprised a roofless open-air enclosure 4'6" high around the whole of the upper deck, with timber lower panels surmounted by plate-glass windows. Fitted to Brush car 78 about February, 1904, it offered partial protection from boisterous Pennine breezes.

Unfortunately, Pennine rains inconsiderately continued to fall vertically, and knowing that Liverpool had successfully fitted permanent "Bellamy"-type covers to some of their trams, Halifax sought permission to do likewise. At first, the Board of Trade were reluctant to allow top-covered cars on a narrow gauge, fearing that their raised centre of gravity might cause them to overturn in strong winds.

Faced with strong protests from the Municipal Tramways Association as well as from Birmingham, the principal user of the 3'6" gauge, the Board relented but reserved the right to inspect all plans and drawings. When the Walsall and South Staffordshire 3'6" gauge operators secured approval for an experimental top cover, Halifax were allowed to try a similar design. One unit was therefore

bought for £61-4s from Milnes, Voss and Co. of Birkenhead in February 1906 and fitted to tram no. 66, whose passengers welcomed the all-weather protection which it provided when it re-entered service in April. However, several structural defects developed, and Milnes, Voss received an invoice for £16 in respect of repairs carried out by Halifax.

Suspecting that locally-constructed products might prove more durable, the Committee placed an order for twelve similar covers with Mr. Richard Turner of Gibbet Street at a cost of £68-10-s per unit, and the covers were fitted to Brush cars 63, 65, 71-77, 79, 81 and 82 between November, 1906, and May, 1907, to the great satisfaction of passengers and staff. The glazed timber structures had a slightly arched roof,

"Turner top" car 71 halts at the "Peacock Inn", Burnley Road, on a summertime journey from Hebden Bridge to Cow Green.
[Courtesy Roy Brook]

and extended over the short end balconies, with a door at the head of the staircase. In view of their much increased height and wind-resistance, the twelve cars were confined to relatively sheltered routes such as Hebden Bridge, Ovenden (only), West End, Savile Park and Brighouse. Also, they were unable to pass beneath the low railway bridge at Sowerby Bridge, and their additional weight adversely affected their riding qualities, with resulting complaints about pitching and rolling on their short-wheelbase trucks.

Like its neighbours in Bradford, Huddersfield, Leeds and Rochdale, the Tramways Department was a progressive undertaking which continually modernised and improved its installations. Thus, when Messrs. G. D. Parr marketed an electricity-operated point controller activated by tram drivers without the need to halt the car and change the points manually, a set was purchased for £75 and installed at busy Wards End. In King Cross Street the Akeds Road crossover was removed to a much more useful location at People's Park. Similarly, a colour-light signalling system was installed as a means of speeding up journeys on the single track and loop sections such as Burnley Road, where signals were installed between Burr Wood and Naylor Lane, Naylor Lane and Luddenden Foot,

Tramcar 66, on a journey from the Post Office to Savile Park, pauses at St, Jude's to allow an official photographer to admire its new Milnes-Voss top cover.

[Courtesy the late R.B. Parr]

Spring Royd and Cold Wind Hall, Mytholmroyd and Bobbin Lane, Bobbin Lane and Fallingroyd Lane.

The overhead line equipment received its share of attention too. In March, 1905, the Electrical Engineer was instructed "to erect an additional pole and an Automatic Trolley Reverser at Bailiffe Bridge terminus", a two guinea royalty being paid to Brecknell, Munro and Rogers for the patent sprung reverser "frogs" (overhead points). Presumably intended for use by the one-man operated demi-cars during their brief sojourn on the Brighouse–Bailiffe Bridge route, the reverser was one of the earliest in Yorkshire (Bradford, Huddersfield and Leeds had none until 1915, c.1918 and 1926 respectively). A year later, similar reversers were erected at Brighouse and Thrum Hall where the presence of bustling crowds had created difficulties for conductors attempting to "swing" the trolleys manually. However, the reversers seem to have been shortlived, as they are not to be seen on photographs, and it may be assumed that as they were designed for the short, steeply-inclined trolleys of the demi-cars, they were unsuitable for the longer booms of the double-deckers, especially those equipped with side-mounted trolleys. In 1908 trolley cords were superseded by bamboo trolley sticks, which when not in use were stowed on hooks at the bottom of the side panels, and in the following year, manually-operated overhead "frogs" were mostly superseded by drop-lever frogs mechanically operated by the trolley head, thus further speeding up the services.

The duties of the senior tramway staff were outlined in October, 1904. Chief Inspector J. W. Bamber was responsible for traffic staff, rotas, timekeeping and tramcar movements, for which he received a weekly wage of 50s and the assistance of two inspectors. On the engineering side, Mr. C.H. Spencer, the Rolling Stock Superintendent, oversaw tramcar maintenance, the depot and the works, with the assistance of 42 works staff, for which he received a surprisingly low wage of 30s. Supervision of the 70 depot staff was exercised by their foreman, Mr. W. Jagger ($7\frac{3}{4}$ d per hour). In the office the chief clerk (Mr. J. Midgley) earned 40s (£2) and had charge of invoices, stores, waybills, correspondence and five clerks, while the chief cashier, Mr. B. M.Bagott, kept a watch on seven staff and the conductors' takings, also for 40s.

The disparity in the wage rates was rectified by the Committee, who upgraded Messrs. Spencer, Midgley and Bagott to 45s (£2-5-0d) and appointed three additional traffic inspectors. Meanwhile Mr. W. Evans (one of the original recruits from the South Staffs tramways) had become Traffic Superintendent at the princely salary of £3, but within a short while he lost the services of his fellow veteran, Chief Inspector Bamber, who impressed the neighbouring Keighley Tramways Committee so favourably that they appointed him as their General Manager in June, 1905; unfortunately he had to resign only four years later after having threatened his depot foreman, who was then appointed as his successor!

Burnley Road, between King Cross and Cote Hill, with 'Turner top' car 77 returning to the Post Office in Commercial Street. The two dogs are untroubled by the approach of the tramcar.

[Author's collection]

CHAPTER 9
SLIPPERY SLOPES

As part of the Department's investigations into the efficiency of tramcar braking, Mr. Nathan Greenwood of Halifax was allowed to fit his newly-patented slipper brake to car 34, but although the drivers liked it, at the end of the trial period he was asked to remove it without receiving any comment on its performance. Unable to market his invention without a testimony from his local tramway operator, he appealed to Ald. Hey, who dismissively replied that the Committee "did not consult their drivers in matters of this nature", — an astonishing response which he may have remembered later, particularly on Sunday, July 1st, 1906, when an unexpected disaster disrupted the tram service, fomented dissension in the town, threw 200 men out of work and undermined the Department's finances.

Relief driver Theodore Chadwick and conductor Wm. Duffy on board tramcar 94 had been performing leisurely Sunday afternoon journeys on the Shelf route. On their sixth journey they left Union Street at 6.15pm and embarked on the return trip half an hour later. The day had been showery, and the rails were wet as no.94 began the descent of New Bank, halting at Prospect Street to allow two ladies to board. On the top deck Conductor Duffy conscientiously kept hold of the trolley rope as the car rumbled across the junction with the Southowram route, but as he was descending the stairs, the tram unexpectedly gathered speed. He quickly applied the slipper brake from the rear platform and closed the saloon door to prevent the passengers from jumping off.

At the bottom of New Bank, P.C. Dixon on point duty had just signalled a Queensbury tram to turn into Haley Hill when he heard no. 94 approaching at speed, its driver frantically applying all his brakes and dropping sand. Calling to pedestrians to keep clear, he ran for his life as the tram skidded round the curve on to North Bridge, wheels locked and sparks flying. After careering on two wheels for a few yards it overturned on the bridge with a thunderous crash, throwing the upper deck passengers into the road and flinging the saloon travellers into a tangled heap. Two died instantly; twelve were injured and only one escaped unscathed as a crowd of people and four doctors rushed to their assistance.

All next day the badly-damaged tram lay across the tracks, preventing the Queensbury, Shelf and Brighouse trams from returning to the depot and obliging them to operate to and from North Bridge only. Predictably, they were little used, as most of their usual passengers chose either to walk or travel by train – not that their confidence in the local railways

was well founded. In 1903 a disaster in Sowerby Bridge railway tunnel had caused one death and 24 injuries; in December, 1904, a goods train hauling 70 waggons had collided at Todmorden with "catastrophic" consequences, while in September, 1907, a runaway train wrecked Holme Station near Todmorden and killed the assistant station master.

Tramcar 94 overturned on North Bridge, July 1st, 1906. Note the elaborate gantry installations from which the tram wires were suspended.
[J.A. Pitts collection, courtesy West Yorkshire Archives, Bradford]

When tramcar 94 had been hauled back to the depot and reunited with its missing parts, it was driven twice down Salterhebble Hill at about 20 mph (five times the statutory speed) and halted without difficulty. Similar tests were enacted on the undulating Hebden Bridge section and the Savile Park line, and again no mechanical defect could be found.

The Board of Trade report, published in September, laid the blame firmly on Driver Chadwick, who, in the stately words of Lt.-Col. Druitt, "did not make use of the means at his disposal in time to check the car"; in other words, he had applied the wheel brake too hard (thus locking the wheels) and the slipper brake too late and too vigorously, thereby virtually jacking the car off the track.

One of the two dead men was never identified but presumed to have been an Irish labourer who had come to England for the hay harvest. When the sad facts were reported locally, no fewer than five women claiming to be his widow came forward to claim compensation!

Driver Chadwick had been suspended on full pay after the accident and then dismissed when the Inspector's findings were published. His case was taken up by the Amalgamated Association of Tramway and Vehicle Workers, who requested his reinstatement. Anxious to avoid confrontation, Ald. Booth, the former Tramways Chairman, offered Mr. Chadwick a post in the Corporation's Weights and Measures Dept., but out of loyalty to the union, Mr. Chadwick felt obliged to refuse. The situation deteriorated. A strike began on August 25th, and scheduled tram services were not fully resumed until late October, during which time replacement staff had been recruited from all parts of the kingdom and much ill-feeling caused in the town. Nevertheless, the dismissal was endorsed by the Corporation's insurers, whose rules demanded that all staff should be reliable and competent men.

The financial effect on the tramways was drastic. Not only had accident insurance claims to be met and tramcar 94 repaired, but revenue had fallen by £1,500 per month during the strike, and workmen's fare concessions had cost £2,670. The year ended in a loss.

A glimpse of Skircoat Road Depot's tramcar maintenance routine was revealed during the strike, when it was noted that there were usually 11 trams in the workshop at any given period, ie., 2 due for re-tyring; 2 with accident damage; 4 awaiting motor repairs and 3 in the paintshop. Everyday maintenance tasks were performed in the "running shed" by the depot staff – washing, cleaning, polishing, greasing of moving parts including the trolley, electrical leakage tests, brake adjustments and replenishment of sand hoppers, and the tram drivers had to ensure that their "steeds" were fit for public service before they took them out of the depot.

By this time the need for fundamental improvements to tramway braking efficiency was being felt in all hilly areas, and on October 11th, 1906, Mr. Spencer attended a special conference at Huddersfield. Hitherto, Halifax's slipper brakes had been applied by means of levers attached to a shaft parallel with the axles and fixed to the truck side, which allowed a certain amount of undesirable elasticity. Mr. C. H. Spencer had therefore devised a firmer structure, with a strong downward pressure taken by four bearings bolted to the truck frame near the axle boxes, reputedly increasing the efficiency by 50%.

Unfortunately, while the new design was being tested, a second tramcar, no. 52, had run out of control down New Bank, this time keeping to the rails and halting without incident, but when Sarah Ann Witham of Shelf claimed that the tram had been sent out with badly worn brakes, she received a £100 out of court payment. Next, on April 15th, 1907, a tram returning from Queensbury ran downhill so swiftly that (in the words of the passengers), "it fair hummed". It did not halt until it had passed the Boothtown penny stage, but prudently the conductor did not venture to collect an extra penny from his shaken cargo!

Improvements were certainly needed, as the Sowerby Bridge and Triangle passengers had for some time been experiencing a series of unwelcome excitements. Within ten weeks of the opening of the route in November, 1902, a fully-laden late-night car had run away down Pye Nest Road and not halted until it reached Wharf Street, the cause being slippery rails and empty sandboxes. Later in 1903 lack of sand caused a similar runaway, and this time the driver was demoted to conductor for having neglected to check the state of the sandboxes. In October, 1906, car 61 returning to Halifax rolled backwards down Pye Nest Road for a distance of 200 feet, snapping its trolley boom and damaging a cart. Snow on the track was blamed for a fourth incident in December, 1906, when a runaway tram was halted by its

Viewed from the "Engineers' Hotel" at the junction of Wharf Street and Stanley Street, Sowerby Bridge, car 64 prepares to make the ascent of Bolton Brow and Pye Nest Road on its way to King Cross and Halifax, with the distant beckoning finger of Wainhouse Tower on the right. On October 15th, 1907, no 64 failed to complete the ascent, and five people died when it ran backwards and was wrecked.

[J. S. King collection]

slipper brake, but not until it had passed at speed through the Wharf Street loop.

Alarming though they were, these episodes were merely the prelude to the great Pye Nest Disaster of 1907, a tragedy which ended the life of five people and had far-reaching consequences for the management of the tramways.

In British tramway circles it was generally considered good practice for all trams to be turned from time to time, as a means of equalising the wear on brakes, tyres and wheel-flanges. Despite the availability of reversing facilities in the depot yard, this seems not to have been done in Halifax in the earlier years, except of course in the case of trams working on the circular services.

For the Sowerby Bridge route Mr. Spencer had set aside six or more Brush cars whose powerful 35 hp motors were well suited to the challenge of Pye Nest, and had arranged for the Westinghouse controllers at the "Halifax" end of the cars to be modified with an anti-run back device indicated by a letter "B" painted on the controller, a refinement not needed at the "Sowerby Bridge" end, where ascending gradients would not be encountered, and runbacks therefore could not occur. The fact that the electric emergency braking systems were thus subtly different at each end of the car was not considered significant. That is, until the morning of October 15th, 1907.

At about 4.30 am on that day, tramcar 64 emerged from the depot under the control of Driver T.H. Simpson, one of the Department's most senior employees, and his 32 year old conductor, Walter Robinson. For reasons never explained or commented on, Driver Simpson drove the tram from the rear platform, using the conductor as a lookout at the front, so that when the tram arrived at Cow Green, both men were already in their correct positions for the outward journey. Descending Pye Nest Road, Driver Simpson cautiously applied a few notches of electric brake, as a light drizzle was falling, and the lines appeared "greasy", being flushed with running water from a nearby hydrant.

Arriving at Triangle, the two men exchanged places before departure for Halifax at 5.25 am. The saloon was soon packed with passengers both seated and standing, and a few others had to huddle on the rainswept open top deck. More passengers boarded at Sowerby Bridge at 5.40, swelling the top deck contingent to a dozen. Slowly and doggedly car 64 began the ascent of Bolton Brow and Pye Nest Road, until at the curve opposite Edwards Road the wheels began to lose their grip and spin wildly. The driver depressed the sand pedal to regain adhesion, but the sudden excess of current being drawn by the motors tripped the overload switches at the power station and cut off the supply.

Driver Simpson promptly turned the controller handle to the "off" position and pulled at the handbrake – but not quickly enough. The car began to roll backwards, and as a second, harder pull on the brake merely locked the wheels, he released it and re-applied it, simultaneously applying the electric and slipper brakes, all without effect. Then the current came on again, and the driver quickly attempted to drive forward again, but the trolley which was now being pushed by the momentum of the tram, sprang from the wire, entangled itself with the centre-pole bracket arm and was wrenched from its mounting.

Again Driver Simpson feverishly applied the electric brake, forgetting (or, as he claimed, not knowing) that the controller at the "Halifax" end of the car was of the modified type on which he needed only to pull the controller handle back to the 5th braking notch, leaving the master key untouched in the "forward" position. Instead, he performed the normal process of switching the key to "reverse" before pulling the controller handle to the braking position, which produced no effect.

Contrary to the regulations governing Pye Nest, Conductor Robinson had been collecting fares instead of remaining on the rear platform. When the top deck lights suddenly failed,

he hurried back down the stairs where he found a passenger wrestling with the brakes. Shouting, "Come out o' th' road!" he pushed the man aside, but at that moment another passenger fell down the stairs and knocked the would-be helper into the road, from whence he watched the car hurtle downhill with passengers jumping off and the conductor shouting to warn pedestrians. At the entrance to the single line in Bolton Brow the tram left the rails with a violent lurch, smashing with tremendous force into a shop between Grove Street and East Parade. The impact sheared the tram into two halves; the top deck floor was completely ripped off, while the lower deck and the truck spun around, overturned and slithered to a halt 30 yards away amid a flurry of violently splintered wood, shattered glass and scattered sand. Conductor Robinson and two passengers were killed instantly.

The resounding crash aroused Sowerby Bridge. Within a short time all the local doctors, St. John's Ambulance Brigade and horse-drawn ambulances were at the scene, and some of the dazed passengers were taken home by cab, though one man resident in Tuel Lane was carted off by his friends in a wheelbarrow. Householders looked after the rest until a special tramcar arrived to convey them to hospital, where two more victims passed away shortly afterwards.

Conductor Robinson's funeral took place two days later at Mount Zion Chapel, Bradshaw; his coffin was conveyed in a suitably-draped demi-car, and the mourners followed in double-deck trams. The Coroner ruled that the Department had been "sadly to blame in sending out a car with a different form of controller at each end", and Lt.-Col. Druitt at the public inquiry agreed with his verdict, adding that the driver had not applied the slipper brake quickly enough, and that the conductor should have remained on the rear platform. Brakesmen were immediately appointed to ride on the rear platforms of trams ascending Pye Nest, New Bank, Haley Hill and Lee Mount, a move which possibly prevented another accident on October 29th, when another fully-laden tram ran backwards on the same gradient, but was halted within 150 yards. Most of the passengers continued their journey on foot.

Drastic action was inevitable. At the first meeting of the Tramways Committee after the November elections and with a new chairman, deepest sympathy and condolences were expressed to the injured and bereaved. That done, the resignations of the Manager, Mr. Fred. Spencer, and his son Mr. Charles Henry Spencer, Rolling Stock Engineer, were accepted as from March 31st, 1908, and December 31st, respectively. Both received handsome presentations and warm wishes on their departure. The timing of their resignations was ironic, as their search for an efficient tramcar brake had succeeded at last. During the year Mr. C.H. Spencer had experimented with a solid 3'3" long slipper brake shoe, which had proved so successful that he

Awestruck crowds inspected the remains of tramcar 64 on October 15th, 1907. The postcard was despatched from No 5, Daisy Street, Hopwood Lane, a fortnight later.

[J.A. Pitts collection, courtesy West Yorkshire Archives, Bradford]

Three special tramcars were provided for Conductor Simpson's funeral. Leading the cortège is car 78 with its patent Mozley upper-deck windguards, with a Milnes car bringing up the rear. The coffin is being loaded into one of the demi-cars.

[J.A. Pitts collection, courtesy West Yorkshire Archives, Bradford]

had patented it on December 5th (Patent 6262). Huddersfield, Oldham, Ashton and the S.H.M.D. tramways adopted it, and eventually the entire Halifax fleet was equipped with it in place of the wooden block brake shoes invented by his elder brother, Mr. C.J. Spencer.

Nevertheless, it was made clear that the makeshift methods inherited from the early, pioneering days would be replaced by more businesslike procedures. Controllers were standardised on each car, and drivers and conductors were to be always the same pair. Driver Simpson was demoted to cleaner, and a similar fate awaited the driver of a Highroad Well car following a runback in Gibbet Street in which the conductor had been pushed off the tram by fleeing passengers. The Board of Trade solemnly warned that Halifax's tramways were "bordering on the limit of possible safe working by electric trams with flanged wheels running on grooved rails, for not only are the gradients steep but the hills are long and with many curves, and the exudations from the soil and deposits from the air and other traffic frequently produce a greasy surface on the rails."

The Tramways Department was thoroughly reorganised. Mr. J.W. Galloway of Rochdale Corporation Tramways and Mr. James D. Caird of Aberdeen Corporation Tramways were appointed Rolling Stock Engineer and Traffic Superintendent respectively. Overall responsibility was given to the Borough Electrical Engineer, Mr. W.M. Rogerson, with the unflattering comment that he had "ample time to devote to the additional duties to be imposed on him", despite which he would not receive an immediate salary increase, "as he must prove his worth!"

He did so, promptly recommending the Committee at a six-hour meeting to invest £6,014 in better circuit-breakers and trolley-heads for the entire fleet, and 35 h.p. motors and new controllers and resistances for 25 of the oldest trams still underpowered at 25hp and used only at rush hours. Unprepared for such expenditure at a time when the undertaking was losing money, the Committee jibbed, and spread the expenditure over three years, beginning in May, 1908, with Westinghouse B49 motors and type T.I.D. controllers for eight cars, with BTH type GT form B resistances. Steel tyres replaced the more fragile iron variety; the cumbersome fare-box system was swept away in favour of Williamsons' bell-punches and tickets, and electricity prices were reduced to 1^3/$_4$d per unit and later 1^1/$_{16}$d, resulting in a £2,367 gain for Mr. Rogerson's Tramways Dept. and a corresponding loss for his Electricity Dept!

In a drive to brighten the appearance of the fleet, the Manager (Mr. Rogerson) arranged for one tram to be repainted in a red and white livery in May, 1908, but having compared it with two trams newly painted in the usual Prussian blue and white, the Committee decided against change.

Christmas Day tram services were operated for the first time in 1906, "commencing from the Town Termini in the morning at 10 o' clock and leaving the Country Termini in the evening at 11 o' clock", with double wages for the staff. The great Yorkshire Agricultural Show held in Savile Park in May, 1908, warranted a special service from Old Station at a 3d fare, and as a means of relieving congestion and delays in Fountain Street and Barum Top, the departure-point for the Hebden Bridge service was removed in November, 1909, from Cow Green to Wards End, to the grave displeasure of passengers thereby obliged to cross the town centre on foot. Side destination displays were provided for a few years on cars serving Savile Park, Skircoat Green, West Vale, Southowram, Shelf and Brighouse, and at the insistence of the Board of Trade in March, 1906, a red light was displayed at the rear of all trams during the hours of darkness, even though they were the most brightly-lit vehicles on the King's Highway.

Meanwhile the resourceful Pye Nest brakesmen, condemned to wait in all weathers at the bottom of the hill in order to ride on each ascending tram and then return to their starting-point, had provided some protection from the elements by constructing an impromptu shelter fashioned from timber, loose stones, branches and linoleum, resembling the abodes of hermits or tramps.

An offer by Swindon Corporation in June, 1909, to sell or exchange three trams was politely declined, as the cars on offer were fitted with reversed staircases and would have been non-standard in Halifax.

CHANGING TIMES

The appearance of motor-cars on the streets of Halifax not long after the opening of the tramways had at first been something of a "nine days wonder" in the town, but by 1907 enterprising motorists were plucking up courage to venture further afield. In April of that year the Tramways Committee authorised the Halifax Automobile Club to affix direction signs to the tram poles at the junctions of main roads leading out of the town centre, but stood firm three years later when asked to remove the quiet Causeway Foot tram terminus to what the motorists considered a safer location; instead, the Club was allowed to erect a "Danger" sign, even though the only danger came from motorists breasting the brow of the hill without due care and attention.

But the tramcars, like the motor-cars, had also scented the lure of far-away places. Since 1907 a Bradford tramcar had been operating an experimental dual-gauge service to Leeds, using a sliding-axle device to make the transition from its native 4 foot gauge to the broader Leeds gauge, and when a full-scale through service was inaugurated in 1909, Northowram and Shelf residents expressed a lively interest in a similar linking-up of the Halifax and Bradford systems. At the Tramways Committee meeting in July, 1909, it was agreed "that the question of the service between Halifax and Bradford and the running of through cars be referred to the General Manager to confer with the General Manager of Bradford City Tramways thereon".

Whether the Bradford manager viewed the proposal with enthusiasm is uncertain, as the steep descents from Northowram to Stump Cross and in New Bank would have called for adjustable slipper-brakes which would have needed to be equally efficient on either gauge – a complex refinement not required on the fairly level Bradford to Leeds route.

However, the scheme was stifled at birth when the Halifax Chamber of Trade foresaw the possibility of Halifax folk patronising Bradford shops – an unlikely prospect, in fact, as the journey would have occupied almost an hour in each direction. Perhaps Halifax folk were content to remain among their familiar hills and dales; indeed, in May, 1902, the Education Committee had been dismayed to discover that several scholarship candidates had known so little of the outside world that they had placed Birmingham, Blackburn and Hull in the West Riding of Yorkshire – a supreme compliment, no doubt, but not a pathway to high marks! Evidently the tramways and electricity employees were more alert and lively than their juniors, as they had formed an active Social, Athletic and Benevolent Committee with a gymnasium in the basement of the depot, where they expended surplus energy in their leisure hours. Employees who preferred more sedate activities frequented rented accommodation in Town Hall Street East, where billiards, reading, smoking and refreshment rooms were opened in February, 1910.

In the busy town centre the layout of the tramways was by this time inadequate and a hindrance to punctuality, particularly in Silver Street, where the single line was

Bull Green in Edwardian days, viewed from King Cross Street towards Silver Street. Halifax favoured poles with extra-long bracket arms in the town centre, where most other operators would have used span-wires, and the example on the left is supporting one of the central area electrical feeders.

[J.A. Pitts collection,
courtesy West Yorkshire Archives, Bradford]

vulnerable to blockages, and when fogs blanketed the town, lookouts had to be posted at the junction with Commercial Street. In May, 1909, the construction of a tramway in George Street was sanctioned for use by trams to and from King Cross, thereby allowing Sowerby Bridge and Triangle cars to enter the town centre instead of terminating in Cow Green, and permitting the Hebden Bridge service to return to Commercial Street.

For similar reasons the Committee wished to double the Northgate line which constituted such a bottleneck for the services traversing North Bridge that the Queensbury, Shelf and Brighouse trams usually departed from Union Street in convoy. Unfortunately, the Board of Trade vetoed both schemes following frontagers' protests, recommending instead the use of modern colour-light signalling, and red-and-white colour signals were therefore installed in Northgate and also on the heights above Boothtown, from the "Punch Bowl" to Crow Point.

Fortunately, the Corporation later succeeded in obtaining Parliamentary approval for the George Street line, and orders were given in January, 1912, for the track to be laid as quickly as possible, with track gangs and paviors working overtime to minimise the effect on trade in the street. When the Union Street tracks were doubled, with an additional crossover, the Southowram loading point was transferred there from Broad Street in August, 1912. An attempt was made to minimise delays in Commercial Street by the laying of a third track to enable through trams to pass other trams loading at the kerbside, but although the necessary points were inserted in 1913, frontagers' objections prevented the completion of the scheme, and the points were removed ten years later without ever having been used. Elsewhere in the town, extensive track doubling was taking place, using BS no. 4 rail, and 200 rail joints were welded by the Tudor

Every inch of advertising space including the stair risers was rented by Almond, owner of Halifax's largest stock of new and second-hand furniture at no. 34, Northgate, when tramcar 58 was photographed about 1912 exhibiting its new canopy top and its Peckham truck which had been rebuilt to house a C.H. Spencer slipper brake. The location was at Salterhebble (Jubilee Road) — note the extra (third) track and overhead wire for the "Zoo Specials". The overhead wires on the main line appear to be of an early grooved-section type – unusual in Halifax, where round-section wire was almost universal. Note also the elaborate H.C.T. motif, typical of the 1910-1920 period.

[Courtesy Roy Brook]

Congestion caused by the single line in Northgate compelled cars destined for Hipperholme, Brighouse, Shelf, Boothtown and Queensbury to set out from Union Street in convoy, as in this view seen from Horton Street, where Queensbury car no., 30 was preparing to follow four other trams. Bonfire Night was approaching, and the "sandwich-board man" was advertising fireworks.

[Courtesy Roy Brook]

Electrical Engineering Co., all of which improved the quality of travel.

In the enterprising decade before the Great War, when parks and pleasure-grounds were much frequented, Halifax boasted its own Zoo in Exley Lane, formally known as the Halifax Zoological Gardens and Amusement Park, whose popularity was such that in June, 1910, a third track or loading siding was laid on the west side of Elland Road, near the "Punchbowl Inn". The 150 yard long siding accommodated five trams, and a special service was run from the Post Office at fares which presumably reflected the Traffic Superintendent's Scotch canniness, as the outward journey cost a mere penny but the inward journey twopence, on the basis that after a long, hot summer afternoon spent gazing at the beasts of the field, families with tired children would gladly pay a high fare rather than toil up Salterhebble Hill!

The two demi-cars, 95 and 96, were converted into covered, open-sided crossbench ("toastrack") vehicles for the Zoo service, subject to Board of Trade stipulations that they must carry a two-man crew and be equipped with approved braking systems. Both cars were provided with newly-introduced roller-blind destination indicators recently tried on one tramcar and gradually applied to the whole fleet in place of the old-style, cumbersome wooden signboards.

The two little cars took up their new duties during the August Bank Holiday, 1910, after which they were stored until Easter Monday, April 17th, 1911, when, as no. 96 was travelling to the Zoo, a gust of wind removed the hat of Mr.

Rothera, a visitor from rural Otley. Forgetting his 72 years, Mr. Rothera leaped from the car in pursuit of his headgear and was knocked down by a tram travelling in the opposite direction. Despite being picked up by the tramcar lifeguard, he suffered a broken hip and died of pneumonia a week later. The "toastracks" were taken out of service, the coroner having criticised the running of cars whose passengers were able to alight at either side. The Manager was instructed to alter them appropriately, but what action he took is unknown, as the cars were not referred to again for several years.

Halifax's south-westerly neighbours continued to crave the benefits of modern transport. Soyland, Barkisland, Rishworth, Stainland and Elland requested extensions of existing tramways, while Mytholmroyd dreamed of a branch line to rural Cragg Vale, but, wary of financial losses, Halifax requested subsidies which the smaller councils could not or would not provide. Soyland UDC suggested a service of "trackless cars" (trolleybuses) from Triangle tram terminus to Ripponden and Rishworth, but as such vehicles were as yet untried in the United Kingdom, the suggestion had to be declined. Nevertheless, the next Halifax Corporation Act, in 1911, empowered the Tramways Dept. to operate trolleybuses in Queen's Road, between King Cross Street and Pellon Lane, run petrol buses inside and outside the Borough, and extend the tramways to Stainland and to Elland via Elland Bridge.

By this time the Department's finances had returned to such a sound state of health that when a profit of £7,837 was achieved in March, 1911, the Finance Committee felt able to siphon off £4,807 for the relief of borough rates. Litter problems caused by discarded tram tickets in the town centre gave rise to criticism, but the Tramways Committee disclaimed responsibility until ordered by the Council to fit used ticket boxes on the platforms of each tram.

Demi-car 96 exhibits its new cross-bench conversion before re-entering service in 1910. Note the newly-fitted roller-blind destination box and the hooks above the first and fourth side bays which housed the bamboo trolley stick. The works car equipped with a telescopic tower can be glimpsed through the fourth aperture.

[Author's collection]

Coronation Day, 1911 – tramcar 89 adorned with flags, bunting, portraits, greenery, coloured bulbs, a red, white and blue trolley boom and the loyal slogan, "Success to our Colonies", stands proudly in the depot yard.
[J.A. Pitts collection, courtesy West Yorkshire Archives, Bradford]

Requests from chilled and rainsoaked passengers led to the provision of a waiting-room on the ground floor of the Conservative Club at Queensbury terminus at the joint expense of Halifax and Bradford, an amicable arrangement which lasted until 1949. At Brighouse the local Corporation's Public Urinals Sub-Committee proposed the conversion of a shop at no. 30, Bradford Road, into a waiting-room and "convenience", but as the rent demanded was thought excessive, no progress was made. More successfully, at the exposed Southowram terminus a local shopkeeper offered a room for a shelter, for which the tramways happily paid £10 a year.

The spectacular Coronation of King George V and Queen Mary in June, 1911, was enthusiastically celebrated. The Tramways Department's contribution to the local festivities was the decorating of cars 89 and 90, which were splendidly bedecked with a myriad coloured lamps, festoons of bunting and arrangements of greenery, which, temptingly, incorporated two large bunches of grapes accompanied by a polite placard:- "Passengers are earnestly requested not to pluck the grapes" – a forlorn hope, one would imagine! Both cars visited each route at double fares during the week from June 17th – 24th, earning a total of £25-8-11d which presumably offset the £240 cost of the decorations and the double wages paid to those who worked on Coronation Day. As the 1911 Act had authorised the Corporation to borrow £6,000 for the purchase of additional top covers, a deputation was despatched to inspect the latest designs offered by the United Electric Car Co., Preston, the Brush Electrical Engineering Co, Loughborough, and Milnes, Voss at Birkenhead, as a result of which twenty top covers were ordered from Brush in January, 1912, and delivered by November for mounting on the Mozley-cover car, 78, the Milnes, Voss cover car, 66, and open top cars 41 to 58.

Unusually, the enclosed portion of the new top covers was only 11'2" long (out of a possible 16'0"), although the canopy roof extended the full length of the upper deck. Thus only 18 passengers obtained shelter from the elements, with two double transverse seats and a 5-seater longitudinal bench on each side of the little saloon. This probably reflected the Board of Trade's continuing concerns about the stability of top-covered trams on narrow-gauge tramways (Burnley had similar covers), and had the additional benefit of concentrating the extra weight in the centre of the car, thereby counteracting the tendency of the trams to pitch and rock on their short-wheelbase trucks. Because of the outdated 90% direct stair arrangement on cars numbered below 83, the top saloon doors had to be fitted into the right-hand side of the bulkhead instead of occupying a central position. Simultaneously the Committee agreed to equip the open-top short canopy cars with balconies as a means of increasing their modest upper deck capacity by 8 seats, twenty cars to be adapted each year.

The progress of track doubling brought about the introduction of two new cross town services, from Highroad Well to Skircoat Green and from Causeway Foot to Savile Park, facilities which were much appreciated by their users, although the Borough Engineer had to reinstate a loop in Manor Heath Road which had been removed only a few months earlier.

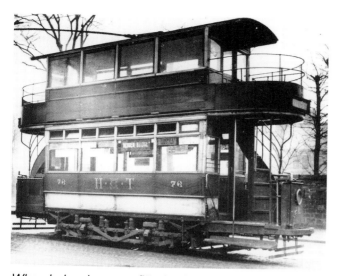

When balconies were fitted to increase tramcar seating capacity, the Turner tops were reconstructed with a central door at the head of the new spiral stairs, an extended roof and a destination box embedded in the new balcony dashplates.   No.76, with upper-deck panels painted blue, was photographed in Skircoat Green Road about 1920.
[Photo: Halifax Corporation Tramways, courtesy the late R.B. Parr]

The important role played by sand in preventing tramcar skids and runaways compelled the Department to seek a better quality of material than that which had been used thitherto. In January, 1907, two consignments of dry sand worth £6 were bought from Bradford, encouraging Mr Galloway to build a sand-drying plant near the salt store in the depot, but initially its success was limited, and damp sand continued to clog the tramcar sandbox outlet pipes. In November, 1911, the Committee accepted a tender from Bradford City Tramways for the supply of tunnel-dried sand available from the city's drying plant at its Bowling permanent way yard. There was, in addition, a small sand store at Pye Nest Farm for the peace of mind of Sowerby Bridge passengers.

For several years the condition of various stretches of route had been causing concern. An ominously–bulging wall near the 'Black Lion' at Luddenden Foot induced Lt. Col Druitt to enforce a compulsory stop for all trams entering the nearby loop (which was used only at holiday times) lest fallen debris should derail a tram and divert it into the Rochdale Canal. Complaints from traders and residents in Bull Green and King Cross Street as to "the noise created by the Tramcars" were echoed by Miss Hartley of Garden Road, Brighouse, who deplored "the disturbance and annoyance she was subjected to by the noise and vibration of the tramcars going over the two sets of points near to her residence". Hebden Bridge UDC, frustrated by Halifax's persistent refusal to remove the tram terminus from the 'dangerous' corner of Crown Street to a point nearer Hope Street, took the opportunity of condemning 'the dangerous running' and 'violent swaying' of the trams between Station Road and Hawksclough, which however was not seen as a cause of concern by the Tramways Dept.

Nevertheless, extensive repairs were carried out in places; a railgrinder was bought in 1905 from the Railway and General Engineering Co., Ltd., and thirty metal plates (at 2s 3d each) were erected at various places to remind drivers of speed restrictions. At Hipperholme the two level crossings had worn out after a life of only seven years, and were renewed in durable manganese steel at the joint expense of the tramways and Messrs. Brookes, owners of the brickworks; surprisingly the new crossings had an even shorter life than their predecessors, and had to be replaced again by Messrs., Edgar Allen at a cost of £65 each. Much alarm was voiced when Messrs Ledgard Naylor of Landsmere Quarries, Northowram, announced their intention of quarrying beneath the highway to Shelf, but the fears subsided when the highway did not!

"Turner top" car 80 leaving the "Dusty Miller" inn, Mytholmroyd, on its way to Halifax.
[Author's collection]

Having at last obtained powers to operate motor-buses, the Tramways Department voted on October 2nd, 1912, to buy three buses at £850 each. On arrival a fortnight later they inaugurated a service to Mount Tabor, and although they were fitful in operation and expensive to run, they enabled the Corporation to begin serving isolated areas where the cost of installing a tramway could not be justified.

Tenders were invited in May, 1912, for six tramcar bodies complete with top covers, to which the Board of Trade raised no objection, and Brush were once again the successful tenderers. Siemens 40 h.p motors and Westinghouse type 90 controllers were purchased, and the Engineer was authorised to build six trucks to a pattern which he had designed to overcome the problems caused earlier by top covered cars on short wheelbase trucks. The new trucks were based on the Peckham type used since 1898, but with stronger frames, short compression springs beneath the leaf-spring cantilevers, a 6'6" wheelbase and C.H. Spencer slipper brakes – a design so successful that eventually most cars were fitted with it. The top decks were of the new full-length canopy and short saloon design, but, surprisingly, with high "decency panels" which matched the height of the saloon panels and imparted a distinctly top-heavy appearance which was accentuated by the livery, as all the top-deck side panels were painted Prussian blue instead of the customary ivory. Numbered 97 to 102 and costing £1,326 each exclusive of the cost of assembly at Skircoat Road, the cars entered service early in 1913.

An early view of Highroad Well terminus, where a canopy-top car is resting near the "Horse and Jockey".
[Photo: the Tramway Museum Society]

Twenty additional top covers were acquired between December, 1912, and October, 1913, so that the benefit of canopy top-deck covers now extended to 46 cars, i.e., 41-62, 66–70, 78, 83–94 and 97–102, and nine of these were re-equipped with 40hp Siemens motors during 1913, to match their speed to that of the new rolling-stock.

Holiday traffic showed a slight but encouraging improvement in 1912; Whitsuntide travel earned the useful sum of £3,099-17-11d, and on July 11th the Tramways Committee supported a gala at the Zoo on the understanding that they would underwrite any loss up to £100 and receive half of any profit. Mr. Bunce, proprietor of the Hipperholme pleasure grounds, was permitted to affix signs to tram standards at Stump Cross and Hove Edge inviting passengers to "Alight Here for Sunny Vale".

The strategic importance of the semi-isolated Brighouse-Bailiffe Bridge tramway was enhanced in 1910 when Bradford received Parliamentary consent to extend their Wyke tramway to meet the Halifax line at Bailiffe Bridge crossroads. In May, 1912, Mr. Galloway discussed with his Bradford counterpart as to whether Halifax's trams "could be adapted to meet the requirements of through running to Bradford", ie., as dual-gauge cars operating from Brighouse or Halifax. Thus, when in January, 1913, Northowram residents once again pleaded for a better tram service, they were told that powers were to be sought for the service of cars between Halifax and Bradford "to be materially augmented and improved". In anticipation of this very desirable objective, Halifax decided to broaden the underframe of certain tramcars to enable them to accommodate wider trucks. This was achieved by the distinctly unconventional expedient of widening the underframe and the lower saloon floor, but not the ceiling, so that the sides of the saloon tapered inwards

slightly. Photographic evidence indicates that cars nos. 47, 65, 72, 77, 86, 88 and 90 were among the cars thus rebuilt.

The fortunes of the Brighouse–Bailiffe Bridge line underwent a dramatic improvement when the first Bradford tram arrived at its new terminus $37^1/_2$ yards short of the Halifax tracks on March 17th, 1913. The two sets of rails were slightly out of alignment and the wires not connected, but the public availed themselves of the new facility with such eagerness that Halifax's takings, hitherto almost the lowest on the entire network at 10.64d per passenger mile, soon rated among the highest – indeed, ten years later they were the highest of all. Within weeks Brighouse Corporation were pressing for an increased tram service as well as a parcels office at the new joint terminus so that parcels could be conveyed directly to and from Bradford. Both requests were granted, and a through service from Halifax (Union Street) was instituted in August at a 15 minutes frequency, each car displaying the destination name, "Brighouse & Bailiffe Bridge", even though inevitably each time the trams arrived at Brighouse the upper deck passengers had to reverse their seat backs if they wished to avoid completing their journey with their backs to the direction of travel.

Sloping-sided" car 86 with three-window canopy top at Pellon Barracks about 1928, when Swan Vesta matches, Hudsons' Soap and Oakey's knife polish, emery cloth and glass-paper were in popular demand

[Courtesy Roy Brook]

Similarly, the Bradford trams instituted a long cross-city service to Thornbury on the road to Leeds.

Meanwhile, a revival of the oft-discussed plan for a 1 mile 6 furlongs extension of the Halifax tramway in the opposite direction, from Brighouse up the steep hill to Rastrick had once again been quashed by the Halifax borough ratepayers at a public poll. Also quashed were the hoped-for dual-gauge services to Bradford: fears of damage to local trade still loomed large, and so the sloping-sided trams never received the dual-gauge trucks which would have made through-running possible.

Less controversial proposals for tram shelters at Stump Cross, Southowram, West Vale and Bradshaw were happily approved, and 10,000 timetable leaflets were supplied by Pickles Bros. of Hopwood Lane for a modest £20. A new scale of conductors' wages was fixed at 5¼d per hour on appointment, rising to 5¾d after 6 months and 6¼d after a year, subject to satisfactory performance. As the Electricity Department was by this time expanding considerably, Mr. Rogerson was relieved of the tramways responsibilities which had been thrust on him after the Pye Nest disaster. Acknowledging his "ability, industry and valuable services", the Committee placed the tramways under joint management in September, 1911, with Mr. Caird as Traffic Manager at an increased salary of £300 per annum, but unfortunate Mr. Galloway was adamantly refused any additional financial reward as Tramways Engineer.

In March, 1913, the Copley Ward councillors requested an extension of the Skircoat Green tramway to the top of Dudwell Lane, and a revival of the dormant Elland scheme was urged by the Halifax Chamber of Trade and the Drapers and Hosiers Association. Conversely, although Luddenden Foot U.D.C. greatly appreciated their well-established tram service, they considered the modest speed limits allowed by the Board of Trade as dangerously excessive, and Halifax courteously agreed to erect "Curve 4 m.p.h." signs at Daisy Bank on tram poles 164, 166 and 173, and a "Gradient 6 m.p.h." sign on pole no. 167. A request from Warley Road residents for the reinstatement of the long-discontinued King Cross–Pellon connection, was granted on the proviso that no

additional trams would be required, whereupon as from May 4th, 1914, a half-hourly service was instituted to and from the Post Office via Gibbet Street, West End and King Cross Street, bringing the Spring Hall Lane and Warley Road tracks back into use once more.

Early in 1914 Hebden Bridge U.D.C. asked Halifax to repair the track between Machpelah and Fallingroyd Bridge. Wary of spending money on permanent way which might ultimately pass out of their ownership, the Corporation somewhat injudiciously countered the request by enquiring whether the U.D.C. intended to exercise their right to compulsorily purchase the tracks in their area in 1921 under the terms of the 1870 Tramways Act, to which Hebden Bridge, not to be deflected from their purpose, bluntly replied that the track was unsafe, and that they were not prepared to discuss the distant future!

The vexed question of trams to Elland had at last been resolved by Huddersfield Corporation, who in January, 1914, had extended their Birchencliffe route down "The Ainleys", and on May 29th opened the final section of the line, via Jepson Lane and Long Wall to a point in Saddleworth Road approximately 100 feet from Halifax's West Vale terminus. Possibly this was the spur that Halifax needed to accede to Stainland U.D.C.'s long-deferred tramway ambitions, and as spring turned to summer, detailed plans were drawn up by the Borough Engineer. A request from Southowram UDC for an extension from Bank Top to the Pack Horse Inn was accepted on condition that the Corporation would be paid a yearly subsidy of £200 for five years and £100 thereafter until the line became profitable – a clause which the UDC found unacceptable.

Meanwhile, some weeks previously in far-off Sarajevo the imperial heir to Austro-Hungary had been assassinated, and unwittingly, Europe was drifting towards war. Almost without warning the crisis deepened into hostility, and on August 4th the United Kingdom joined the conflict. Patriotic enthusiasm was immediate and far-reaching: within days the tramway ranks were depleted as loyal Halifax lads queued to enlist. The world was about to change, and although no one suspected it, to change beyond recall.

Tramcar 87, fitted with a canopy top in 1913 and seen descending Godley Lane, is about to pass the Stump Cross section–breaker and feeder-point which are indicated by the white band on the tram standard, and the adjacent junction box. The Northowram line ascends the steep hill (centre right), but car 87 is due to bear right past the Museum Hotel ("Stocks' Ales") and head for Hipperholme and Brighouse. The wooden hut (left) houses H. Smith's confectioner's, baker's and tobacconist's shop as well as a Tramways Parcels Office, and the Stump Cross Inn is located centre left.

[Photo: Lilywhite Ltd.]

Chapter 11

GREAT WAR

The spirit of patriotism which pervaded the whole nation affected the Tramways Committee also. On September 21st 1914, decisions were made to allow the military authorities to place recruiting advertisements on the trams, to prepare an illuminated tramcar for the same purpose, and to allow Northern Command to commandeer the old Mile Cross depot. Knowing that H.M. Government wished to buy surplus petrol-buses for use as troop carriers, they contributed 3 guineas (£3.3s) to the Electric Vehicle Committee of the Incorporated Electrical Association to promote the use of battery propulsion, and a few months later offered to exchange their petrol buses for battery-powered vehicles. Fortunately the latter never materialised, as they would have been totally unsuited to Halifax hills.

Some Belgian refugees who had been obliged to flee their war-ravaged homeland found refuge in Halifax, where the Corporation offered them free travel until the end of the year, and provided a special Sunday morning tram from and back to Causeway Foot for use by those billeted at Ogden who wished to attend the Roman Catholic church at Halifax.

Faced with a prohibition on unnecessary capital expenditure and a rapidly-worsening shortage of men and materials, the Tramways Department had to discontinue track improvements and large-scale renewals, only the most essential repairs being allowed. In February 1915, the possibility of night-time air raids by German Zeppelins brought about the imposition of a 'blackout' whereby street lamps and tramcar lights were 'darkened' or masked to avoid detection from the air, and eighteen months later white bands were painted on the tram standards to render them more visible to pedestrians after dark. The need for these precautions was emphasised by a 'Zeppelin scare' on April 14th 1915, followed on February 5th, 1916, by an even more serious alarm when the mill 'buzzers' (hooters) sounded an urgent warning and the power was switched off, bringing the trams to a standstill. Fortunately, no actual raid materialised. The manpower shortage compelled the Committee to depart from all known precedents: they recruited 'Lady Tram Conductors' (but not more than ten!) in November, 1915, and even (in February, 1917) appointed Mrs. O. Smith as a Lady Inspector. In order to assist the ladies in their task, the Department replaced the last of the cumbersome destination boards on the trams with modern roller blinds, supplied by the Equipment and Engineering Co (ECO).

Wartime emergencies did not diminish Yorkshiremen's habit of 'plain speaking', and the longstanding friction between Hebden Bridge U.D.C. and Halifax Corporation provided another opportunity for frank discussion in April, 1915, when the U.D.C. requested a tram shelter at the terminus and simultaneously refused to extend Halifax's operating powers beyond 1921 unless Halifax carried out their promise to build the Whiteley Arches extension. The U.D.C. were promptly informed that the shelter would not be provided unless the operating powers were extended, and there the matter rested until October, 1917, when at the U.D.C.'s request Halifax, Todmorden Corporation and Todmorden Rural District representatives once again discussed ways of linking the tram terminus at Crown Street with the nearest Todmorden bus terminus at Sandbed. Unfortunately, nothing could be done until the war ended.

For several years the tramways had been free from serious accidents, thanks to the efficiency of the C.H. Spencer slipper brake. There was consternation therefore when two trams inexplicably ran downhill out of control and overturned. The first accident occurred to tramcar 89 on a cross-town journey from Causeway Foot to Savile Park on May 22nd, 1915. On the gradual descent of Ovenden Road

No reason could be found for the overturning of tramcar 89 at Lee Bridge on May 22nd, 1915, but the photograph provides a clear view of the car's underframe, lifeguard equipment and the C.H. Spencer slipper brakes mounted between the wheels.
[Photo: Halifax Corporation Tramways, courtesy the late R.B. Parr]

the car halted without difficulty at several tram stops, but as it began to move away from the compulsory halt at Shroggs Road, the leading wheels unaccountably left the rails, causing the car to veer unsteadily across the setts and slowly overturn, almost completely blocking the narrow road between the two mills at Lee Bridge, fortunately without

Although the photograph does not convey the impression of an English summer day, the date was nevertheless July 15th, 1917, when tramcar 99 ran away and overturned at Ambler Thorn. Against a background of wild hills an open-top tram is preparing to ascend Priestley Hill on its way to Halifax.
[Photo: Halifax Corporation Tramways, courtesy the late R.B. Parr]

A backward glance towards Queensbury and the loop which no.99 entered at excessive speed.
[Photo: Halifax Corporation Tramways, courtesy the late R.B. Parr]

injuries. On examination, the tram's brakes and its newly built 6-foot wheelbase Halifax-style Peckham truck were found to be in excellent condition, and the driver was absolved from blame.

The second incident took place at the height of summer, July 15th 1917, when a Mrs Easton and her husband, a carter for Luddenden Foot Co-operative Society, had decided to take advantage of the fair weather and enjoy a tram ride to Queensbury, a place which they had never visited. Together with about 40 other passengers they later boarded tram no 99, one of the newest in the fleet, and like most of their fellow-travellers they settled down on the open balconies for the return journey. As the tram approached the Ambler Thorn loop at about 9.15pm several ladies began to make their way to the rear platform in readiness for alighting at Roper Lane, but to their consternation the car failed to halt, and entered the loop at excessive speed, causing it to leave the rails and rattle over the setts. At the curved end of the loop the wheels dropped back into the rail grooves, and the

sudden shock and change of direction caused the tram to sway violently and topple on its side. Mrs Easton was fatally injured, and 36 others were despatched to hospital. Once again no mechanical defect could be found, and as the driver appeared to have acted properly, no conclusion was reached. In addition to the insurance claims and repair costs, the Department suffered the loss of £5-2-0d from the conductor's cash bag during the commotion.

By the beginning of 1916, monetary inflation was beginning to undermine municipal finances, and the parcels charges had to be increased substantially, e.g.

Not exceeding 5lb. – 2d for 2 stages, 3d for 6 stages and over;
To Bradford – up to 7lb: 4d; up to 56 lb: 8d.
To Heavy Woollen District (via Bradford) — up to 7lb : 5d;
— up to 56lb : 9d.

During the year the shortage of staff and serviceable tramcars compelled the Department to reduce all services and eliminate various stopping-places, although the Council rejected proposals for a 50% fares increase. Wounded soldiers sent for treatment in the area were allowed free travel to and from the Elland V.A.D. Hospital at West Vale, and as the casualty lists lengthened, the West Vale service had to be augmented despite the shortages.

The wartime munitions drive necessitated the laying of a third level crossing at Hipperholme where Brookes' Chemicals Ltd. were installing a railway connection to their explosives department. Messrs. Edgar Allen provided the necessary trackwork at a cost of £96. Unfortunately, for other, non-essential purposes, new rails were unobtainable, and short lengths of rail from rarely-used loops were retrieved for re-use elsewhere. However, when the 19 year old track in Gibbet Street wore out, it had to be replaced from the Department's fast-dwindling stocks, and so desperate was the shortage of labour that the Borough Engineer was authorised to hire tracklayers at whatever wages they would accept!

In December, 1917, the Board of Trade proposed the setting-up of a national Tramways Control Board, and despite natural misgivings, the Corporation sensibly made use of it to press for immediate powers to increase fares beyond the limits imposed by the local Acts. Such was the sense of urgency that from January 14th, 1918, the Tramways Committee abolished transfer tickets as well as the lightly-used Warley Road service. Perversely, the Council insisted on February 18th that the Warley Road Circular be resumed, and within a few weeks Mr Caird, unable any longer to bear the strain of insistent demands and dwindling resources, was obliged to take four months' rest and a 'change of air'.

For his remaining colleagues there was no respite. Under pressure from the Board of Trade, services were reduced even further from June 10th; private hire was discontinued, and 'the one-man car' was confined to Horton Street (Ward's End – Old Station) at a penny fare. The other demi-car, no. 96, casually referred to as 'the old tramcar now used as a travelling kitchen', had been pressed into service for the benefit of the hungry. Horse-meat for human consumption had been on sale in the town since November, 1916, and in

(above) A clearer view of the Ambler Thorn loop, showing how a typical Halifax straight-entry and dog-leg exit loop straddled the highway. The device on the tram pole bracket arm appears to be a semaphore signal controlling access to the loop.

[Photo: Halifax Corporation Tramways, courtesy the late R.B. Parr]

January, 1918, Ald Spencer was co-opted by the Ministry of Food as its Director of National Kitchens. No doubt at his suggestion no. 96 was loaned in May, 1918, to the Local Food Control Committee, who paid its working costs and the cost of alterations. Briefly glimpsed in a wartime cine film, the grey-painted 'kitchen' offered a bill of fare which augmented meagre wartime rations, i.e.,

> Pint of Soup or Dumplings or Potatoes – 1d
> Vegetable Pie 4d., Rice Pudding 1½d and
> Ginger Pudding 2d (with custard, one hopes!)

Predictably, the impressive power consumption of the travelling kitchen and its ovens caused problems in outer areas, particularly Mytholmroyd, where tram drivers were asked to proceed with caution when it was in their vicinity lest the soup should "go off the boil"!

On routes not provided with a substation or "booster", the distance from the generating station caused voltage drops which gave rise to the jocular observation that Halifax's trams were like horses – the nearer they were to the stable, the more lively was their performance! However, the restricted voltage played a useful role in tramcar timekeeping after dark. For instance, whenever a tramcar climbing towards Queensbury passed under the Boothtown section-breaker and feeder-point, the perceptible dimming of the lights in the other tram standing

at Queensbury terminus warned its driver that departure time was nigh, and as soon as a subsequent increase in brightness told him that the approaching car had reached the summit of the hill, he set off, so that the two trams would conveniently pass in the loop at Catherine Slack.

By this time, supplies of high quality coach paint and gold transfers had long since dried up, and in common with most other operators the Tramways Dept. had to resort to plain, unadorned battleship grey and white. A few cars appeared in pale blue and white, and as the Corporation continued to insist that all advertisements should conform to the colours of

Demi-car 96 after conversion to a "National Communal Kitchen " in 1918.

[J.A. Pitts collection, courtesy West Yorkshire Archives, Bradford]

the tramcar on which they were displayed, rather than in the advertisers' own "house colours", familiar advertisements were to be seen in a variety of unfamiliar hues.

"Battleship grey" was applied also to the Tramways Department's contributions to "Tank Week" in April, 1918. Inspired by a visit to Blackpool made by Mr. Galloway, the resourceful Skircoat Road works staff disguised demi-car 95 and a bus to resemble tanks, which they patriotically named "Duke of Wellington" and "Havercake Lads" in honour of Halifax's famous and ever-popular regiment stationed at Pellon Barracks.

The Halifax Corporation Act of 1915 had renewed the Stainland tramway powers and had also authorised the Corporation to construct a 'railless' (trolleybus) route, not in Queen's Road as envisaged in pre-war days, but from Pellon New Road to the moorland settlements of Mount Tabor and Wainstalls. Optimistic that electrically-driven 'railless' cars might prove more reliable than the petrol buses used thitherto, the Tramways Department purchased from Dundee Corporation two Railless Electric Traction (R.E.T) cars which had briefly been used on the Clepington Road route from 1912 to 1914. The two vehicles were delivered to Skircoat Road depot on Monday, February 14th, 1918, but could not be used for their intended purpose until hostilities ceased, as depot foreman Jack Naylor recalled.

"My workmates and myself parked them in the tramcar body shop, where they stayed for several weeks. Later, the joiners removed the seats and installed welding equipment in the interior, making them mobile welding plants. Owing to the shortage of new tram rails, the Department was having a very difficult task keeping the tramcar services in operation. These difficulties were (partly) solved by welding new strips of metal on to the existing rails where the check rail had been broken off. For this reason, one of the mobile welding plants was placed on the Hebden Bridge section, while the other was taken by myself to the Mytholm (level) Crossing (at Hipperholme). The Permanent Way staff utilised these two cars for various jobs until hostilities ceased", drawing power from the overhead tram wire via one of the trolley booms and completing the electrical circuit by means of an iron shoe placed in the groove of the tram rail.

In the autumn of 1918 the war suddenly began to draw to a close, and national pay scales mounted alarmingly. Weekday overtime, Saturday and holiday working in excess of 9 hours qualified for "time and a quarter" and the working week was officially reduced to 47 hours. Hostilities finally ceased at 11am on November 11th 1918, when war-weary Halifax paused for a few hours of heartfelt rejoicing.

"Sloping-sided " car 90 in its wartime guise – plain grey and white livery, and placards advertising that the "maximum number of passengers allowed to travel on the upper deck is 38", all of whom were requested to have their fares ready for collection. On the dashplate can be seen the postbox bracket (right) and (next to the fleet number) the long-disused trolley-rope holder. The handbrake and slipper-brake wheel (left) are mounted separately, and – a sign of wartime lack of maintenance – the destination box appears to be about to drop on to the driver's white-topped summer uniform cap.

[Courtesy Roy Brook]

Chapter 12

INTERLUDE

"New Boy at the Orphanage" by R.C. Scriven. (Reproduced by courtesy of the "Halifax Courier")

In 1918 when I was 11, all I knew about Halifax, Nova Scotia, was where it was. What I didn't know about Halifax, Yorkshire, could have been written in a schoolboy fist, on the back of a penny stamp.

In those bad, old, faraway, inefficient days if you put a penny stamp on an envelope and addressed it to Pough-keepsie or Penzance it would be delivered first post the following morning without fail. Even I, young and ignorant as I was, knew that.

I was an orphan. My father's eldest brother, my uncle James, was the guardian of myself and my brother Neville, four years younger. As it was wartime, my uncle in his wisdom decided to confine us to the care of Iron Ann, a farmer's wife who lived at Low Moor Farm, North Rigton.

Ann was a disciplinarian of the old school. She disciplined us and fed us on good plain, wholesome food — podge, lumps included.

In late August 1918, my uncle took me out of Iron Ann's care, left her in charge of Neville and took me to Leeds Central Station. All he said was: 'You're going to a new school'.

The locomotive that drew our train was in the black livery of the old Lancashire and Yorkshire railway. It snorted like a dragon. It climbed towards the hills, it chanted a song:

"To Lancasher, to Lancasher to buy
a pocket Hankasher."

I pressed my nose against the cold window pane and watched the world go by, as boys do.

Presently we came to a station, Low Moor. In my guileless innocence I supposed that it had been named after Low Moor Farm, though its black, steep hills looked very different from the flat green fields I knew.

On snorted the dragon, up, up, up into the hills. There were exciting tunnels, through which the dragon roared and snorted. Tunnels which smelt thrillingly of sulphurous smoke through which ruby red sparks floated.

Eventually the dragon panted to a halt in a strange wild station called Halifax. The platform where we got out had a kind of long toothed green wooden fringe. On the other side was a mountain. 'Beacon Hill' said my uncle. In the lee of this terrific mountain was a huge building called Mackintosh's Toffee.

Grabbing my hand, my uncle marched me over a square of cobblestones and we boarded a tram.

There are two sounds which all who knew Halifax as it used to be will never forget. One is the sound of iron-rimmed clogs battering the pavements. The other is the deep, whining sound of Halifax trams

No trams in all the world could match the trams of Halifax. They rolled, they lurched, they swayed and they bucked like bronchos. "Ee-whine, ee-whine, ee-whine;" they droned and sang. Ours, like all the others, climbed implacably upwards. Enchanted by this marvellous chant I pressed my nose against the cold glass. I saw a giant's wood of tall chimneys belching smoke. I saw the station, the town, Mackintosh's toffee factory, rows and rows and rows of houses dropping behind us.

Free School Lane, Halifax.

Car 63 has just passed St.Jude's Church on a return journey from Savile Park about 1913.
[J.A. Pitts collection, courtesy West Yorkshire Archives, Bradford]

Still the tram climbed, it seemed to me, towards the sky. "Ee-whine, ee-whine" it sang. It passed a broad almost green expanse of grass; I saw ahead the most magnificent palace I'd ever seen, bigger, blacker, grander than Leeds Town Hall.

Beyond it rose a slender, fairy tower like the ivory minaret of Gibb's tooth-paste, except that it was black, not ivory.

The tram stopped. "Come along, Ronald", said my uncle. He struck off at an angle across the rough almost green grass.

My uncle took me along a tessellated corridor to a terminal door on which he knocked. A resonant voice said; "Come in".

We entered the study of G.B. Newport MA (Cantab) the headmaster of the Crossley and Porter Orphan Homes and Schools. As my uncle closed the door, symbolically he closed the prison gates behind me. One of the most momentous journeys of my life had ended. I had arrived in Halifax.

21912

THE ROYAL INFIRMARY, HALIFAX.

Car 85 ascending Free School Lane on a journey to
Savile Park about 1913, is seen outside the Royal
Infirmary.

[J.A. Pitts collection,
courtesy West Yorkshire Archives, Bradford]

Fireworks at the Zoo and the virtues of Farr's Nervine
('Cures Tic and all Nervous Pains') were being
advertised by car 33 when it was photographed at Pye
Nest on a journey from Sowerby Bridge to Cow Green.
[Courtesy Roy Brook]

CHAPTER 13

RECONSTRUCTION

The return of peace enabled the Corporation to turn their thoughts to the formidable and daunting task of renewal and reconstruction. Four years of enforced neglect had taken their toll – many miles of heavily-worn track, overworked trams and many hundreds of tram poles in need of repainting. Brighouse and Mytholmroyd were complaining about the permanent-way in their areas, and Triangle passengers were protesting against reductions to early morning and workmen's services.

In a more constructive vein, Stainland were pressing Halifax to make early use of the powers granted (or re-

and Bailiffe Bridge sections who had observed the gradual modernisation of neighbouring fleets, the Tramways Committee in April, 1919, resolved to equip one tramcar with glazed platform vestibules for the better protection of staff and passengers. The favoured vehicle was canopy-top car 50, which returned to service in 1920 with neat Bradford-style angular wood and glass vestibules which achieved instant popularity.

An AEC chassis for the motor tower-wagon was bought for £1,006 from the West End Motor Co. and the question of the vacant Mile Cross Depot was solved in May when Messrs. W. Asquith purchased it for £6,500 subject to the

Car 16, seen here at King Cross in 1932, had been completely rebuilt with square-topped windows and Bradford-style platform vestibules complete with half-lights above the platform entrance. The old-style Peckham truck had been strengthened to accommodate the C.H. Spencer slipper brake, and the coat of arms was of the miniscule 1928 variety.

[Author's collection]

granted) in the Halifax Corporation Act, 1915, and, surprisingly, in view of their heavy commitments and their prolonged hesitation in pre-war days, the Corporation undertook to build the Stainland extension as soon as labour and materials became available and the grossly-inflated price of steel had subsided.

Five hundred tons of rails at £17-15-0d per ton and a corresponding quantity of fishplates at £21-17-6d per ton were ordered from Walter Scott, Leeds, in May, 1919, this being the first bulk purchase permissible since 1914, facilitating the total renewal of the decrepit track between Lee Bridge and Athol Mount, Ovenden. At Skircoat Road the renovation of the tram fleet began in earnest, and no doubt at the request of drivers on the West Vale, Queensbury, Shelf

removal of the rails, pointwork and overhead equipment. A much-appreciated revival of a colourful pre-war custom came in June 1919, when several trams were decorated and illuminated to mark the longed-for Peace Celebrations.

A detailed survey of the proposed extension from West Vale to Stainland having been undertaken, in July 1919, the

Committee invited tenders for the necessary materials, thereby arousing the attention of Soyland U.D.C. in the adjoining Ryburn valley who continued to hanker after bus services connecting Triangle tram terminus with Rishworth, Ripponden Bank and West Vale via Barkisland. Although Ripponden Bank was considered too steep for buses, Halifax offered a bus service to Slitherow Bridge, Soyland, provided that the U.D.C. would install street lighting at the terminus and agree to a loss guarantee of £200 per annum – at which point Soyland lost all interest.

Gradually, the tramcar fleet began to regain its smart pre-war appearance, with gleaming Prussian blue and ivory vehicles emerging from the Skircoat Road paintshops, and wartime shortages faded into history. Sowerby Bridge now felt justified in complaining about the cost-saving practice of reversing alternate trams in Wharf Street instead of continuing to Station Road, but although the practice officially ceased in March 1920, from time to time one or two top-covered cars travelled as far as Wharf Street at rush hours – but not beyond, as they would have suffered instant decapitation by the low railway bridge.

Much of the tramcar equipment had now 'come of age', and was due for replacement. Late in 1920 six trams were re-equipped with motors and controllers supplied by the Metropolitan Vickers Electrical Co. of Manchester at a cost of £726 per car, and a year later two dozen sets of 'Metrovick' motors and English Electric type DB1 controllers were bought at an increased price of £760 per tram. An offer from Sheffield Corporation of old single-deck trams previously used on the hilly Walkley route was courteously considered but wisely declined, as Halifax had sufficient old tramcars already.

When the tracks across North Bridge were renewed in June/July, 1920, the town terminus of the Boothtown and Queensbury trams was temporarily removed to the foot of Haley Hill, while the Brighouse, Shelf and Southowram cars operated from New Bank.

The problem of tramway finances was beginning to reach epic proportions, as the Tramways Committee needed to increase revenues in order to build up a reserve fund which would pay for large-scale track renewals and wipe out the loans still outstanding on the original, worn-out installations.

They faced formidable problems:-

---

1) serious inflation and consequential wage demands;

2) industrial depression which was reducing the patronage of the trams;

3) the unwillingness and often the inability of many passengers to pay higher fares;

4) the querulous attitude of some of the smaller local authorities, particularly in the Calder Valley, who, having no financial liability towards the tramways, felt free to criticise Halifax's apparent indifference to the worsening state of the track.

Even within the Halifax Council Chamber the Committee were often unable to impress upon their colleagues the seriousness of the situation. In November, 1919, they attempted to increase income by imposing a fare scale of 1d per mile, thereby raising the Hebden Bridge fare to an unheard-of level of 7d. Then, in July, 1920, they proposed to double the 1d fare and introduce intermediate $1\frac{1}{2}$d stages, but were overruled by the Council, who allowed the 2d minimum fare but rejected the experimental $1\frac{1}{2}$d fare designed to mollify passengers who boarded at points between the fare stages. Understandably, the increases aroused opposition.

Next, the Committee requested that ownership of the permanent way be transferred to them from the Highways Committee. But that, too, was rejected. Patiently persevering, the Committee resolved to fill the long-vacant post of Tramways Manager by upgrading Mr Galloway, the engineer. The Council referred the matter back for further discussion, but the Committee insisted that the appointment was necessary for the efficient running of the undertaking. Unimpressed, the Council rejected the motion again after a heated two-hour debate, whereupon the frustrated Tramways Committee chairman (Ald.C.F. Spencer), his deputy (Coun A Bradley) and the chairman of the tramways special sub-committee (Coun R Stirk) angrily resigned their posts.

Ald Spencer bluntly reminded his recalcitrant colleagues that if the backlog of track repairs were to be overcome, the Corporation would need to renew 6 or 7 miles of track every year at a cost of £15,000 per mile, and that repeated delays would merely compound the problem. Until 1915 the tramways had been one of the Corporation's most prosperous undertakings, but now the situation was daunting. For two years the Council had refused to allow fares increases, so that the coffers were now depleted at a time when track renewal ought to be a priority; there was little point in placing new or overhauled trams in service if after a few days they suffered broken axles or similar damage because of track defects. The undertaking needed to be restored to a commercial, businesslike and vigorous condition, with permanent-way repairs under the direct control of the Tramways Committee. The health of the Traffic Superintendent (Mr. Caird) had been seriously undermined by the prevailing stressful conditions (he had to resign shortly afterwards and died three years later at the age of 49). Mr. Galloway deserved promotion, as he was a strong leader (a trait of which not all the councillors approved) and was thoroughly experienced in the technical and commercial aspects of the undertaking.

Under the temporary chairmanship of the Mayor (Ald. Hey) the shaken Tramways Committee resumed its duties, and this time the Council, though still reluctant, were more conciliatory. Permanent-way responsibilities were duly handed over, with Mr. E. H. Dolling from Rochdale Corporation appointed as engineer, and the depot was extended to provide additional space for tramcar maintenance as well as the construction of much-needed new vehicles, it having been estimated that the Department could design and build trams at two-thirds of the cost of commercially-manufactured products.

The thornier (and costlier) problem of track renewals aroused much more opposition, and at first the Council could not bring themselves to approve a three-year programme involving a substantial Government loan:-

Causeway Foot	£72,412
Pellon	19,504
Hebden Bridge	95,885
West Vale	55,421
	£243,222

Common sense prevailed eventually, although the programme was destined not to be achieved within the desired three years.

The Committee's only significant rebuff at the hands of the Council in 1921 stemmed from a request for the Finance Committee to increase the Borough rates by a shilling (1/-)

it before April, the Easter holiday tram service beyond Mytholmroyd had to be restricted.

In an enterprising endeavour to reduce the price of tram rails, the Corporation pressed the Municipal Tramways Association to consider bulk buying, but other municipalities would not accept the principle.

Meanwhile, the Tramways Department's Parcels Service was quietly continuing to provide a quick, cheap and popular public facility. Goods despatched via Bradford to Leeds and the Heavy Woollen District (Batley, Dewsbury etc.) now cost a minimum of 9d (3lb weight) and a maximum of 5/- (2 hundredweights), although perambulators, bicycles and "ordinary sewing machines" cost 3/- each to transport. The

At 3-5p.m. on a sunny day in the 1920s a canopy- top car rumbles across North Bridge against a background of mills, tall chimneys and the steep hills which impressed Daniel Defoe two centuries earlier. New Bank begins its ascent on the right of the tram.

{Courtesy: Roy Brook }

in anticipation of a loss on the year's operations, a novel ruse which the municipal treasurers declined to entertain. In the event, the net loss turned out to be a mere £618-2-9d brought about by industrial depression and a consequential loss of 2,472,364 passengers, and the wages bill represented a 246% increase over 1914 levels. Even the weather had frowned on the trams; rain had fallen on 191 days, discouraging families from frequenting their much loved 'beauty spots' at Hardcastle Crags, Sunny Vale, Ogden Moors, Cragg Vale and the parks. However, the trams continued to be the Electricity Department's favourite customer, as they consumed one third of its total output! Embarrassingly, the output in the upper Calder Valley was abruptly reduced in February, 1921, when the Hebden Bridge rotary converter failed, and as the General Electric Co. were unable to repair

work of loading all these items on to the trams (driver's platform only of course!) and then trans-shipping them to the Bradford cars was considerable, and as a means of simplifying the process, Bradford City Tramways were invited to run their "Electric Battery Vehicles" through to Halifax, but as the vehicles (Bradford's two original trolleybuses converted to goods wagons) were fully occupied in making deliveries in their own area and to Leeds, the suggestion was not pursued.

Premises were purchased in Powell Street (between Fountain Street and Rawson Street) for use as a central parcels office and tramways inspectors' kiosk linked to the departmental telephone network.

Chapter 14

GALES AND GALAS

The morning of Friday, December 3rd, 1920, was wild and windy, obliging Halifax folk to hold on to their hats as they struggled to their places of work. By early afternoon a full-scale gale was raging over the town and its surroundings, and on the encircling heights the force of the storm was terrific – nowhere more so than at Stocks Gate on the Queensbury route, where, to quote the 'Halifax Courier', "this particular portion of the road is the most exposed on the whole of that bleak route. It is at the height of the hill and open to the full force of the wind from all directions. It forms a gap in which the gales collect and rush over it with the full might of their concentration".

At about 2pm top-covered tramcar no. 50 left Union Street for Queensbury, halting at intervals on the ascent of Haley Hill and Boothtown Road to allow passengers to alight, so that when it set off from the Boothtown fare stage only two

car sideways, lifting one side off the rails, and before it had time to right itself, a second blast toppled it on its side across the down track. Wrenched from the overhead wires, the flailing trolley boom struck the nearest wall while the passengers and staff were flung across the saloon.

Both adult passengers lay injured, but the agile boy scrambled out of the tram and was not seen again. Summoned by the lineside telephone and scarcely able to believe that a ten-ton tramcar could be toppled by the elements, Mr Galloway and Inspectors Drinkwater and Lumb hurried to the scene and sent for a breakdown gang, but not surprisingly it proved impossible to raise no. 50 in the teeth of the gale.

Meanwhile on the Queensbury side of the loop, two Halifax-bound trams had been waiting for some time, and when the wind had abated somewhat, the first of these, no.

Car 98 and vestibuled car 50 lie side by side at Stocks Gate, Catherine Slack, after having been toppled by gales, while a works car presumably laden with jacks and other lifting equipment waits for the wind to abate. The surroundings, photographed towards Halifax, are little changed eighty-four years later.
[Copyright: Halifax Courier Ltd.]

adults and a boy remained on board. Partially sheltered by the glazed platform vestibules fitted to the tram only a few months earlier, Motorman Lumb and Conductor Midgley were at first unaware of the increasing violence around them.

However, when the tram came to rest in the Stocks Gate loop, waiting for a car from Queensbury to pass in the opposite direction, they were assailed by the shrieking and buffeting of the gale. A sudden tremendous blast rocked the

98, was allowed to venture over the points, using the outward track as a means of circumventing its capsized companion. At that moment another tram arrived from Halifax, but was promptly sent back whence it came, and as soon as it had moved off, no. 98 began to follow it. A malicious gust of wind then sprang up and blew the trolley off the wire – a very unusual occurrence – and before it could be retrieved, no. 98 too was blown over, to the astonishment of the tramway officials.

At that, the breakdown gang abandoned the unequal struggle, leaving the two tramcars lying side by side with the third tram standing in the shelter of the nearby houses until next day. Needless to say, no trams ventured beyond Boothtown until calmer weather returned, and when they did they were all open top cars which presented much less wind resistance. This action was approved on behalf of the Board of Trade by Major G. L. Hall, R.E., who advised the installation of an 'anemometer station' (wind-gauge) which would automatically transmit wind velocities to the Tramways offices at Skircoat Road. Suitable equipment was located in June, 1921, and installed on one of the tram poles, and H.M. Meteorological Dept, ("the Met. Office") in London contracted to provide 24 hours forewarning of winds likely to exceed 40 mph.

It was not long before Queensbury U.D.C. were pressing for the reintroduction of top-covered cars and suggesting the provision of an extra loop in a more sheltered area so that trams would not have to linger at Stocks Gate. Halifax agreed to lay a new 600 yard extension of the Stocks Gate loop as far as the 'Cavendish Hotel', and with the approval of the West Riding County Council (the road being a County highway) the work was begun in April, 1922, but surprisingly not completed until June 18th, 1923. Covered-top trams finally re-appeared at Queensbury in June of that year. It should be added that although the Bradford trams serving Queensbury from the opposite direction never suffered the same fate as their Halifax colleagues, their conductors were ordered as a precaution to open all the upper deck windows when gales were blowing, but the passengers always adamantly closed them again.

Catastrophes such as the above have always tended to linger in popular memory and thus obscure the humdrum, day-to-day work which the Halifax trams performed during their forty year lifespan, and it is worth recording that during that period, they transported no fewer than 820,000,000 passengers with only 19 fatalities – a proud record for trams tackling such a difficult terrain.

While the folk of Queensbury had been agitating for the return of covered-top trams, the residents of Stainland had been looking forward to trams of any kind, as the press revealed early in 1921 – "Stainlanders belong to that class of people who are never contented until their dreams are realised. For many months the coming of the Halifax trams to the village on the hill has been the cause of feverish and restless expectancy", and, shortly afterwards, "The eager minds of the villagers are now fixed at Easter; will the cars be climbing the hill in time for the holiday?" Steady progress had been made; all the poles had been in place since June, 1920, and by November the rails had reached Little Bradley. Two months later the Tramways Department agreed to Stainland's request that as soon as the tramway had been completed as far as Holywell Green, the West Vale service should be extended to that point.

And so it was that on the morning of March 16th, 1921, the villagers delightedly beheld the arrival at the Station Hotel, Holywell Green, of tramcar no. 50, newly released from the Works following its Stocks Gate ordeal but shorn of its covered top, bearing the official inspector, Major Mount, who declared himself satisfied with what he had seen. A pleasant Spring day then heralded the inauguration of the public service on Thursday, March 24th, when a special tramcar conveyed the Mayor (Ald. Hey), Town Clerk, Borough Engineer, Borough Treasurer (did he collect the fares?), Tramways Engineer (Mr Galloway), the Chairman and Clerk of Stainland U.D.C. and a complement of councillors. A minute or two before midday, the tram rolled into West Vale

and halted before venturing on to the new line. Flags were flourished, schoolchildren cheered and millworkers spared a few minutes from their dinner-time to hear the Mayor declare the extension open and present free tram tickets to the children.

Having digested a celebratory "meat and two veg" repast at Stainland Mechanics' Institute, the U.D.C. expressed thanks to Halifax for having "kept faith", and for their unfailing courtesy. "Stainland has a church, four chapels, its own waterworks, sewage works, golf links, capital Council offices and a public debt of only £2,000", they declared proudly. "So if anyone ought to be happy, it is the Stainlander!"

The happiness was slightly marred by the revelation that the tram fare from Commercial Street was to be 7d, or 3d from West Vale. After negotiation, the through fare was reduced to 6d, and extra late-evening cars were run to Salterhebble and West Vale to ensure that the longer-distance Stainland revellers were not crowded off their trams by short-distance riders.

The final section of the new line, from Holywell Green to Stainland, was opened on Saturday, May 14th. Regrettably, the extreme narrowness of the long main street prevented the trams from proceeding beyond Crossfield at the entrance to the village, but this deficiency had no effect on revenue, which quickly established itself at a very satisfactory 29.08d per car mile, to the chagrin of the local railway branch line,

Photographs of Stainland trams are extremely rare. In this view, car 52 on a journey from Stainland to Halifax and West End has halted at the West Vale fare stage, with the railway arch in the distance and signboards advising passengers to "Stand Here for Stainland" and "Stand Here for Halifax" visible to the left and right of the tram. The tramway between West Vale (Saddleworth Road) and Stainland was the only section equipped with overhead span-wire construction throughout.

which saw its patronage vanish overnight. There were a few grumbles, of course; with a half-hourly frequency it was found that each tram had a 13 minute layover period at the terminus, a cause of some congestion in the narrow highway, but when the time–table was adjusted, the complaints disappeared, and a new feeder cable laid from the power station to the overhead section feeder at Prescott Street near Ward's End boosted the tramcars' speeds very satisfactorily.

The long-simmering policy dispute between the Tramways Committee and the Borough Council was finally resolved when the latter consented to reinstate the long-vacant post of Tramways General Manager, and six prominent applicants were interviewed:-

1) Mr. A. C. Baker, Assistant Engineer, Birmingham Corporation Tramways,

2) Mr. J. S. Hamilton, General Assistant, Leeds City Tramways,

3) Mr. Ben Hall, General Manager, Wigan Corporation Tramways,

4) Mr. J. W. Galloway, Tramways Engineer, Halifax Corporation Tramways,

5) Mr. F.A. Fitzpayne, Deputy Tramways Manager, Edinburgh Corporation,

6) Mr. T. G. Richardson, General Manager and Engineer, West Hartlepool Corporation Tramways (ex Colne Corporation Light Railways).

Mr Baker achieved eminence a few years later when he was appointed General Manager of the large Birmingham Corporation undertaking and Mr. Fitzpayne ultimately became the innovative General Manager of Edinburgh Corporation Transport, but for the Halifax Tramways Committee on March 18th the choice was Mr Ben Hall, at a salary of £900 per annum.

A new, experienced hand was certainly needed, as operating expenses at 26.284d per car mile were not being matched by an average income of only 25.347d. The West Vale – Highroad Well service was achieving the best results at 29.73d, with Brighouse and Bailiffe Bridge not far behind at 29.29d and Stainland at 29.08d. Of the rest, only Triangle at 27.92d and Queensbury at 26.55d could be considered profitable, with Hebden Bridge (25.46d), Shelf (25.23d), Skircoat Green to Pellon (22.8d), Savile Park to Causeway Foot (22.36d), the West End Circular (21.27d) and Southowram (20.01d) unprofitable, although the densely-populated sections from Town to Pellon and Ovenden were obviously 'money-spinners' when considered in isolation. The Old Station section at 7.66d was as usual beyond redemption. Most of the loss was attributable to the prevailing industrial depression as well as to resistance to the fares increases, but better times were expected.

Sadly, the better times seemed to be like desert mirages – always receding out of reach, and at the annual municipal budget meeting Halifax's ratepayers were advised to "clench their teeth and go on". Towards the end of April, 1921, a national coal strike curtailed electricity and gas supplies as well as tramcar frequencies. The number of trams in daily service had to be halved; weekday services commenced one hour after the normal time and ceased half an hour earlier; Sunday services were suspended and all street lighting extinguished. Gloom descended.

The Tramways Department hastily arranged for a skeleton Sunday service to be provided by privately-owned 'motor coaches' – a euphemism for solid-tyred charabancs, tiny petrol buses and ex-army chassis fitted with primitive bodies. The service, which began on April 17th and operated from Barum Top to the outer termini, was eagerly welcomed by the vehicles' owners, who for the first time tasted the lucrative delights of regular public service operation. However, their delight did not extend to the purchasing of the necessary licences, and when the Highways Committee requested a payment of 15/- per bus, the owners, led by Oliver and Charles Holdsworth, aggressively withdrew their services and encouraged the public to lay the entire blame on the Corporation. Fortunately, the coal strike began to flag; weekday tram services returned to normal on July 2nd and full Sunday services resumed in mid-September.

The welcome accorded to the trams on their return to full-time working was not, however, shared by the Borough Chief Constable, who bemoaned "the total obstruction of Commercial Street at the points of the Pellon tram terminus" near the foot of Crown Street. The Tramways Department did not complain, however, as they needed all the income on which they could lay their hands. The Ovenden track was under reconstruction, and parts of the Salterhebble track were being patched up, and when the new Ministry of Transport was approached for a loan to replace the inward track from Salterhebble (Heath Junction to Dudwell Lane) and Gibbet Street (Cow Green to Spring Hall Lane), only £13,869 was made available, repayable over 20 years, leaving the Corporation to find £9,631 from their meagre resources. To assist with the renewals, a hydraulic rail-bender was bought for £54-10-0d from A.H. Hardisty & Co of Huddersfield, and a replacement rail grinder (No. 2 Patent Electric Model) acquired for £140 from George Robson and Co, of Sheffield.

An indistinct view of King Cross in tramway days. Tramcar 72 is returning from Hebden Bridge by way of Burnley Road (centre, background) and has just crossed the junction with the Warley Road route (right). To the left of the motor-cycle and sidecar and the tiny branch office of the Yorkshire Penny Bank, Rochdale Road branches off towards Pye Nest.
[Copyright: Halifax Courier Ltd.]

Short-time working in the local textile and engineering works caused a temporary reduction in early-morning tram services in September, 1921, but some of the tram stops eliminated during the war were reinstated where necessary.

Thrum Hall 'football special' tram fares were increased to 2d (from the Post Office) and 3d (from Old Station), and private hire of tramcars was resumed at double fares after midnight, before 4 a.m. on weekdays and before midday on Sundays.

The useful work performed by the two ex-Dundee railless or 'trackless' cars as mobile welding units had come to an end in late 1919, when, as recorded by Mr. Jack Naylor, the depot foreman, they had returned to Skircoat Road depot. "The welding plant was removed, and (later) a complete overhaul made, so that once again they became public service vehicles. After the completion of the overhaul they were given fleet numbers 103 and 104 at the end of the tramcar fleet series."

Quotations for the supply of railless overhead equipment were sought in July, 1919, and by June, 1920, rows of poles supplied by Stewarts and Lloyds had been laid on the verge of Mount Tabor Road. The task of planting the poles, stringing up the overhead wires and energising them was completed in the Spring of 1921. Meanwhile the body of no. 104 had been condemned and a replacement built at Skircoat Road, the reassembled vehicle being licensed as CP 2020 on April 3rd. The other railless car, 103, was licensed on May 3rd as CP 2021, and no doubt both were immediately tested on the new route. On the afternoon of June 3rd one of the cars was used for driver-training purposes.

Major Mount on his formal inspection on July 18th returned to London somewhat shaken and breathless, as the rough, unmade highway had buffeted the vehicle and its occupants. Observing that repair bills would be high unless the roads were improved, he recommended improvements between Stocks Lane and Sandy Ford and road-widening between Cross Street and 'the blacksmith's shop' to prevent passing vehicles from having to mount the pavement.

No overhead equipment was provided for the railless cars on their journeys between the depot and Pellon; instead, they set out each morning from Skircoat Road with one trolley on the tram wire and a trailing iron shoe in the groove of the tram rail to complete the electrical circuit, to the delight of local children, who enjoyed the arcing and sparking thus created. Power for the Wainstalls overhead line was fed from the tramway supply at Pellon New Road, the return current being conveyed to the tram track.

Railless car 104 was re-numbered 1, either to signify the beginning of a new fleet series or in anticipation of an expansion of the tramcar fleet, although the date is uncertain.

The Wainstalls service commenced on July 20th at a 4d fare, with 2d stages and 3d intermediate stages, and, aware that both the railless cars could conceivably be out of service simultaneously through damage caused by the rough roads, the Department obtained Ministry permission for emergency use of petrol buses at railless fare scales – a wise precaution, as the incessant ruts and potholes wrought havoc with the springs. The hardy folk of Mount Tabor and Wainstalls nursed their bruises and looked forward to better roads and pneumatic tyres.

Excitements of a similar nature befell the passengers of old open-top tramcar no. 1 which contrived to run out of control from Club Lane, Ovenden, on June 24th, 1921. Leaving the rails abruptly at Nursery Lane, it upended a horse-drawn cart belonging to a pot-hawker, damaging his crockery beyond all hope of repair.

In the workshops at Skircoat Road depot, the rehabilitation of the tramcar fleet was making good progress. Five cars, nos. 9, 11, 17, 71 and 73, were withdrawn from service, and Mr Hall was authorised to design and construct replacements. The first of these, which took the vacant numbers 17 and 64, comprised sturdily-built lower saloons with enclosed platforms of a design similar to that of Mr Hall's former Wigan fleet. Both were mounted on Halifax-style Peckham cantilever trucks, with smaller (30 inch diameter wheels) and some of the 40 h.p. Metrovick motors bought earlier in the year. Being open-top cars intended for the Sowerby Bridge/Triangle service, they probably made use of two of the stock of second-hand trolley standards recently purchased from the London County Council at a cost of £217-7-0d

No.17, the first of the "Ben Hall" cars, displays its neat lines, smart livery and Halifax-designed Peckham truck.

[Photograph: Halifax Corporation Tramways]

The two new tramcars created such a favourable impression that further examples were authorised in December, 1921. Four of these were built during 1922 – vestibuled open-top cars 9 and 11 on old style, unmodified Peckham trucks, and canopy-top cars 71 and 73. The top covers were a new 4-window design which matched the length of the lower saloon, and wisely, in view of the increased side-wind resistance, the balcony panels were only half the height of those fitted to cars 97 to 102. Possibly for purposes of comparison, no. 71 sported a Bradford-style angular wood-panelled platform vestibule, but no. 73 and all future vestibuled cars were built to Mr Hall's "Wigan" design. In common with most municipal operators, Halifax had developed a distinctive style of tramcar which marked them out from all others, and numerous minor design features crept in as the years passed. The surviving 'Turner' top covers, on cars 63, 65, 72, 74-77, 81 and 82, were converted into neat 4-window canopy tops during this period.

The time was now approaching when, under the terms of the Tramways Act, 1870, the smaller councils would be entitled to compulsorily purchase the tramways which Halifax had built in their areas, a possibility which alarmed the Tramways Committee, especially in November, 1921, when Brighouse Corporation declared its intention of acquiring the Bailiffe Bridge line and transferring it (after re-gauging) to Bradford Corporation.

A conference was duly held at Bradford Town Hall on December 6th, when Halifax, Brighouse, Hipperholme and Bradford representatives discussed terms. Brighouse were determined to have a direct tram service from Bradford into their town centre, and Bradford were willing to provide it. The 'Brighouse Echo', enthusiastically but not realistically, proposed that Bradford should 'take over the tramway (i.e. as it stood), buy two Halifax trams and run the service for the time being'. Hipperholme U.D.C. were keenly interested too, and took the opportunity of persuading Bradford to install an electric street lamp (fed from the tram wires) at Bailiff Bridge terminus, a facility which Halifax had refused ten years earlier.

However, Halifax had no intention of losing the tramway, and, advised by their shrewd Town Clerk, they invoked a clause in the 1870 Act to insist that if Brighouse and Hipperholme wished to compulsorily acquire the Bailiffe Bridge line, they must also acquire the portion of the Halifax – Brighouse tramway which lay within their boundaries – a tramway in which Bradford could not possibly be interested. The fateful day — February 6th, 1922 – therefore came and went with Halifax still in possession. Bradford did not abandon hope, and offered to undertake a lease which would not have expired until 1963, but Hipperholme U.D.C. felt so frustrated that they compelled Halifax to spend £2,000 in repairs to the Bradford Road track.

The other councils "lay low", aware that the cost of tramway repairs and reconstruction in their districts were beyond their slender means. In view of Bradford's lack of success, it was ironic that Huddersfield Corporation succeeded in reaching Brighouse from the other direction in March, 1923, their 4'7¾" gauge tramway reaching to within less than 100 feet of the Halifax track. Brighouse now enjoyed the attentions of two tramway operators, but continued to hanker after the third.

Back in Halifax, track and other improvements occupied much time and expense in 1922. On the Causeway Foot line the section between Nursery Lane and Illingworth was earmarked for renewal; 180 yards of track doubling was carried out between Cousin Lane and Pharaoh Lane, and at Ovenden a new substation with rotary converter and transformer was commissioned just in time to provide extra power for the convoys of trams which conveyed crowds of holidaymakers to the moors at Whitsuntide. A special Permanent Way and Rolling Stock Sub-Committee comprising the Mayor and four councillors was set up to consider how to pay for the reconstruction of trams, overhead line and tracks in the light of the tramways' fragile finances. Their conclusion, published in May, was that an outlay of £56,914 over five years and an additional £10,000 for 'special work' (points and crossings) would be a sound investment, provided that a Ministry loan of £60,510 could be obtained.

A renewed proposal to extend the Skircoat Green tramway 250 yards through the cutting hewn out of the rock twelve years previously, was again rejected, but other, more tangible plans were approved – an additional loop at West End (Long Lover Lane), fifteen tons of BSS No. 40 curved-section rails for the Commercial Street/Silver Street junction, and the repositioning of track in Huddersfield Road where road-widening was due to take place. Old equipment superseded by recent purchases was disposed of: Darwen Corporation Tramways bought six BTH GE 58 motors in July, and twelve further 'old tramway motors' were advertised for sale six months later. And when passengers in the lower saloons of the old open-top cars complained of leaky ceilings, the upper deck floors received new canvas and planking. In December, 1922, yet another request for an extension of the Southowram tramway across the Borough boundary 'into the area of Southowram U.D.C.,' i.e., to the village itself, had to be declined, as the village streets was still too narrow, while at Hebden Bridge the twenty-year old dream of trams to Whiteley Arches was for the last time debated and quietly forgotten.

It was at this crucial time in the redevelopment of the tramways that there appeared on the horizon the proverbial 'small cloud no bigger than a man's hand'. In May, 1922, Sowerby U.D.C had noticed that Mr F. Bateson, haulage contractor, had commenced to run a small petrol bus at certain times of the day between Rishworth and Sowerby Bridge, along the route used by the Triangle trams. Mr. Bateson had not troubled to buy a licence or publish a timetable, but was picking up the millworkers who would normally have walked between Ripponden, Soyland and the Triangle tram terminus. As the bus was still plying for hire in October, Sowerby discussed the situation with their neighbours at Sowerby Bridge, when they learned that unless Mr. Bateson cut back the service to avoid competition with the trams, Halifax might withdraw the Triangle tram service and run their own buses up the Ryburn valley – a threat which, however, the two local councils did not treat seriously.

As 1923 dawned, the gloom of post-war industrial depression began to lift, and the demand for late-evening trams began to quicken, especially on Saturdays. Late cars were therefore operated as far as Salterhebble, West Vale, Sowerby Bridge, Stump Cross, Hipperholme, King Cross and Ovenden (Nursery Lane) as well as evening 'extras' to Pellon, West End, Savile Park, Skircoat Green and Southowram, to the great delight of cinema and theatre goers and Halifax folk who were more energetically addicted to quickstep, foxtrot, tango and "Charleston".

When loan sanction was sought for track renewal at Boothtown (Woodside Road to the 'Punch Bowl'), the Ministry of Transport advised the Corporation to widen the highway and double the track above Ploughcroft Lane. The Corporation agreed, but in view of the prevailing cross-gradient decided to widen the carriageway at the expense of the causeways, thereby creating a minimum clearance of 9'6" between the kerb and the outermost rails. The work was completed by March 1924, with reinforced concrete foundations "on account of the tendency of the road to slide" on the steep hillside – an unsettling possibility, one would imagine!

Bought as an open-top, open platform tram in 1902, car 72 had been greatly transformed by the skilful staff at Skircoat Road. After the Great War its "Turner top" had been converted into a canopy-type cover with half-light ventilator windows, and the fenders had been extended to prevent collision damage to the "bay window" plant on" vestibules which now enclosed the platforms. Seen here in the 1928-style livery, the tram was preparing to set out from Union Street to Boothtown.

[Courtesy Roy Brook]

Chapter 15
THE ROCKY ROUTE

<hr>

Along the winding Calder Valley there was deepening dissatisfaction with the condition of the long tramway to Hebden Bridge, and not only the local councils but also the West Riding County Council Highways Department were demanding remedial action.

At a conference of all the interested parties in December, 1922, it was agreed that the highway itself should be straightened, levelled and (where possible) widened to a maximum of 60 feet, as numerous stretches were little more than 12 feet wide, with several dangerous blind corners. Halifax Corporation, who had already renewed the track curves within the Borough boundary, at Whitty Lane and Causeway Head, were prepared to embark on the much greater task of entirely reconstructing the 4 miles 1,610 yards of tramway outside the boundary, from Tuel Lane to Hebden Bridge, with additional loops and extensions to existing loops. All the loops were to be of the normal "parallel point" type instead of the "straight run in and dogleg exit" form previously preferred by Halifax, which no longer conformed to modern traffic requirements, as it caused the trams to veer disconcertingly as they approached the points.

The first section to be attended to was from Brearley to Hebden Bridge (2 miles 682 yards) at an estimated cost of no less than £33,180, and the local councils were earnestly requested to ensure the success of the venture by refraining from licensing private bus services.

When the news reached the ears of the chairman of Todmorden Corporation Transport Committee, he was openly scornful in conversation with his Halifax counterpart. "You might as well throw the money into the Calder!" he said bluntly. Demonstrating how flexible his buses were in comparison with the trams, he extended his bus service through Hebden Bridge town centre from Mytholm to Crown Street on January 19th, 1924, thus saving passengers a ten minutes walk and creating a Yorkshire – Lancashire link: it was now possible to travel from Liverpool to Leeds by a succession of trams and buses, provided that one had two days to spare!

The Todmorden chairman was not alone in holding such radical views about the future of public transport. Mr Saxon Walshaw, a Halifax solicitor, had recently spent a whole fortnight's holiday on a tour of the country by tram and bus, the highlight of his odyssey being a 15 mile 'nightmare' journey on a Nottinghamshire and Derbyshire company tramcar between Nottingham and Ripley, which, he claimed, was "worse than Hebden Bridge" – the ultimate comparison, one assumes! Having thus sampled the relative speed and comfort of the bus, downhill and on the level at least, Mr Walshaw speculated why Halifax were preparing to relay tram tracks when for a quarter of the capital outlay they could install buses. But as the buses had a life expectancy of only a quarter of that of the trams and less than half their carrying capacity, the advantage was perhaps not all that Mr Walshaw imagined.

In official Halifax circles there was no doubt where the future lay, and the announcement in May, 1923, that nearby Keighley had decided to replace their small worn-out tramway with a system of modern trolleybuses failed to shake their confidence. Mr Ben Hall, who had been Keighley's assistant electrical and tramway engineer only a few years previously, was adamant that trams would not be superseded in industrial or populous areas. Trolleybuses were, in his view, suitable for outlying areas such as Wainstalls, but not on heavy gradients, narrow streets or Halifax's excessive cambers, while petrol buses were prohibitively costly. " There is no other passenger transport vehicle on the road that can compare with the tramcar", he declared. "Now that operating costs are gradually being reduced and conditions becoming more favourable, the tramcar is proving superior to all other types of vehicle."

All were agreed, however, that the Burnley Road improvements needed to be completed without delay, as tramcar derailments were occurring at almost monthly intervals. In June, 1924, a tram left the rails at the bottom of Redacre Lane, Mytholmroyd, headed across the road and collided with a wall overlooking the River Calder, to the passengers' dismay. "The evil condition of the Hebden Bridge tram track has become almost a byword", complained the press. "However, Halifax has no monopoly of sections which cause trams to behave like rocking-horses. On the Bradford system there is a stretch of line between Queensbury and Horton Bank Top which will take some beating, but as the Bradford fares are lower, a little extra tossing there is excusable!"

The reconstruction work was carried out on the basis that Halifax would lay the rails and the concrete foundations up to the statutory 1'6" width beyond the outer rail; all other foundations would be laid by the County Council, and the cost of a modern tarmacadam road surface would be borne pro rata by both parties. The Halifax firm of Bradshaw & Co., asphalters, were then awarded a contract at 8s 10d per square yard plus a five years' free maintenance guarantee, and work began at Hebden Bridge in July, 1924, whereupon Luddenden Foot U.D.C. loyally rejected an application from a Halifax firm for a Halifax to Luddenden Foot bus service licence.

Another new tram body was built in 1923 as a replacement for scrapped car 81. With its Ben Hall-style vestibuled lower deck it closely resembled the previous Skircoat Road-built products except that the windows of its neat four-window canopy top had no quarter lights, the structure being a reconstruction of a 'Turner' top cover.

However, Mr. Hall was increasingly convinced that nothing short of a radical change of design would be able to protect the trams from the threatening onward march of the motor-bus. Accordingly, in February, 1923, he presented the Tramways Committee with a plan for a modern, 35 foot long single-deck tram seating 24 passengers in the saloon and 6 in

A 1920's transport revolution. Singledecker 103 was designed as a fast, stable, high-capacity tram suitable for all routes, with luggage compartments near the entrances. As the saloon and platform floors were on the same level, the height of the platform steps obliged all passengers to be unusually nimble. The photograph is said to have been taken at West End.
[Photograph: Halifax Corporation Tramways, courtesy the late R.B. Parr]

end compartments capable also of housing luggage, bicycles, perambulators and parcels. Designed to be capable of speeds considerably greater than anything that the existing double-deck fleet could aspire to (buses were not legally permitted to exceed 12mph), the car was approved by the Ministry and built at Skircoat Road by the Department's own skilled craftsmen.

Emerging in a blaze of publicity in June, 1924, and proudly sporting a new Indian Red and Ivory livery, it bore a "family resemblance " to Mr Hall's former Wigan single-deckers, except that it was mounted on a long-wheelbase Halifax-style Peckham cantilever 4 wheel truck and powered by two 45hp Metrovick motors. Trial runs having proved it 'very suitable', the novel vehicle, No 103, was put to work on the Queensbury route where double-deck operation was still subject to 'Met. Office' forecasts.

The construction of two further single-deckers was immediately authorised, but, conscious that conventional double-deckers would always be needed for the town routes, Mr Hall had already laid plans for an improved type, the first of which emerged from the Works only a few weeks after no. 103. Designed to achieve a lower centre of gravity and reduced wind-resistance, it had a lightweight top deck with low balcony panels, a single-skin domed roof and full drop oak-framed windows without half lights, and its platform vestibules were of the now-standard Ben Hall type. Numbered 104 and powered by two 40 hp Metrovick motors, it had a turn of speed which endeared it to its passengers, although in later years it was remembered as a fairly noisy car.

The fleet now comprised 104 tramcars in various stages of modernity:-

9	old open-top cars without canopies or vestibules,
22	old open-top cars with canopies but no vestibules,
13	old open-top cars with canopies and vestibules,
49	covered top cars without vestibules,
9	covered top cars with vestibules,
1	demi-car (no. 96),
1	"long single-deck car, enclosed", i.e. no.103.
104	
also:-	
1	welding car (converted demi car no. 95),
3	permanent-way trucks,
1	overhead line truck,
1	motor tower-wagon,
1	horse-drawn tower-wagon,
1	pole carrier,
8	Works cars

Alderman Hey was justly proud of his tramcars, whose 'comfort in travelling and greater carrying capacity' exceeded those of their rubber-tyred competitors. The many small traders in the district appreciated them too, as they could use them for the conveyance of small quantities of goods both conventional and distinctly unusual. One of the local electricians had an informal agreement with the tram crews that whenever he needed to transport lengths of conduit, he would be allowed to lash them to the bamboo trolley stick which lay on hooks along the bottom of the rocker panel of the tram on which he was travelling, a practice which would assuredly invoke the hostility of present-day

Designed by the General Manager and soundly constructed by the skilled craftsmen at Skircoat Road Works, no. 104 embodied a lightweight top deck with stylish wind-deflecting domed roof and neat vestibules, serving as a prototype for later double-deckers.
[Copyright: Halifax Courier, Ltd.]

A last view of demi-car 95 in its final form, photographed from the interior of a Dennis bus in Skircoat Road depot yard about 1925.
[Photo: Halifax Corporation Tramways]

Health and Safety inspectors and European bureaucrats. Sadly, the arrangement was terminated abruptly one day, when the string snapped and the conduit became jammed in the tramcar brake gear!

Other electrical matters occupied the Committee's attention. A new automatic point-controller was bought at a cost of £65 for the Beacon Hill junction, and in the Spring of 1924 modern span-wire construction attached to new J Spencer and Co. poles replaced the handsome Pye Nest centre-poles which had become an obstruction to motor traffic.

Unfortunately, a complete lack of electricity brought the trams to a standstill on Saturday, August 9th, 1924, when a fire erupted at the Electricity Works in a cable subway which housed 61 distribution cables. Cinemas ceased to function; shops and houses which had been converted from gas to electric lighting were plunged into twilight; all the tramcars rolled to a standstill, and the town's entire stock of candles was bought out.

It was providential that the breakdown occurred at the end of Halifax Wakes Week, by which time most of the local holidaymakers had already returned home. Nevertheless, many trams were filled with passengers travelling into town for their Saturday evening's entertainment; for some time they confidently expected that the unusual delay would soon end. When realisation spread that the situation was somewhat more serious, most travellers accepted it philosophically and either set out on foot, walked to the nearest railway station or hailed one or other of the charabancs which by that time were returning home after having conveyed a fresh batch of holidaymakers to Blackpool. A few grumblers demanded but did not receive a refund of their tram fare.

While Mr Rogerson, the Electrical Engineer, hurried to supervise repairs to the damaged cables, Mr Hall, the Tramways Manager, organised a distribution of oil lamps and candles to the marooned trams before night fell. Drivers were instructed to remain with their cars, although some conductors were allowed to return home if two or more trams had come to rest in proximity to each other. Mr Hall then contacted the Huddersfield Corporation (for whom he had

worked from 1903 to 1914), who instantly agreed to install emergency links between their neighbouring tramway overhead wires and tracks at the West Vale and Brighouse termini. Curiously, no contact was made with Bradford, whose installations at Queensbury and Shelf were much closer to the Halifax wires and rails than were those of Huddersfield.

The borrowed current began to flow at 4am next morning, when despite the very considerable voltage drop incurred by the 8 mile distance from Huddersfield's power station, the trams were enabled one by one gingerly to make their way back to depot, a process which was completed within three hours. Then, as soon as new cables had been spliced in at the Halifax power station, the traction current was switched on again, and the tram services resumed at 1.45pm, although until damage to the high-tension feeder to the Hipperholme sub-station was rectified on the Wednesday morning, the Brighouse and Bailiffe Bridge sections had to be fed, somewhat inadequately, from the Stump Cross feeder.

Subsequently the entire tramway feeder system within the Borough was reorganised on the advice of a consultant from B.I.C.C. (British Insulated Callenders Cables) of Prescot, Lancs., from whom the Corporation periodically purchased copper trolley wire. Prudently, Halifax and Huddersfield then installed a permanent emergency link between their power stations, which was completed and tested in February 1927.

At the start of its long journey to Brighouse and Bailiffe Bridge, tramcar 78 passes the top of Woolshops, whose timber-framed building dates from 1670. "Driver's Market" belongs to John S. Driver, the high-class local grocery chain. Ahead lie Northgate and North Bridge.
[Photograph: Gregory, Wolverhampton]

The economics of tramway operation continued to furrow civic brows. Almost a year previously, the Council had asked the Tramways Committee to lengthen all penny stages by 25% and reduce all fares over 1d by approximately the same percentage. Pointing out, however, that they could not afford to take such fundamental risks with the fare scales, as they needed to set aside £30,000 each year for renewals, the Committee decided instead to try a six-months' experiment with books of prepaid tickets ranging from fourteen 1d tickets for a shilling (a saving of 2d) to fourteen 6d tickets for 6 shillings (a saving of one shilling). The average length of a penny stage was 1,191 yards, approximately two-thirds of a mile.

Next, an agreement was reached with the Electricity Committee for a reduction of 1/4d (a farthing) per unit, which would save the Tramways Committee £6,000. On learning of this, the Borough Council again demanded fare reductions, but the Committee stood firm, even when Shelf U.D.C. reported that Bradford's fare scales were so favourable that Shelf shoppers now preferred to shop in Bradford. In such circumstances it was fortunate that there still remained one sphere of tramway operation that could still score victories: in April, 1923, the Rugby Team triumphantly trounced their Salford counterparts 21 points to nil.

The wretched condition of the roads on the Wainstalls railless route brought about some highway widening and the re-siting of 36 poles, and the manager sampled Birmingham's Nechells route where double-deck railless cars had recently replaced trams, but unlike his fellow-manager at Keighley, he returned unimpressed. Nevertheless, as the ruts and unevennesses of Mount Tabor Road had shaken his two railless vehicles almost to pieces, he sought tenders for an additional car. The successful tenderer was Tillings-Stevens Motors Ltd for a 2 to 2 1/2 ton chassis with twin 25h.p motors at a cost of £763 plus £28-16-0d for its licence (CP 3457), valid from June 1st, 1924. With a neat, Skircoat Road-built body similar to that of no. 1 but one bay longer, it entered service a few days later as car no. 2, after which no. 103 was probably relegated to part-time use, and may have been renumbered 3 when the tramcar fleet expansion began.

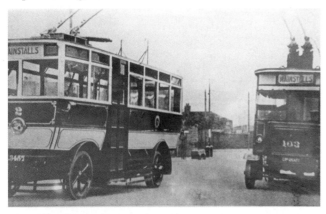

"Trackless Trams" _ new Tillings - Stevens trolleybus no. 2 sharing overhead wires with ex-Dundee 103 at Pellon (New Road) terminus.
[Photo: Halifax Corporation Tramways]

Experiments in lengthening the life of the permanent way were made with in-situ "Sandberg" rail-surface hardening at a cost of 18s per mile of single track plus 2s 6d per yard for labour. A mile of new-style extra-durable cadmium copper trolley wire was bought from Richard Johnson and Nephew, but as the price was 11.437d per lb., compared with only 9.625d for the normal hard-drawn copper, the experiment was not repeated.

Competition from private bus companies was now beginning to cause serious concern, and the Municipal Tramways Association had discussed it at their annual conference held at Southport. Todmorden found themselves locked in a life-and-death battle with Ribble Motors of Preston, who had attempted to destroy the municipal service

by operating buses free of charge, and the Ministry of Transport had banned the company from plying for hire in the area. Halifax and their municipal neighbours hurriedly formed a Joint Control Committee to co-ordinate counter-attacks. "The motor bus is knocking at our doors!", the press warned ominously.

The brothers Oliver and Charles Holdsworth were not wasting time knocking at doors – they were too busy studying maps. Originally fish and fruit salesmen in and around Halifax, they had inherited their father's furniture removal business about 1917, expanding into the role of funeral directors shortly afterwards. When the war ended and ex-army lorry chassis flooded the market, they introduced petrol-driven hearses and, as seen above, took advantage of the 1921 Coal Strike to taste the more lucrative opportunity of transporting living beings. The antipathy towards licences which had brought them into conflict with the Corporation in 1921 had not deserted them: by November, 1924, their map-reading skills had enabled them to introduce services for which no one had ever seen a need, e.g., Halifax to Bingley via the Causeway Foot tramway, and Brighouse via the Southowram tramway, and needless to say, they did not neglect to pick up anyone whom they saw waiting at tram stops.

Although Mytholmroyd U.D.C. retained sufficient loyalty to refuse (by a narrow 5 to 4 margin) licences for a Halifax – Hebden Bridge bus service, despite criticisms of Halifax's high fares and not-yet-renewed tram track, their member Coun, A .A. Jackson claimed gleefully that,

"Halifax have got the wind up, and if by seeming to encourage Holdsworths we can put more wind up them, it will be all the better!"

Halifax Tramways Committee were so concerned at the ease with which unlicensed and undisciplined competition was spreading that the chairman, Ald. Hey, requested the Mayor to convene a special Council meeting for a frank discussion of fares, track and transport topics in general. Ironically, the meeting took place on December 15th, 1924, two days before the running of nearby Keighley's last tramcar. The debate lasted 2 3/4 hours, of which no less than 1 hour and 36 minutes were taken up by Ald. Hey in a frank and wide-ranging explanation of his Committee's policies.

He began by observing that although a few small tramway systems had recently closed down, circumstances naturally varied from town to town. Were Halifax to discard their tramways in favour of buses, the volume of traffic using the highways would double. Buses were complicated machines which required a great deal of maintenance; they were prone to skids in bad weather, and their top decks (if they had one) were unusable whenever it rained. Trams by their very nature moved in an orderly and predictable path, whereas buses darted hither and thither. Unfortunately, trams were burdened with costly statutory requirements from which buses were almost free; indeed, the buses helped to destroy the road surface hich the tramway owners were compelled to maintain. Capital outlay on the tramways since 1898 amounted to £517,566, of which £286,946 was still to be repaid (with interest) either from tram fares or from the Borough rates.

Continuing, Ald. Hey questioned Parliament's irrational attitude to public transport. Publicly-owned gas, electricity and water undertakings were guaranteed a public monopoly in the areas they served, so why not public transport? If Parliament genuinely believed in free competition, municipal and private operators should be placed on an equal basis, because if the present unfair competition were to continue, small private operators (and, he could have added, small municipalities) would eventually be squeezed out by large private combines. Trams continued to be the most economical users of road space, and modernised track layouts such as those in Burnley Road would improve speed as well as safety. Halifax's smaller neighbours were exhorted to continue their support for the trams, as it was they who had asked for them in the first instance, and they derived direct benefit not only from the rates paid by Halifax but also from the regular, reliable tram service itself.

Turning to the insistent demand for lower fares, Ald. Hey pointed out that even when trade had been good and fares 25% lower than at the present time, the number of passengers carried had been no greater, which indicated that a fares reduction would merely diminish the income without a corresponding increase in patronage. Comparisons with other towns were misleading, as larger centres such as Huddersfield and Bradford had much higher population densities, the most extreme example being South Shields, Co. Durham, with 32,000 inhabitants per square mile, compared with Halifax's 4,500. In the Halifax area, even one additional passenger for every car mile operated would turn a loss into a profit.

Looking to the near future, Ald. Hey announced that they would soon be operating buses to Elland, Holmfield and Bradshaw as well as a jointly-worked bus service to Huddersfield. Elsewhere, the trams had always been profitable, and would still be serving the district in twenty years' time. In the meanwhile, there were 35,000,000 passengers to be carried every year, and if the Corporation did not carry them, who would? (A dissentient voice – "Holdsworths!"). Loud and appreciative applause greeted Ald. Hey as he resumed his seat, and, impressed by his fluency and expertise, the Council approved the purchase of six Dennis 26-seat motor-buses, and authorised him to carry out the previously-disapproved 280 yard extension of the Skircoat Green tramway through "Dudwell Cutting" at a cost of £1,800.

The new buses, delivered six weeks later, were urgently needed, as Holdsworths were no longer knocking at the door: they had invaded the house itself. Their bold attempt to launch bus services within the Borough were fended off by the previously-announced Corporation bus services from Crossley Street to Holmfield, Holdsworth and Bradshaw; also, Inner and Outer Circulars via the Hopwood Lane, Warley and Norton Towers areas were instituted as a precautionary measure. Further afield, Greetland U.D.C. were now hosts not only to Holdsworths but also to Yorkshire Woollen, the North West Road Car Co. and Todmorden Corporation as well as Halifax's trams and buses. Huddersfield and Halifax were actively negotiating with their nearest Lancashire neighbours in Rochdale and Oldham for jointly-operated municipal bus services across the Pennines. The world was changing rapidly.

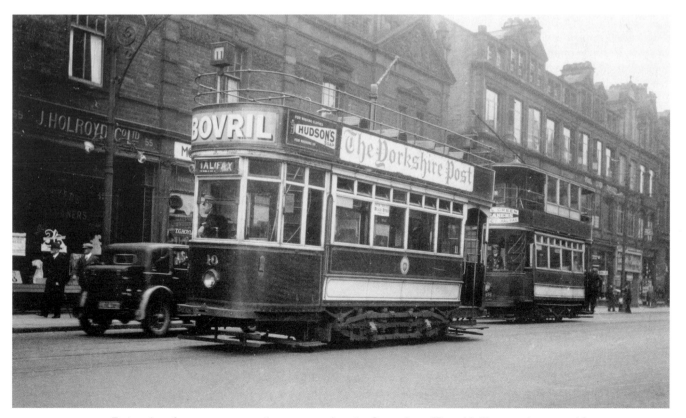

Returning from a summertime excursion to Ovenden, "Ben Hall" open-top car 10 (ex 76) passes Pellon-bound "sloping-sided" car 68 in Commercial Street, 1932.
[Courtesy Roy Brook]

Chapter 16

WEATHERING THE STORM

While battles raged in bus company boardrooms and Corporation debating chambers, the Tramways Committee decided to attempt yet another bold fares experiment at the request of the Council. Commencing on April 1st (an unwise day, surely?) 1925, the books of pre-paid tickets were discontinued, and, despite Ald. Hey's forebodings, all fares were reduced by approximately 25%. The risk was great, because if patronage did not increase proportionately, the annual income would plunge by as much as £28,000.

It did. Within eight months the previous year's net profit of £11,626 had been transformed into a loss of £24,757-13-7d. Although passenger numbers on the 1d stages had increased slightly, the 2d and 3d stages which provided the bulk of the tramways' passengers had declined. The experiment was abandoned.

Meanwhile, the more down-to-earth enterprise of renewing the Calder Valley tramway had begun at last in mid-January, 1925, near the Grove Brewery at Brearley, where Corporation workmen were renewing the foundations, re-laying the tracks and re-siting them where appropriate, while the West Riding Highways team were widening and levelling the carriageway and the contractors were laying a new surface, mostly in tarmacadam but on gradients such as Pismah Hill in new granite setts. At the outer end of the route, other teams were progressing inwards from Hebden Bridge. The intended rate of progress of 100 yards a week failed to satisfy Luddenden Foot, who complained that the improvements would not reach their area for a year! Obviously, they failed to realise that whereas in the relatively traffic-free days of 1901/2 the laying of the original tram tracks had been continuous and uninterrupted, the need to maintain modern traffic flows was bound to cause delays.

It was unfortunate that by this time the Halifax press had become so enthusiastic for the new era of the motor-bus that, brushing aside all arguments, they consistently condemned the Hebden Bridge re-laying scheme and the municipal minds which had conceived it.

In a cynical vein they predicted that despite the fact that the scheme had been approved twelve months previously by Halifax Borough Council ("in an easygoing way as they do with important projects"), it was probable that "...some Rip van Winkle on the Council will want to point out some weakness or anomaly in the scheme, and will feel quite injured when he is told that he has already given his approval!" (Coun. Law of Mythdmroyd U.D.C. did so: even at this late stage he was proposing the impossible dream of a sleeper-track alongside Burnley Road as a means of segregating trams from other traffic).

"As a matter of fact", the press unkindly added, "the whole proceedings of Council are carried through too perfunctorily, and some of the members seem to have only the foggiest notion..." this being a pointed reference to Coun. Carter of Halifax, who, having approved the relaying project and the awarding of the necessary contracts, was now urging that

work be halted to permit a trial with motor-buses.

The work continued nevertheless, and inevitably the single-line sections of track had to be severed from time to time, with two or three trams maintaining a shuttle service on the Hebden Bridge side of the gap. In these circumstances it was difficult to maintain normal timetables, a factor which soon provoked an irate letter to the press.

> "Every day this week", the correspondent wrote, "you could see a long line of would-be passengers walking from Tuel Lane top to King Cross, mostly with stiff necks through constantly turning round to see if the tram was coming. They were teachers, clerks and men and women of other salaried professions who don't get out of bed till they can see to put their stockings on."

Many had walked to the bottom of Tuel Lane to catch one of the more frequent trams from Sowerby Bridge, and not a few would have welcomed the sight of a competing bus. However, by October, 1925, the section within Hebden Bridge U.D. was complete, and for the first time the highway presented a smooth, unbroken surface resembling a racing track. The local councils were so impressed that they informally agreed to refuse all private bus licence applications. Four months later all the new installations west of Brearley were completed and in use, except that awkward, narrow Fallingroyd Bridge was still to be rebuilt by the County Council.

The next section, eastward from Brearley to the Borough boundary at Tuel Lane, was then begun at a cost of £22,360 to the Corporation and £33,180 to the County Council, although this time granite setts were to be used between the tramlines, and from the 'Black Lion' to the boundary the highway was to be widened and the tracks re-aligned at an additional cost of £2,448.

By mid-August, 1926, the entire 3½ mile section from Hebden Bridge to Luddenden Foot (Mill Lane) was complete and in use. Motorists marvelled at the quality of the new, level road surface, and tram passengers revelled in the long-forgotten pleasure of gliding along almost noiselessly on smooth, welded steel rails. Unfortunately, the ever-changing contours of the landscape had prevented any possibility of a uniform road width, and new road signs had to be erected to warn of dangerous corners, "tram pinches" and the need for vigilant driving.

The wisdom of these precautions was demonstrated on August 10th, a day on which rain had been falling heavily. At the controls of Halifax-bound tramcar 78 as it approached the sweetly-named Evercream Toffee Factory at Brearley, Driver Myers espied a small bus approaching, and cautiously halted his tram in order to enable the bus to pass on either side, as there was limited clearance on the curve. The front of the bus, a 14-seat 20h.p "Graham" vehicle belonging to Mr. J. W. Crossley of Siddal, passed without difficulty, but the rear wheels skidded, bringing the tail of the bus into violent contact with the tramcar front platform. The bus chassis continued on its way, but the body dropped into the road, with resulting inconvenience to the passengers whose planned excursion to Blackpool was abruptly terminated. Measurements showed that although the distance between the kerb and the outer rail was 7'6", the 6'4" wide tram overhung the track by 1'5" on each side, leaving a gap of only 6'1", through which the 5'7" wide bus could not squeeze in safety.

Tramcar 52, evidently in need of repainting in the attractive new Indian Red and white livery, stands proudly at the Skircoat Green terminus about a year after the route had been extended through "The Cutting". When the cloche-hatted lady and her two small children have boarded the tram, it will depart for Pellon, allowing time for its trolley to negotiate the automatic reverser suspended from the bracket arm and attached to the pole (right). When no trams are in sight, intending passengers can wait in the Huddersfield-style shelter (left), which lasted 80 years
[Courtesy Roy Brook]

More congenially, the much-debated extension of the Skircoat Green tramway opened without ceremony on June 12th, 1925, when Mr Hall drove the first tram out of the depot at 3.50pm and arrived at the new terminus at the top of Dudwell Lane about 8 minutes later, to the cheers of residents and the children of All Saints' School. Lt. Col. Mount of the Ministry of Transport gave his formal approval on July 31st, and the local residents' pleasure at their new facility was crowned by the erection of a splendid Huddersfield-style tram shelter at the terminus, which lasted 80 years as a memorial to 1920s municipal enterprise.

Additional passenger comforts were provided by two new trams built in the Works during the year. Car 105, the second single-decker, was basically similar to no. 103 except that the platforms were lower, thus providing easier access, and the interior arrangements were simpler – two compartments (smoking and non-smoking) separated by a central bulkhead with double sliding doors; driver's and conductor's platforms integrated with the compartments, and folding jack-knife doors at all four corners. When it joined no.

103 on the Queensbury route, orders were issued that because of their extra overhang, the two long vehicles must not attempt to pass on sharp curves such as the North Bridge/Haley Hill junction.

In overall appearance the other new car, double-decker no. 76, resembled no. 104 introduced the previous year. Its lower deck was a copy of tram no. 17, except that it sported one-piece flush-panelled sides and was 6" lower, giving an overall height of 15'3". It was soon in regular use on all routes except, of course, Sowerby Bridge and Triangle, which top-covered cars could not reach. Although the County Council were improving the levels of Wharf Street, Sowerby Bridge, while Halifax were relaying the tracks, the problem of the low railway bridge could not be solved.

Modern trams and up to date track layouts merited better speed limits than those authorised in Edwardian days, and in December Lt. Col. Mount approved a series of speed relaxations, although, somewhat perversely, Luddenden Foot complained that the existing speeds were "excessive". The next few years were to prove, however, that "speed was king".

Increasing congestion in Halifax town centre encouraged the Corporation to plan better loading facilities for the trams as a means of speeding up traffic flows. Taking advantage of a property clearance scheme in Bull Green at the junction of King Cross Street, Barum Top and Fountain Street, the Tramways, Improvement and Watch Committees agreed in June 1925, on an £11,520 plan for kerbside loading, new double tracks, sidings and junctions, the work to commence when the Ministry approved the project.

The eventful year of 1926 began auspiciously with the proud unveiling of Mr Hall's third single-deck tramcar, no. 106. Like its predecessors, it accommodated 36 seated

The second of the new singledeckers, no. 105, embodied two design improvements – larger saloons and drop-frame platforms which made boarding and alighting easier. The location is thought to be Martin's Nest, between Brighouse and Bailiffe Bridge, a route often served by the single-deckers.
[Copyright: Halifax Corporation Tramways]

passengers in two compartments, with sufficient "leg-room" for 20 standing passengers, but otherwise it embodied several forward-looking innovations. The height from rail to floor was reduced by 4 inches by the adoption of small 25" diameter wheels, thus allowing shallower steps and easier access. From a mechanical viewpoint the tram was revolutionary, as it embodied a worm and cardan drive system designed by a Mr. Bostock of Leeds in place of the traditional spur gearing, with lightweight motors mounted in line instead of transversely. With roller bearings and a 50% weight reduction over its two predecessors, no. 106 proved to be comfortable, smooth running and silent; indeed, the spinning of the trolley wheel created more noise than the tram itself.

(above) Passenger comfort, 1925-style – polished wood seating in two compartments (smoking and non-smoking) separated by a central bulkhead with double sliding doors, and overhead strap-handles for standing passengers. Because of the abundance of platform doors at the end of the saloon, the resistance cabinet (centre) had to be sandwiched between the driver's controller (centre left) and the brake equipment (centre right), and the heat emitted by the resistance must have been welcome in winter but a sore trial (to the driver's stomach!) on a summer's day. The woodwork was stained and polished and the ceilings white, with carbon-filament electric light bulbs. Two notices are visible: "At the town terminus or at the request of the conductor, passengers may leave the car at the driver's end", but, "Passengers boarding or leaving the car while in motion do so at their own risk". The photograph appears to have been taken at Southowram terminus.
[Copyright: Halifax Corporation Tramways]

(below) Lightweight singledecker 106 had an almost flat roof without a ventilating clerestory, and was propelled by high-speed motors and worm-drive. The location is uncertain, but may be at Mytholmoyd.
[Copyright: Halifax Corporation Tramways]

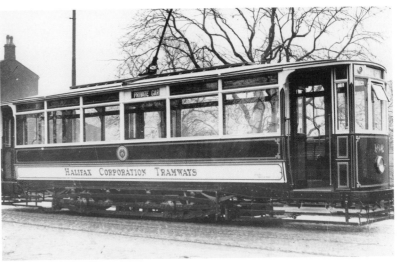

"Ben Hall" car 76, the second car to bear the fleet number had a lightweight top deck with a roof frame rebuilt from the remains of the storm-damaged roof salvaged from no. 50, and with one-piece side panels. Seen here at King Cross in 1932, the tram is about to return to town from West End and Gibbet Street.
[Courtesy Roy Brook]

After having been demonstrated to Area D (Yorkshire, Lincolnshire and North Derbyshire) of the Municipal Tramways Association during the week commencing January 15th, 1926, no. 106 took up service on the Queensbury route where it scaled the heights of Boothtown at unprecedented speeds.

One minor defect quickly manifested itself; as the roof was flat instead of being surmounted by a raised clerestory, the overall height of the car was less than that of nos. 103 and 105, and the upward pressure of the trolley proved to be inadequate, resulting in unheralded dewirements, but the provision of a small steel gantry mounted on the trolley plank was sufficient to raise the height of the sprung, swivelling trolley base and thus solve the problem. Considered to be "the car of the future" by its proud designer, the "Hall-Bostock car" was the Manager's pride and joy.

Mr Hall's enjoyment proved to be short-lived, however, as on March 14th he tendered his resignation, having been appointed General Manager of Portsmouth Corporation

Tramways, whose committee had visited Halifax and approved of what they had seen. After taking up his new post in June, Mr. Hall designed a modern double-deck tram (no.1) for his new employers, which was mounted on a standard-gauge version of the novel truck used under no. 106.

With the minimum of delay, the Halifax committee interviewed three candidates for the vacant post:-

> 1) Mr. D. P. Morrison, deputy manager of the Gateshead and District Tramways Ltd.,
>
> 2) Mr. J. A. Bromley, general manager and engineer of York Corporation Tramways (previously at Keighley),
>
> 3) Mr. W. T. Young, general manager and engineer of Dundee Corporation Tramways.

The choice fell on Mr Young, who accordingly assumed control on July 4th. Mr. Morrison subsequently consoled himself with the management of Hull Corporation Transport, while Mr Bromley emigrated to Durban.

A native of Aberdeen, Walter Theodore Young had entered the Aberdeen Tramways Dept. in 1898 where, under the tutelage of the manager, Mr. R. Stuart Pilcher, he had attained the rank of Traffic Superintendent, subsequently holding similar positions in Oldham (1912-1914, during which time he had applied for the managerial post at Keighley), West Ham (1914-1918) and Belfast (1918), graduating to Assistant General Manager in Edinburgh in 1919 (again under Mr. Pilcher) and to General Manager and Engineer in Dundee in 1921, where he had taken a keen interest in the repair and construction of tramcars, notably the neat, sturdy "Walter Young" cars which survived in daily use until their premature withdrawal in 1955.

Mr. Young quickly established himself in the social life of Halifax, as a member of the Borough Club and the Rotary Club, and of course, as president of the Tramways Club. Serving on the Tramways and Transport Association (which he represented on the Joint Industrial Council), he was widely respected in the industry.

Mr Young inherited all his predecessor's problems, notably those created by Holdsworths. In August, 1925, the company had received licences to operate buses to Brighouse via the Southowram tramway at a minimum 6d protective fare, but as they regularly flouted their licence conditions, pleas for a reduction of the fare were rejected. By February 1926, the boldness of their infringements had reached such a degree that the Town Clerk was instructed "to adopt any course that he could recommend to the Committee to protect the tramway service". Sad to say, the law provided few remedies, and the depredations continued.

> "It will soon be difficult to remember all the different motor-bus services in existence in Halifax and district, as they have sprung up like mushrooms in the last few months",
> the press complained.
> "The great misfortune is that Halifax did not bestir themselves when pressed to so do, and to launch out with buses into the outlying districts, as it would have been much better to have the vehicles under the control of one authority."

Not surprisingly, the financial year ended disastrously competition and unwise fare reductions having converted an £11,000 profit into a £9,369 loss. In an effort to minimise the impact, electricity prices were reduced by a further $1/8$d per unit. Times were hard.

An elegant side view of car 106 seen at West Vale on a trial run.

[Copyright: Halifax Courier, Ltd.]

Chapter 17

STRIKE AND AFTERMATH

In May, 1926, the Corporation Tramways and Electricity Departments found themselves "grappling with the Great Strike". A long-simmering dispute in the coal industry had induced the trades unions to call a unilateral General Strike, which paralysed the municipal tram and bus services throughout the country.

The private bus companies could scarcely believe their good fortune. On May 7th, while fourteen Halifax trams manned by inspectors and volunteers were attempting to provide a skeleton service, the Watch Committee had to invite the companies to step into the breach, which they did with alacrity. Within a few hours hordes of buses and charabancs were operating from a central terminus at Ward's End over each of the tram routes and further afield, to Rishworth and Bradford. By arrangement with the companies, tramways inspector Harry Whittingham, a familiar and highly respected figure in his normal role of Commercial Street traffic controller, struggled to create order out of chaos and confusion, but the strain proved too great, and only a few months later he died at the age of 49.

Within a week the Strike began to fade. On May 13th the tramways employees sought and received reinstatement without recrimination on either side, and on the following afternoon all the Corporation tram and bus services recommenced. For a few weeks longer the evening services had to be curtailed until coal stocks at the power station returned to their normal levels, but local industry quickly settled back into its accustomed pattern. The Tramways Department hoped to do likewise. "The reintroduction of the tram services has dispensed with the need for the emergency motor-bus and chara service which has been appreciated during the last few days", the press commented optimistically.

Unfortunately, their optimism was misplaced, as the private companies had no intention of surrendering their unexpected gains, as the press belatedly realised a fortnight later:-

> "If the Halifax Tramways Committee had launched out wholeheartedly into motor-bus traffic… instead of systematically pouring cold water on that form of locomotion, what a harvest they would be reaping. Instead of that, they have allowed private enterprise to step in and take the profits. Messrs. Holdsworth and others deserve the thanks of the community for displaying the vision our councillors lacked. Buses are running regularly to Bradford, Leeds and Bingley, and the ventures are paying, despite all the restrictions against picking up in the Borough."

The press omitted to mention Holdsworths' determined disregard of agreements, licence conditions and speed limits or the Corporation's inability to venture outside the Borough boundaries without the consent of Parliament, the local councils or the County Council. Nevertheless, the Tramways Committee were determined to fight back. By July, they had secured agreement with their neighbours for Corporation bus services to Bradford via Shelf, Leeds via Shelf and Dudley Hill, Keighley via Causeway Foot and Rochdale via Ripponden, and the last-mentioned service began on August 28th in conjunction with Rochdale Corporation. A second trans-Pennine service, to Oldham, followed shortly afterwards. But the West Riding County Council, custodian of county highways and a resolute opponent of all forms of municipal expansion, disapproved of the ventures, and the proposed Bradford, Keighley and Leeds services had to be postponed indefinitely in the hope of reaching agreement.

A permanent casualty of the Strike was the provision of the Pye Nest brakesmen or 'pilots', who had diligently ridden on the rear platform of every tram which had ascended Pye Nest since 1907. Greatly-improved braking systems had long since made them unnecessary, and despite Sowerby Bridge protests, the Ministry upheld the decision. Another casualty was the Wainstalls railless service, which ceased on October 24th, bequeathing an impressive £5,989 debt from its short-lived operation. Assuming that the original vintage railless cars had survived until the closure, it is a minor irony of trolley-bus history that they had escaped from redundancy in Dundee only to be scrapped in their second home by an ex-Dundee manager, a fate which they shared with the two-year old Tillings-Stevens car no. 2. Other relics were disappearing too: 48 old tramcar controllers and 30 low-powered motors were offered for sale. In a more forward-looking vein, Mr. G. E. Canning, general works foreman at Skircoat Road, was appointed Rolling Stock Engineer in September, 1926, in succession to Mr. Galloway, who had resigned previously.

The prestige of the Tramways Concerts at the Victoria Hall soared to new heights in November, when Heddle Nash, the popular tenor, Peter Dawson, the celebrated bass, and Miss Rachel Norton from the National Opera Company sang to appreciative audiences; Yorkshire folk have always been renowned for their musical tastes, and Halifax's tramwaymen never fought shy of culture.

Others sought different forms of enlightenment: the Boys' Club from All Souls' Church, Haley Hill, had the good fortune to be conducted around the depot by Mr. Canning, who courteously explained how two trams were overhauled each week, a process which always culminated with a thorough brake test on Salterhebble Hill before they re-entered service. Mr. Canning had 106 trams and 29 buses under his control.

Faced with endless complaints about high fares, e.g. Queensbury, Shelf, Triangle and Causeway Foot 4½d, Stainland 5d, Brighouse 6d and Hebden Bridge 9d, the Committee analysed the income derived from each fare value:-

1d	— 14.8%	4d	— 2.9%	6½d - 7d	— 0%
1½d	— 45.4%	4½d	— 7.7%	7½d	— 0.4%
2d-3d	— <u>23.9%</u>	5d	— 1.0%	8½d	— 0%
	84.1%	5½d	— 0.6%	9d	— 0.4%
3½d	— 0.9%	6d	— 2.0%		<u>100%</u>

In other words, fares above 3d. attracted only 16% of the revenue, and substantial fare reductions on the longer routes would probably win back custom without seriously endangering the income. On the other hand, attempts to increase income by raising short-distance fares would encounter resistance.

Nevertheless, on April 1st 1927, all 1½d fares were raised to 2d and all 2d fares to 3d, with a maximum 4d fare (6d return) to Hebden Bridge. Within the first three days receipts had risen by £240 – but Holdsworths promptly reduced their fares, and once again a substantial loss could not be avoided. Determined nevertheless to secure fairer competition, the Corporation reiterated their vow to challenge every breach of licence conditions by their rivals, even though the fines imposed by the magistrates were seldom more than a derisory £1.

foot in the side-streets, the horse waited in Haley Hill, where the carriageway was so narrow that one of the cart-wheels overlapped the tram track. Determined to avoid delaying the Boothtown and Queensbury tram services, whenever the horse espied a tramcar, it glanced both ways to ascertain whether the road was clear, then pulled the cart to the other side of the road, returning as soon as the tram had passed – an accomplishment which passers-by often stopped to admire.

During all this time, the ambitious scheme for the Bull Green area had been taking shape. The objective was to relieve Commercial Street of the volume of trams which used it as the central terminus and reversal-point for no fewer than eight services – Pellon, Highroad Well, Causeway Foot, Savile Park, Skircoat Green, Hebden Bridge, Sowerby Bridge and Triangle, and West Vale and Stainland.

New north-south and east-west track connections were therefore laid in Bull Green and Barum Top, with a double curve into Fountain Street, another double curve from Horton Street into Union Street and a three-quarters "Grand Union" (see map) in Ward's End at the busy intersection of Fountain, Horton and Commercial Streets and Skircoat Road. A siding was laid in Powell Street (on the west side of Fountain Street) as a loading-point for Sowerby Bridge and Triangle cars, while neighbouring Harrison Road

GEORGE'S SQUARE. HALIFAX.

COPYRIGHT.
HFX 431

LILYWHITE LTD
TRIANGLE HALIFAX

The oft-repeated claim that trams were obsolescent tended to overshadow the fact that an even older form of conveyance – the horse – was still in regular use for haulage and local deliveries. Being sagacious creatures, horses adapted themselves to changing times, the best-known local example being the animal which hauled a milk-float at Woodside. While the milkman was delivering his orders on

George Square about 1925, with (left) cars 41 and 17 about to make their way uphill. In Commercial Street an unidentified car is proceeding towards King Cross and West End, preceded by car tramcar 58 still in the pre-1920 livery.

[Photo: Lilywhite Ltd.]

received a siding accessible from Barum Top where spare cars could wait in readiness for the peak-hour. Unfortunately, the Harrison Road business men (who were evidently not readers of the local press) rose in anger when tracklayers made what they considered to be an unpublicised and illegal appearance in their thoroughfare, and although the Town Clerk stoutly maintained that all was perfectly legal, by February 1927 half the siding had been removed, and the remainder was rarely, if ever, used. In all, nine double movable points, one pair of right-hand movable points and a pair of left-hand open points were bought from Edgar Allen Ltd of Sheffield for this major scheme.

New cross-town services were planned, and cars from King Cross were to reach Old Station via Fountain Street, allowing the circuitous Silver Street and George Street tracks to close (the Silver Street rails were lifted in February, 1927 although George Square was retained as a storage siding for spare trams). The Highroad Well to Circular Route cars were to remain in Commercial Street, as a track curve out of Cow Green into Gibbet Street would have been impossibly sharp. Accordingly, George Street was last used by regular services on December 4th 1926, and on the following day new services were introduced: -

> Powell Street to Sowerby Bridge and Triangle;
> Old Station to Inner circle (via King Cross, West End and Gibbet Street),
>
> Old Station to Hebden Bridge (peak hour only; at other times the Hebden Bridge cars departed from Commercial Street),
>
> plus new cross-town services which reduced reversals in Union Street: -
>
> Brighouse and Bailiffe Bridge to Skircoat Green,
> Southowram to Causeway Foot and Bradshaw,
>
> and other cross-town services to minimise reversals in Commercial Street: -
>
> Old Station to Ovenden;
> Stainland to Highroad Well.

Probably the new arrangements merely dispersed congestion rather than curing it, and Fountain Street in particular became thronged with trams and other traffic, notably the Hebden Bridge cars which had a heavily-used

picking-up and setting - down point there, and the Sowerby Bridge/Triangle trams which had to sidle into and out of Powell Street. In June, 1927, instructions had to be issued that incoming trams should halt at Victoria Hall and not Ward's End.

As soon as the Union Street track had been doubled and the new double-track curve laid into Horton Street, further cross-town services were introduced on November 1st :-

> Queensbury to Triangle,
>
> Shelf to Hebden Bridge,
>
> Outer Circle via Savile Park and Pellon.
>
> Simultaneously, the existing cross-town services were re-shuffled:-
>
> Skircoat Green to Highroad Well,
>
> Stainland to Causeway Foot,
>
> Southowram to Inner Circle,
>
> West End via Gibbet Street to Brighouse and Bailiffe Bridge.
>
> Services to Old Station were discontinued.

However, Mr Young's enthusiasm for cross-town services, so successful when he was manager in Dundee, proved unequal to the limitations of the single-track and loop arrangements prevailing on most of the routes, and following angry complaints from inconvenienced Pellon and Highroad Well passengers, the pack was shuffled once again: -

> Southowram to Hebden Bridge,
>
> Stainland to West End,
>
> Skircoat Green to Causeway Foot

as from February 8th, 1928, while simultaneously the Old Station line was reopened as a terminus for Inner Circle cars. The Queensbury, Shelf, Brighouse and Bailiffe Bridge cars terminated once more in Union Street, allowing service reliability to return to normal.

Realising that their long-suffering passengers were by this time somewhat confused and disorientated, the Tramways Committee yielded to the manager's oft-repeated plea for route numbers to be displayed on all the cars except the oldest of the "open-toppers" which were retained for special duties only. Displayed as black numerals on white linen roller-blinds, the apparatus was mounted on the upper-deck railings of open-top cars and the underside of the roof canopy of covered-top cars as from February, 1928

Route no.	
1	Stainland – West End via Old Station & Gibbet St
2	West Vale – Highroad Well
3	Halifax – Brighouse and Bailiffe Bridge
4	Outer Circle (Pellon – West End – Savile Park)
5	Halifax (Powell St) – Triangle
6	Halifax (Powell St) – Sowerby Bridge
7	Southowram – Hebden Bridge
8	Halifax (Union St) – Queensbury
9	Halifax (Union St) – Boothtown
10	Skircoat Green – Causeway Foot
11	Skircoat Green — Bradshaw and Ovenden
12	Halifax (Union St) – Shelf

Even so, slight adjustments had to be made, so that by the end of the year the Outer Circle (Savile Park – Pellon – West End) service had been renumbered O, and a Savile Park – Pellon (only) service had started as route 4.

The worn-out condition of the outermost stretch of the Keighley Road tramway (Ratten Clough to Causeway Foot) encouraged the Corporation to seek a Ministry of Transport grant towards highway works, re-siting of tracks and provision of an additional loop, so that for an outlay of only £2,191 from its own funds the Borough obtained a wide, tarmacadam highway with new tram tracks and modern overhead span-wire construction. The extra loop proved particularly useful at holiday times, as hitherto the long stretches of single line had obliged the Department to despatch the trams in convoys so that they did not meet between loops.

The phenomenal growth of motor-bus services which had so seriously affected Halifax since the General Strike had had its effect in all the surrounding areas too. Brighouse found itself overwhelmed with buses belonging to the Hebble Bus Service (i.e Holdsworths), Yorkshire Woollen District, Calder Bus Co, County Motors, Huddersfield Corporation and Ideal – a far from 'ideal' situation which at

Luxury in a tramcar: car 107 proudly displays its clean lines, handsome livery and long-wheelbase truck at Skircoat Green in April, 1928.
[Photograph: Halifax Corporation Tramways courtesy the late R.B. Parr.]

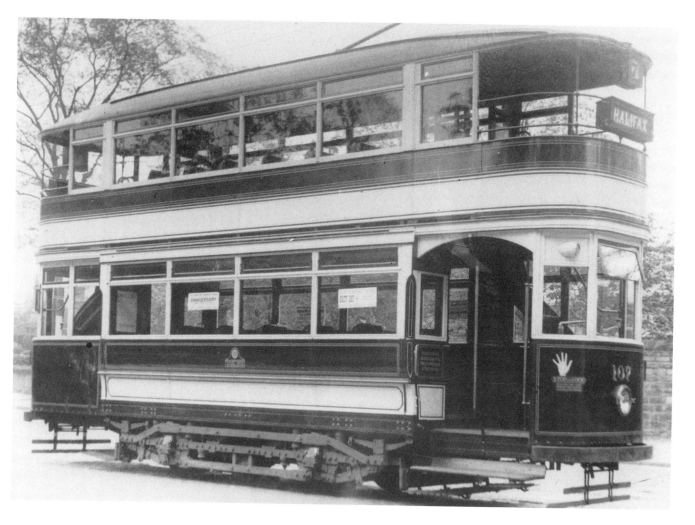

last compelled Halifax Corporation to review the future of the Bailiffe Bridge branch tramway which Bradford had coveted for so many years. As most of its passengers had been filched by the buses, the Tramways Committee conferred with their Bradford counterparts in April, 1927, agreeing a few weeks later that the future of the line should be delegated to the Chairman, Vice-Chairman and Coun. Crabtree, upon whom was conferred the grand title of "The Bailiffe Bridge Section of Tramway Sub-Committee".

Before long the parties had agreed on a sale price of £7,500, for which sum Halifax would alter the gauge, link up the tracks at Bailiffe Bridge, renovate the overhead equipment and provide mixed-gauge arrangements in Brighouse town centre between Bonegate Road and the terminus at the "George". Thus, uniquely, Brighouse would play host to trams operating on three different gauges – 3'6" (Halifax), 4'0" (Bradford) and 4'7¾" (Huddersfield). The necessary clauses were included in Bradford Corporation's latest Parliamentary Bill.

Another protective measure emerged in June, 1927, when Halifax and Todmorden reached agreement on through tickets available on the Halifax – Hebden Bridge trams and the Hebden Bridge-Todmorden buses, although it was six months before the scheme was launched.

A further batch of second-hand trolley standards was bought for £81 in June from Messrs. E. J. Walsh, dealers, and one of them was probably used in the construction of the last of the so-called 'Ben Hall' cars – a posthumous description in this instance – no. 22, an open-topcar with platform vestibules, which entered service after another replacement tramcar, no. 75, which sported a canopy top cover with distinctive quarter-lights above the side windows.

In Mr Young's opinion, however, the survival of the tramways called for something more appealing and striking than new bodies built on traditional lines. On June 26th, 1927, he revealed details of an interview with the Ministry of Transport in connection with plans for "a single saloon tramcar on the lines of plans already submitted", subject to guarantees "that the use of the car would be limited to the setting back of kerbs at corners to gain the necessary clearance between the footpath and the tram, with a further guarantee that no two cars shall be allowed to pass each other on a corner or radius which could be too acute for safety."

This appeared to imply a fourth single-decker, but in fact Mr. Young was planning a long-wheelbase double-decker, for which English Electric tenders were accepted in September for motors, controllers and magnetic brakes for the sum of £578-10-0d. The equipment was delivered in January, 1928, at the same time as a set of upholstered tramcar seats from Siddal and Hilton, Ltd., of Sowerby Bridge, worth £134-10-0d, for "the new tramcar" already under construction at Skircoat Road.

The development was timely, as the future of British tramways was becoming less certain as the months passed. Salford, Colne, Rawtenstall and the S.H.M.D. Joint Board now favoured buses, and it was openly said in Halifax that as passengers had declined by 3,000,000 in two years, some of the loss-making routes might have to be handed over to buses in due course.

There was dismay in Brighouse Town Hall in early March, 1928 when it was learnt that negotiations for the sale of the Bailiffe Bridge tramway had broken down. Despite keen probing by the press, no explanation was forthcoming from either Halifax or Bradford. Possibly Halifax had begun to suspect that if Bradford's trams were allowed to reach Brighouse, Bradford's buses might soon follow, and Bradford's subsequent purchase of Bailiffe Bridge-based Calder Buses deepened suspicions even further.

Whatever the reason, Halifax's trams continued to plough an increasingly unremunerative furrow along Bradford Road, accompanied now by gadfly swarms of buses. In nearby Hipperholme village centre (Whitehall) eight competing private buses often arrived simultaneously, to the detriment of the trams, whose fares had been reduced to a mere penny, while on Burnley Road the fare to Cote Hill had been cut to 2d in a drive to retain passengers.

However, the battle was far from lost. On April 20th, 1928, the "Halifax Courier" announced with obvious approval the completion of Mr. Young's latest experiment:-

> "A special tramcar has been built at Halifax tram shed and is to be run on the Hebden Bridge route. It is no. 107. The car is handsomely painted and furnished, the seats in the lower saloon being upholstered in tapestry (it was actually wool cut moquette) and those on the upper deck in leather. Instead of having a long seat on either side of the lower saloon, the seats are fixed two on one side and one on the other, with an aisle between. If the tramcar can be given an appreciable increase in speed, it may recover some of the patronage lost to buses."

Such was, of course, the hope of the Tramways Committee, who inspected the car on the same day and gave it their enthusiastic approval.

Nineteen-twenties tramcar décor: dark polished woodwork, white ceilings adorned with gilt designs; bright electric lamps in glass holders; a clock on the bulkhead and the borough arms on the opposite corner; dark red patterned upholstery on the 2 and 1 (double and single) seats, and definitely "No Smoking allowed inside the car"

[Photograph: Halifax Corporation Tramways]

Trial runs probably began on the following day, and no. 107 created something of a public sensation, as it was the most handsome and best designed tramcar that had ever appeared in the streets of Halifax and district. The platform steps were wide and easy to negotiate, and in recognition of the reduced height and wind-resistance (as pioneered by trams 63 and 104) the Ministry had sanctioned Mr. Young's bold attempt to enclose the upper deck as much as possible, i.e., the balcony sides were raised to the level of the upper deck side windows to provide better protection from the weather, in addition to which the balconies were partly glazed at each side, leaving only the ends open – a far cry from the spartan three-window short-saloon canopy tops fitted to most of the older cars. Also, the neatly-enclosed platforms gave excellent protection to drivers and conductors at a time when many of their colleagues were still exposed to the elements and obliged to wear oilskins and 'sou' westers' in wet weather. The teak-framed lower deck structure was sturdy and indestructible, and the only detectable design fault was a series of small,

On test: car 107 framed in afternoon sunshine, possibly at Martins' Nest, Brighouse, in April, 1928. The Rolling-Stock Engineer, Mr Canning, by no means a tall man, was dwarfed by the motorman (driver). The "warning hand" sign on the dash was accompanied by the advice , "Stop and look behind the car before proceeding across the road" – an indication of the increasing presence of motor traffic.
[Photograph: Halifax Corporation Tramways courtesy the late R.B. Parr]

floor-level vents on the upper deck which allowed melted slush from passengers' shoes and boots to drain away instead of lying in pools on the floor, but also admitted chilly, ankle–height draughts.

Proudly placed in service on the long Hebden Bridge to Southowram service, no. 107 was an instant success. Gone was the leisurely, unhurried "Ee-whine, Ee-whine" of the older cars; in its place there was a strong, purposeful hum and rumble coupled with a certain amount of flange-squeal on sharp curves. The speed, quietness and steadiness of the tram on its long-wheelbase truck were a revelation to passengers, who promptly dubbed it " the De Luxe car". Equally delighted were the Tramways Department, who discovered that the takings on no. 107 were 2d per car mile higher than on its older, slower companions; moreover, it consumed less current. Comparative tests made with tramcar 82 (with two 35 h.p motors) and no. 107 (with two 50 h.p motors) over the same route from 7a.m. until 9 p.m. demonstrated that whereas no. 82 consumed $206^{1/2}$ units, the new tram used only 188 units while starting and re-stopping 100 times more, and saving I hour 40 minutes on the journey time. The pro-bus press wavered. "If all the trams were like this, the buses wouldn't have a chance!" they admitted.

The Tramways Committee agreed, and debated ways of pressing home their advantage. Most of the fleet was very far from modern; nos. 1—43 had been in service so long that they were wholly debt-free, and no car numbered between 1 and 94 was less than 23 years old, apart from the 'Ben Hall' cars which embodied an unknown quantity of parts from scrapped trams. The cost of new tramcars was formidable, and even though the cost of building no. 107 in the Department's own workshops had been only two-thirds that of a commercially- produced vehicle, the expenditure had still been £1.882-9-2d.

Nevertheless, its undoubted success and popularity emboldened the Committee to sanction ten identical trams, although in view of the limited capacity of the workshops only three were to be built there. The remainder were to be constructed by the English Electric Co. on Halifax-style Peckham cantilever trucks, and English Electric also won the contract for the electrical equipment and the electro-mechanical track brakes required for the three home-built cars. Realizing that the speed of the new rolling-stock could be enhanced even further by the fitting of quick-action air brakes, the Committee (and Council) authorised the following expenditure in October, 1928:-

7 complete trams to be built by English Electric with E.E. equipment and Maley & Taunton air brakes, @ £2142-17-0d per car	£15,400
Equipment for the Halifax – built cars:-	
3 sets of E.E. motors, controllers and magnetic brakes @ £579 per car	£ 1,737
3 sets of Maley and Taunton air brakes @ £190 per car	£ 570
	£17,707

In addition, trucks for the three Halifax-built cars had to be assembled from parts fabricated under licence as well as items such as gearwheels supplied by the Peckham Truck and Engineering Co.

In preparation for the new rolling-stock, work on the Hebden Bridge tramway installations continued apace. At Luddenden Foot an electrical sub-station was built at a cost of £4,390 as the relaying of the track, provision of extra passing-places and re-positioning or lengthening of the existing ones had reduced journey times from 1 hour to 45 minutes, and it was calculated that a further 15 minutes could be saved if the power supply were augmented, especially at weekends when the trams were in great demand. As soon as the renewal of the Burnley Road track outside the Borough was complete (apart from Fallingroyd Bridge), the Corporation pressed ahead with the relaying of the Causeway Head to Warley Springs section and the re-positioning of the Tuel Lane to Causeway Head track in the centre of the improved highway.

Other routes continued to receive their share of attention during the year when Highroad Well, Causeway Foot,

The delightful rural setting of old Fallingroyd Bridge is beautifully illustrated in this 1928 view, with "De Luxe" car 107 specially posed for the photographer. The conductor is conversing with the driver of the motor car, and to the left of Hirst & Batty's Mineral Waters lorry the grim warning, "Death Trap", is mounted on the tram standard.

[Copyright: Alice Longstaff Gallery Collection, Hebden Bridge]

Northgate and the downhill track in lower New Bank were visited by track repair gangs. Significantly, however, the Corporation sought to protect its long-term interests by seeking Ministry approval for the operation of motor-buses on all its tram routes outside the Borough, and in September, 1928 joined Huddersfield, Bradford and Brighouse representatives in discussions about the running of Halifax buses to Brighouse (via Slead Syke) and Bailiffe Bridge (via Lightcliffe).

Even more significantly, the continuing losses on the tramways prompted the Finance Committee to appoint a Committee of Investigation, whose major recommendation was that the Electricity and Tramways Departments should in future have separate committees. A new Tramways Committee was therefore formed in November, 1928, with the retiring Mayor, Ald.A .H. Gledhill, as Chairman, and well-deserved tributes were paid to Ald. Hey, who had guided the combined Committee through fourteen years of tumultuous change.

The incoming Chairman's profession – cash register manufacturer – was to serve him in good stead in his new drive to redeem the tramways' finances. Aware that the railway companies had obtained Parliamentary powers for the operation of buses as a means of avenging the loss of railway passengers to the competing buses, he initiated discussions with the L.M.S. and L.N.E. railway companies with a view to joint operation. The outcome was far-reaching.

Early in 1929 an agreement was sealed whereby the ownership and operation of buses within the Borough (Zone A) would remain with the Corporation; the surrounding area,

within a maximum radius of 14 miles (Zone B) would be transferred to a Joint Committee of Halifax and railway representatives, with joint finances and an alternating chairman, while Zone C (the longer distance bus services) would be handed over to Hebble, who were bought out by the railways in May, 1929. Thus, after only four years of predatory operations, the Holdsworth brothers reaped a rich harvest, chiefly at the expense of the Corporation. Indeed, it could be said that the name of their original operating base – Gibbet Hill – was well chosen in view of their impact on the borough which unwillingly harboured them.

Bradford paid a heavy toll too: the price of their ambition for operating buses to Brighouse and Huddersfield was that they had to pay Halifax £7,500 to close the Bailiffe Bridge tramway, as well as purchasing the Calder Bus Co.

Events then moved swiftly. In February, 1929, the Tramways Committee had sealed an agreement with the landlord of the Punch Bowl Hotel at Bailiffe Bridge terminus for the use of his outside lavatory by the tramway employees for a modest charge of 10s per annum, but little use was made of the new facility, as on Wednesday, March 27th, Halifax Corporation announced that,

> "By arrangement with the Bradford Corporation and with the concurrence of the local authorities, the Halifax Corporation will discontinue the running of trams from Brighouse to and from Bailiffe Bridge, after the 30th inst."

In recent years, many journeys on the route had been carried out by one or other of the long single-deckers, which were well suited to the almost straight, level 1½ mile stretch of double track, but the last journey, on the evening of Saturday, March 30th, was performed by double-deck tram no. 104, and on the stroke of midnight the still-shining tramlines nominally passed into Bradford's hands.

Next morning saw a greatly-changed pattern of services. Bradford buses ventured for the first time into Brighouse and (in conjunction with Huddersfield and Hebble) to Huddersfield; the new Halifax Joint Omnibus Committee (JOC) were running to Lower Edge and (via Hipperholme) to Bailiffe Bridge; Huddersfield continued to run buses to Bailiffe Bridge and trams to Brighouse; Calder Buses had vanished, but Yorkshire Woollen and County were working much as before.

The demise of the trams did not pass un-noticed, especially as the 1d single/1½d return tram fare had been replaced by a 1½d single bus fare. The passengers' reaction was plain and blunt. "We want them trams back!", they said. "AZ" added anonymously that, "We would jump for joy if we could see a tram running along, but

alas, no!". "A User" protested that Brighouse and Hipperholme district residents had been betrayed by their councils, and "Tram Man" (driver Whiteley Lumb) penned an anonymous lament:-

> "Fare thee well, for I must leave thee,
> I have loved thee many years;
> Deem me not both weak and foolish
> If I shed some childish tears".

It must be pointed out, however, that although tramcars, apparently ageless and immutable, were capable of arousing strong emotions among their users, Yorkshiremen are rarely given to tears!

The redundant overhead wires were soon dismantled, and six months later Peels of Greetland were paid £450 for the removal of the tram poles and bracket arms and also for the scrapping of ten 1898/9 vintage trams (2, 4, 7, 8, 13, 14, 30–32 and 35). At the same time the Corporation paid the County Council the sum of £4,515 (part of the £7,500 received from Bradford) for the removal of the abandoned track and reinstatement of the highway. Other hallowed institutions disappeared also. Bailiffe Bridge railway station burned down in March and was not rebuilt (passenger services ceased on September 14th, 1931), and although Bradford's tram service to Bailiff Bridge survived until June, 1944, after 1932 it was a peak-hour and Saturday morning facility only. South west of Halifax the Rishworth and Stainland railway branch lines closed on July 6th and September 21st, 1929, respectively, having been superseded by road transport. More progressively, "talkies" made their first appearance at a Halifax cinema on September 22nd.

The disposal of the ten old trams was brought about not only by the route closure but also by the completion of the three Halifax-built "De Luxe" tramcars ordered in the

Bailiffe Bridge shortly after the closure of the tram service, 1929. The overhead wires have been cut down, but in the foreground the track, poles, bracket arms, trolley wire hangers and ears are still in place. In the distance Bradford tramcar 119 wistfully surveys the abandoned track to Brighouse which it had hoped to use if the 37½ yard gap between the two sets of metals could have been bridged.

[Copyright: Water Scott, Bradford]

previous year. Car 108 had already entered service in December, 1928, being later followed by 109/110 and by E.E. built nos. 1, 6 and 15. All were instantly allocated to the Hebden Bridge route, which thus underwent a dramatic transformation, with quiet, comfortable modern trams operating on smooth, new tracks at speeds which at last enabled the Department to achieve its goal of reducing the journey time to a mere 35 minutes. At first, nos. 107 – 110 had to rely on the hand and magnetic track brakes, but the fitting of Maley & Taunton air brakes later in 1929 allowed them to match the performance of the seven E.E. cars, 1, 6, 15, 20, 28, 33 and 95.

The gleaming "De Luxe" cars presented a striking contrast with the oldest trams which now appeared only at rush hours and holiday periods, and whose paintwork was distinctly shabby. Some were retired as soon as all the new cars were in use, and Mr. Young undertook to speed up the normal repainting programme so that eventually there would not be a "dirty" car in the fleet. As ever, the press claimed that something more than paint was required to make the trams compete effectively with "the more speedy and commodious buses" on the out-of-town services.

By this time, the new chairman believed that he had mastered the subject of tramway finance, and, declaring that, "We cannot afford to sell pennyworths on our tramways", he persuaded the Council to abolish penny fares and thus increase revenue by £30,255. He proposed three zones, Urban, Suburban and District, with minimum fares of 2d, 3d and 4d respectively, 3d return fares over all the former 1d stages, and a maximum 7d return fare on the Hebden Bridge route. His financial confidence was misplaced, however, and an alarming loss of short-distance passengers compelled him to replace the 2d single and 3d return fares with a more acceptable 1½d single. Working expenses were tackled next: the two-shift system which necessitated a good deal of costly overtime was replaced by a three-shift system which reduced expenditure despite employing four extra men.

The link between All Souls' Church and the Tramways Dept. was strengthened in May, 1929, by a visit from the Young Men's Bible Class who enjoyed the pleasant privilege of inspecting the repair shops, stores and body-construction department at Skircoat Road. Their guide proudly informed them that 21 "De Luxe" cars would eventually be in stock, providing a quality of travel matched only by the Sheffield and Birmingham tramways.

Evidently Ald. Gledhill did not attend All Souls', as his enthusiasm was reserved for Halifax's first double-deck buses, a batch of A.E.C. "Regents" which entered service early in 1930. Praising their "striking success", he asserted that, "If they could be introduced on every route, the doom of the tramways would be sealed". His colleague Ald. Law disagreed fundamentally, pointing out that the trams, unlike the buses, used British steel and British coal. "If they scrapped the trams", he warned, "They would be sending their money to Mesopotamia and throwing their own people out of work" — a clear message which has been continually repeated and repeatedly ignored in the United Kingdom for more than seventy years. Predictably, the condescending press dismissed Ald. Law as "courageous but pathetic".

However, Stainland Council had not yet succumbed to the lure of the buses: they asserted that, "There is no Corporation in the West Riding or even in the country that is running such abominable buses as Halifax!", citing in particular bus no. 40 which had shaken its passengers unmercifully with an engine "open to the inside" that had filled the saloon with suffocating fumes and stalled so frequently that the driver had asked passengers to board and alight while the bus was still moving. No doubt the depot mechanics worked overtime when they learned of the complaint, as Coun. Gledhill (now no longer an alderman) could find no fault when he sampled the bus!

The Chairman's vigilant eye next alighted on a curious seasonal fluctuation whereby every year the tramway receipts fell by almost £3,000 in April. Attributing the cause to Halifax housewives' age-old habit of "spring-cleaning", he authorised fares concessions for the month in question. Other seasonal occurrences were less easy to resolve: traditional Whitsuntide processions in towns and villages often disrupted the tramway schedules so severely that journeys to Hebden Bridge could take up to 1¾ hours, while on the Causeway Foot line even the colour-light signalling system and the custom of despatching trams in convoys at holiday periods proved incapable of preventing trams from meeting on the single line sections.

While their 'betters' were debating the long-term future of the tramways, the employees continued to keep the undertaking in good shape. The Sowerby Bridge permanent way was being upgraded, with renewal and re-alignment between Tuel Lane bottom and Wharf Street and from King Cross to Pye Nest, but plans to double 150 yards of track at West Vale were rejected by the Ministry on account of the narrowness of Stainland Road. On July 19th, 1930, the Ovenden short-workings on the Causeway Foot route were reorganised so that most cars reversed at Mason's Green instead of Nursery Lane. However, no doubt on the grounds of economy, the Permanent Way Department was transferred back to the Highways Department on a net cost basis.

Pleasingly, the success and popularity of the "De Luxe" cars encouraged the Committee to place orders for seven identical trams in September, 1929, i.e., three complete trams from English Electric at a cost of £2,303 each, and English Electric motors, controllers and magnetic brakes as well as Maley & Taunton air brakes for four cars to be built at Skircoat Road.

Thus the Department achieved its goal of twenty-one splendid vehicles whose speed and comfort could now be shared with the lengthy Shelf, Stainland, Queensbury, Brighouse and Causeway Foot routes, leaving the older, lower-powered top-covered cars to serve the town routes and the open-top trams to work the Sowerby Bridge/Triangle route. Like all the trams, the "De Luxe" cars underwent periodic brake tests on Salterhebble Hill; also, they provided occasional peak-hour journeys as far as Wharf Street, Sowerby Bridge.

As delivered, the first seven English Electric trams had been allotted the random fleet numbers 1, 6, 15, 20, 28, 33 and 95 vacated by scrapped cars, but before long the batch of ten cars was numbered 114-123 in between the two sets of Halifax-built trams 107–113 and 124-127.

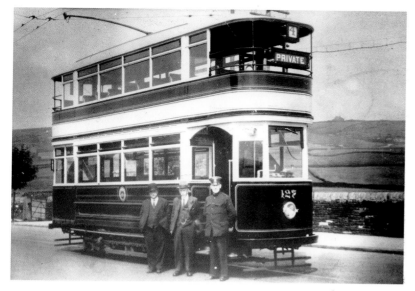

Tram no. 127 was the last of the twenty-one "De Luxe" cars to enter service, in March, 1931, by which time the livery had been slightly amended, with Indian Red rocker panels and a reversion to the full coat of arms on the waist panel. The identity of the elderly gentlemen flanked by Mr. Canning (left) and the tram driver (right) is not known; it could be Ald. Hey, although he had ceased to be Tramways Committee Chairman in 1928.

[Copyright: Halifax Corporation Tramways]

It could be claimed that the "De Luxe" cars were the safest vehicles in the kingdom, as they possessed no fewer than eight braking systems:-

(1) Hand/wheel, (2) Hand/track, (3) Air/wheel, (4) Air/magnetic track, (5) Air/wheel and air/track combined, (6) Rheostatic emergency brake, (7) Automatic runback brake, (8) Reversing the controller key and thus the motors – a last resort! Not surprisingly, no "De Luxe" car ever experienced braking problems.

In the financial year ended March 31st, 1930, the trams managed to achieve a small profit of £379 which was promptly swallowed up by an £11,180 deficit on the buses, but, confident that the future of the buses under the co-ordination scheme would be a bright one, on July 19th the Chairman persuaded the Committee that certain lightly-loaded or outlying parts of the tramway network ought not to be renewed when the tracks wore out. His recommendation was based on the formidable capital costs:-

	ORIGINAL DEBT STILL OUTSTANDING	COST OF RENEWAL
Skircoat Green	£ 2,995	£ 12,500
Savile Park	1,514	16,020
Warley Road (Outer Circle)	1,418	7,930
Southowram	2,845	7,740
Sowerby Bridge to Triangle	8,119	13,350
Stump Cross to Brighouse	9,547	35,980
Stump Cross to Shelf	4,112	17,320
Boothtown to Queensbury	10,939	12,220
	£41,489	£123,060

Accordingly, on December 13th the Committee agreed to a two month experiment with buses in place of trams on the Southowram and Savile Park routes.

A happier fate was planned for the more profitable routes, as the Council were asked to authorise large-scale track renewals when the need should arise:-

	ORIGINAL DEBT STILL OUTSTANDING	COST OF RENEWAL
Halifax to West Vale (a)	£ 37,739	£22,880
Halifax to Tuel Lane (b)	42,901	28,000
Cow Green to Highroad Well	2,814	10,300
King Cross to Sowerby Bridge	15,096	7,260
Halifax to Ratten Clough (c)	21,710	21,630
Grand Theatre to Boothtown	23,407	8,750
(Punch Bowl)	£143,667	£98,820

(N.B., the tracks from (a) West Vale to Stainland, (b) Tuel Lane to Hebden Bridge and (c) Ratten Clough to Causeway Foot were relatively new and not in need of attention, as was the Pellon route.)

In view of the healthy income being generated by the above routes, Coun. Gledhill considered it sensible to spend £98,820 on renewals rather than to "throw a deadweight of £143,667 on the rates", a recommendation endorsed 29 to 24 by the Council. During the debate, however, it was revealed that the recent Royal Commission on Transport had advocated the replacement of trams by trolleybuses or motor-buses, a policy enthusiastically supported by the local press.

Coun. Gledhill dismissed any notion of wholesale abandonment, which would incur a total liability of £357,182 — equivalent to a supplementary rate of 11s 8d in the £ — an intolerable burden for Halifax people at a time when national and international trade depression was causing serious unemployment and short-time working in the district. "We are fighting a retreating battle", he admitted. "But the general of an army does not run away or leave his guns for the enemy to capture; he gradually draws in his exposed salients, and converges upon a solid front". When the Outer Circle closed, the Pellon service would be extended to West End, and if the "temporary" bus substitutions on the Savile Park and Southowram sections were successful, 15 obsolete trams would be replaced by 18 buses.

The opposing "general", Coun. Leach, expressed concern for the Electricity Department which was heavily dependent on the tramways, and forecast that when the newly-approved Road Traffic Act abolished local licensing authorities and replaced them with Regional Traffic Commissioners, some measure of protection for the trams might be obtained. While it was true, for instance, that "the fearful state" of the Brighouse track and fierce competition from the buses had caused the Brighouse revenue to plummet from 20.28d per car mile in 1925 to 13.25d three years later, the situation could be remedied if the track were to be renewed.

Indeed, Halifax's buses were no more popular in Brighouse than the trams, and when the Joint Omnibus Committee (JOC) licences expired at the end of 1930, Brighouse Corporation refused to renew them in protest against "the wretched condition" of the buses entering their borough via Slead Syke. The town has become the "dumping-ground for derelict buses", they complained; they were "dirty, unreliable, full of rattles, uncomfortable, unsafe and generally unfit". But as Halifax Corporation possessed parliamentary authority to operate the buses they continued to do so, licensed or not.

A welcome opportunity of acquiring almost-new rolling stock at low cost came when Exeter Corporation offered for sale their four most modern tramcars, nos. 1 to 4, ordered by them in 1928 for a planned route extension to Whipton which had not materialised. In use since March, 1929, the cars, like all West Country trams, were "open-toppers", but were otherwise modern, with vestibuled platforms, upholstered seats in the lower saloon, up-to-date Peckham P35 flexible-axle trucks with high powered motors, magnetic track brakes and small-diameter wheels which ensured lower step height and easier access. Unusually, the rocker-panels were of metal instead of seasoned timber, and the extra length of the saloon – 17'4" instead of the traditional 16'0" – inspired the cars' builders, the Brush Co., to provide three half-width side windows interspersed with two of full width, probably to facilitate standardisation of glass sizes.

After the Manager, Mr Young, had inspected the trams at the Exeter depot, in January, 1931, the Corporation agreed to buy them for £200 each plus £38 for spare parts, and in February the L.M.S. Railway transported them northwards for £146-17-10d. Thus, for a total outlay of only £992-11-1d (which included the Manager's hotel and travel costs), compared with over £8,000 for new vehicles, Halifax acquired four very useful vehicles which, when overhauled, repainted into the Corporation's Indian Red and ivory livery and numbered 128 to 131, brought a welcome touch of modernity to the Sowerby Bridge and Triangle route on entering service in August.

Their comfort and speed soon endeared them to their regular users, who happily claimed them as their own. Only one instance has been recorded of an ex-Exeter car straying from its now-accustomed paths; at the height of the football season, car 131 found itself scheduled to perform a "Thrum Hall" special duty, but despite its regular success in scaling the heights of Pye Nest, it unexpectedly jibbed at the gentler gradients of Gibbet Street. Undaunted, the burly football supporters insisted on pushing it up the hill and into Thrum Hall Lane siding as a means of ensuring that it would be available for the return journey!

Ex-Exeter tram no. 131, the highest numbered vehicle in the fleet, waits in the Powell Street siding before setting out for Triangle in 1932.

[Courtesy Roy Brook]

By this time, all the "De Luxe" tramcars were in service too, the final payment to English Electric having been authorised in May, so that a quarter of the fleet now comprised high-quality cars capable of competing with the buses on equal terms, especially on Halifax's gradients. In addition, the newest of the pre-war trams, nos. 97–102, were rehabilitated and partly modernised: nos. 97, 100, 101 and 102 received "bay window" platform vestibules and no. 99 complete new "De Luxe"-style vestibules with full-width sprung fenders, while nos. 99–102 also acquired the luxury of upholstered seats in the lower saloon. The only exception was no. 98, which had never regained its top cover since overturning at Catherine Slack in 1920, and still retained its Bradford-style angular vestibules. Three of the sturdy "Ben Hall" tramcars received attention too: no. 64 was given a top cover from a scrapped car, while lucky nos. 17 and 80 acquired not only second-hand top covers but also comfortable upholstered transverse seating in the lower saloon.

When the new, realigned Fallingroyd canal bridge opened in October, 1931, and much of the track between Granny Hill and Warley Springs was re-sited as previously agreed, the Hebden Bridge renewal programme finally drew to a close. When it had begun, in July, 1924, tramcars had reigned supreme, but now the future was cloaked in doubt, especially as a predicted profit of £1,022 had just materialised as a loss of £12,465 on the trams and £13,359 on the buses.

Ex-Exeter car 131 had been in service only a few months when it was photographed at Sowerby Bridge (Station Road) on a return journey from Triangle, July 10th, 1932, with the driver (left) and conductor standing near the platform step. No. 131 was probably one of the last trams to be painted in the 1927-style livery with white rocker panels and miniature coat of arms, and details of its modern P. 35 truck and magnetic track brakes are clearly visible.

[Photograph: the late H.B. Nicol, courtesy the National Tramway Museum]

(right)The Burnley Road improvements and track relaying had reached Warley Springs at the foot of Cote Hill when tramcar 107 was photographed on its way to Hebden Bridge in 1931.

[Copyright: Halifax Courier. Ltd.]

(below) A fine study of 1913-vintage car 99 at Pellon terminus (Barracks), opposite Spring Hall Place. The conductor had just hooked the bamboo trolley stick into the loop at the end of the trolley for the purpose of swinging it to the opposite end of the tram for the return journey as for some reason there was no trolley reverser at Pellon. The photograph, taken on July 14th, 1937, by H.B. Priestley, showed the tramcar in its final state, with "De Luxe"-style vestibules, full-width sprung fenders and the 1932-style mostly-red livery.

[Courtesy the National Tramway Museum]

Chapter 18

TACTICAL RETREAT

The implementation of the 1930 Road Traffic Act in the Halifax area proved to be something of a disappointment, as it did little more than formalise the existing situation, and a traffic census taken at the foot of Salterhebble Hill revealed that the trams which passed every 7½ minutes on their way to and from West Vale and Stainland were still locked in mortal combat with a 4 minutes frequency bus service.

Nevertheless, the Corporation was fighting back, with varying degrees of success. An experiment with cheap off-peak and afternoon tram fares attracted 126,915 extra passengers and £69-4-3d additional income in the first month, despite bad weather and worsening unemployment. The trams tasted their first encounter with automation on January 6th, 1931, when futuristic traffic lights ("robots") were switched on in Northgate. A fortnight later, Inspector Binns was appointed successor to the late Chief Inspector Drinkwater.

In November, 1930, it had been agreed that Brighouse Corporation should be allowed to attach street lamps to the bracket arms of the tram standards in their area for a fee of 2s 6d per lamp, but within a few weeks Brighouse embarked on a programme of highway widening and levelling which

led to a recommendation on February 18th, 1931, that the tram service from Halifax should be discontinued, thus enabling the Corporation to remove the rails between Hove Edge (Upper Green Lane) and the "George". This was, of course one of the sections which Halifax had decided not to retain, and in any event it would not have been possible to provide a modern track layout without much road widening, particularly in Bonegate Road, where Brighouse-bound trams travelled on the 'wrong' side of the narrow carriageway.

Agreement was quickly reached. For a payment of £1,775 by Halifax, Brighouse would (i) waive all liability for rates after March 31st, and (ii) assume responsibility for road reinstatement and the redundant tram standards. Halifax undertook to remove the overhead wires, bracket arms and feeder section boxes by May 21st, and ultimately the West Riding County Council carried out the whole of the track-lifting and road reinstatement in Brighouse. The intention was to cut back the tram service to Hove Edge (junction of Brighouse Road and Upper Green Lane) on April 21st, reserving the right to continue operating as far as St. Chad's School in Upper Green Lane for a further six months, although

Two mayors, five top hats and a few hundred townsfolk gathered to witness the departure of the last tramcar from Brighouse terminus on May 6th, 1931. Alongside "De Luxe" car 125 stands the decorated single-deck bus which had transported the official party from Halifax. On the right a large poster proclaims the proud words, "Miles Better, and British!" — a final tribute to the Brighouse trams, perhaps?

[Author's collection]

in fact the Hove Edge cars were to run on weekdays only, until 6 p.m., all other journeys terminating at Hipperholme.

A delay in the delivery of new buses gave the trams a brief reprieve, and a dispute arose with the newly-appointed Traffic Commissioners, who refused Halifax's application for a reduced bus fare which would equate to the tramways workmen's fare. Halifax therefore undertook to provide a temporary bus shuttle service between Hove Edge and Brighouse at a 3d return fare, thus permitting a 6d return fare to and from Halifax.

The changeover was arranged for the afternoon of Wednesday May 6th, 1931, when the Mayors of both boroughs, the Tramways Committee, officials and guests partook of lunch at the Old Cock Hotel, Halifax, before setting out in a single-deck bus. The last tramcar journey was to be performed by Driver Whiteley Lumb, who had joined the Department in 1901 and had been a regular Brighouse driver since the outset. (In private life he was founder of the Calder Valley Poets' Society, a deacon of Park Congregational Church and vice-president of King Cross Adult School.)

Paying a farewell tribute to the trusty trams, which had carried 45,000,000 passengers without a fatal accident, Coun. Gledhill observed that there was "nothing so permanent as change" and that in the previous 6 years Halifax had undergone a superabundance of such "permanence". Replying, the Mayor of Brighouse complimented the Tramways Chairman and Manager on "their youthful vitality and enthusiasm", and solemnly pronounced that "the days of trams were going", whereupon Driver Lumb, in charge of "De Luxe" car 125, cautiously began to move away from the dense crowds at Brighouse terminus before negotiating the awkward curve into Bonegate Road and climbing up the winding ascent to Hove Edge, where the truncated tram service from Union Street, Halifax, was already in operation.

Two unusual incidents caused delays in busy Fountain Street, Halifax, that year. On April 11th a bracket arm became detached from one of the tram standards so that, instead of supporting the overhead wires, it was supported by them, to the detriment of a Triangle tram whose trolley became entangled in it. Then, in November, an incorrectly-set facing point opposite the Halifax Club unexpectedly diverted a tram travelling downhill towards Old Station, causing it to collide with an outward bound Triangle car which had just turned out of Powell Street, The downward car was forced off the track, while the Triangle tram sustained damaged axle boxes. Until the two cars had been removed from the scene, the Sowerby Bridge/Triangle service had to terminate at Bull Green, while the Hebden Bridge cross-town service had to operate in two halves.

For the splendid Bradford Historical Pageant of 1931, a 10d return through fare was provided on the Queensbury and Shelf trams of both authorities, and from September the dogs of Halifax and district were permitted to ride on the trams at a penny fare – but not on the seats! Regrettably, dogs resident in Southowram and Savile Park never benefited from the new concession, as the experimental operation of motor-buses on their routes had already begun.

When the last Southowram tramcar made its final, steady descent of Beacon Hill Road on the evening of July 21st, 1931, the famous spectacle of the "tramcar in the sky" faded into memory and legend, and next morning the Hebden Bridge trams established a new cross-town connection with Shelf, via Horton Street and Union Street. The success of the "experimental" Southowram motor-buses must have been unusually swift and convincing, as on the very day that they commenced operation, the Tramways Committee resolved to remove the tram tracks and remake the road.

Ten obsolete 1898/9 vintage cars, nos. 3, 5, 25-27, 29, 36 –38 and 40 were then offered for sale, enabling no. 27 to fulfil a long-forgotten dream when it was deposited in Wheatley Lane as a bus shelter: Wheatley had achieved its trams at last!

Only one week after the Southowram closure, the elegant suburb of Savile Park with its spacious Victorian residences and tranquil open spaces bade a dignified farewell to its own tramcars which served Free School Lane and the Royal Halifax Hospital as part of the Outer Circle route. This time, the experimental bus service was not reviewed until the end of the agreed trial period, when the Chairman had to concede that the loss on the tram service had been a mere farthing ($^1/_4$d) per car mile, although he was quick to add that if the tracks were to be relaid, the loss would rise to $3^1/_2$d. However, as the buses were achieving a 4d profit, the abandonment was declared permanent on September 23rd, not without opposition. The rails were to be removed, and the tram standards handed over to the Electricity Dept. for street lighting purposes.

Lighting of a more decorative kind adorned a tramcar which was specially illuminated for the Halifax Publicity Campaign from October 10th to 21st. Its special 4d fare also gave free admission to the Exhibition and contributed $2^1/_2$d towards costs, while the multicoloured lights and coats of arms of Halifax and the West Riding displayed on the tram "made a brave show".

"Standard Costs and their Influence on Tramway Policy" formed the subject of a learned lecture delivered by the Chairman in September, when he revealed that the "De Luxe" cars would be able to pay off their capital debt if they

Commercial Street, in 1932, with the elegant dome of the National Provincial House in the distance and tramcar 42 (or 47) on its way to Stainland.

[Photo: S.L. Smith]

increased their average speed by 1% — a feat of which they were perfectly capable, provided that track layouts and Ministry speed restrictions allowed them to do so. Permanent-way costs were a considerable burden. Even though the Shelf and Triangle tramways were near the end of their life, they were still incurring interest and sinking-fund charges of 2.02d and 1.97d per car mile respectively, while the much newer Hebden Bridge installations necessitated a 4d charge, all of which had to be paid for out of tram fares.

Some of the latter were adjusted once again in the face of mounting losses: the 7d maximum return fare on Burnley Road was replaced by single fares of 4d to Mytholmroyd and 5d to Hebden Bridge, which the Chairman considered long overdue, as the service was still incurring a loss of 3$\frac{1}{2}$d per car mile, while

Tramcar 92 at Skircoat Green terminus shortly before the closure of the route in 1932.

[Courtesy Calderdale M.B.C. Libraries, Museums & Arts]

on the Shelf section new 1$\frac{1}{2}$d single or 2d return tickets were available between the fare stages at St. Thomas Street, Stump Cross, Watering Trough, Northowram and Stone Chair.

In view of the recent route abandonments, the supporters of the trams (who included the incoming Mayor, Ald. Rufus Stirk) were heartened by an announcement that £88,897 out of the total of £98,820 agreed in December, 1930, was to be spent on the renewal or re-positioning of tram tracks at West Vale, Highroad Well, Boothtown and the Causeway Foot route (Old Lane – Broad Tree Inn and Ratten Clough – Pharaoh Lane). However, on January 20th, 1932, they were placed in a dilemma when the Committee agreed to discontinue the Skircoat Green service while at the same time partly re-opening the Free School Lane line as an extension of the Pellon service along Warley Road and past

Tramcars 83 to 94 were supplied as open-top, open-platform cars on Brush "A" trucks by the Brush Co. in July/August, 1903, but by the time they were photographed in Skircoat Road depot yard in 1932, no. 86 (left) and no. 92 had been considerably altered. Both had been re-mounted on Halifax-style Peckham trucks with Siemens 40h.p. motors, and had acquired Brush 3-window canopy-top covers. The lower deck of no. 92 had been rebuilt to a reduced height, with early 1920's-vintage vestibules. Both were advertising Queensbury's world-famous Black Dyke Mills Band, but whereas no. 86 displays its destination indicator above the driver's head and bears the small, 1928-style coat of arms, no. 92 prefers the full coat of arms and a destination box attached to the balcony rails.

[Courtesy Roy Brook]

Modernised open-top car 39 prepares to begin the steep ascent of Pye Nest Road in 1932. Surburbanisation has overtaken the old-world charms of Pye Nest Farm, and the roof of Bolton Brow Primary School can be glimpsed (right), while the road studs (bottom left) mark the junction with Bolton Brow. Ahead of the trolley wheel is the "skate" on the overhead wire which will switch off the colour-light signals for the single-line in lower Bolton Brow (behind the photographer) when the trolley makes contact with it, and to its right is the corresponding skate which will switch it on again when the next downward car passes. Did Typhoo Tea actually cure indigestion?

[Photograph: the late M.J. O'Connor, courtesy the National Tramway Museum]

"The Rocks" as far as the junction of Skircoat Green Road. As the Free School Lane area was already covered by three bus services, the restoration of the tram service would merely add to the losses.

Nevertheless, the Skircoat Green route closed "experimentally" on January 31st, 1932, when the last car left Dudwell Lane corner for a final voyage through "the cutting" on tracks laid only nine years previously, and next morning Free School Lane echoed to the sound of tramcars once again. But not for long. Only fifty passengers per day made use of the service, and commencing April 1st, the Pellon trams terminated in Warley Road, King Cross. The Skircoat Green bus service was then made permanent, except that until the next delivery of new buses, "school specials" to Bermerside School near the terminus were worked by tram.

The country was now in the depth of a serious economic crisis; a National Government had been formed, and in common with their colleagues elsewhere, the tramways staff patriotically agreed to a wage reduction for the space of a year. The recent changeovers had improved motor-bus revenue by £11,000 at the expense of the trams, whose income had fallen by £18,000 — an ominous reversal of fortune, as the burden of outstanding debt and the slight operating loss were now falling on a decreasing number of trams. The Manager therefore appealed to the people of Halifax to support their own trams in preference to other people's buses. Seventeen more redundant trams nos. 41-49 and 51-58, were sold in February for further use as bungalows and hen huts.

Nostalgic reminiscences of better days were recalled at the annual reunion of employees who had joined the Department between 1898 and 1904. One of the long-retired drivers described with some gusto his former expertise in driving a tram from Queensbury to Skircoat Road depot in a mere eleven minutes – an incredible feat which met with the retort that in present-day conditions the tram would leave the track altogether. It has to be said that when one considers the number of passing-places, curves and junctions to be negotiated, as well as the precipitous descent through Boothtown, the exploit was not only astonishing but remarkably foolhardy, representing an average speed of 24mph without stops!

Forward-looking plans for the widening of busy King Cross Street from Bull Green to West Parade were unveiled in April, 1932. In the new carriageway, the tram tracks were to be re-laid sufficiently far apart to allow the provision of pedestrian refuges incorporating centre poles supporting the tram wires and street lighting. The new uphill track was duly brought into use in September, 1933, when work on the downhill track began. On the condemned Triangle, Shelf and Hove Edge sections, some unavoidable repairs had to be carried out, and following the closure of the Mansfield District tramways in October, 1932, 150 redundant tram standards were bought for £4 each from Messrs. E. J. Walsh of that town, followed in January, 1933, by additional poles and finials worth £168-15-0d. The installation of modern traffic lights at the junction of North Parade and Orange Street allowed the Department to dispense with the "Board of Trade" compulsory tram stops which had existed there since 1899.

In June, 1932, Messrs. Brecknell Willis, suppliers of overhead line equipment, were paid £27 for the "the fitting of trolley reversers", of which examples soon appeared at Hebden Bridge, Sowerby Bridge, Highroad Well, Pellon, Commercial Street, Causeway Foot, Bradshaw and the Ovenden shortworkings such as Club Lane. Apart from a home-built reverser which had existed at Skircoat Green (Dudwell Lane) terminus from 1925, none had been seen since the short-lived 1905 experiments, and none were provided at Old Station, in Powell Street or on routes due for early abandonment, such as Triangle, Queensbury, Shelf or Hove Edge.

An eminent link with the heady days of late-Victorian enterprise and ingenuity was broken by the death of Mr. Michael Holroyd Smith on July 1st, 1932, at the age of 84. Born in Wade Street as the second son of Mayor Matthew Smith, Mr. Smith had trained as an engineer and taken up

residence in London in 1887 to further his career. After his Blackpool and Bradford exploits, his greatest achievement was the electrification of the City and South London Railway, and although he never subsequently resided in Halifax, he maintained a lively interest in local matters, and often visited his brother, Mr. George. F. Smith, at "The Gleddings".

A bleak scene in Commercial Street at the bottom of George Square (left), the town terminus of the Pellon and Highroad Well services. A "sloping-sided" car stands in front of the unidentified "De Luxe" car, and the photograph may have been taken at the start of the severe snowstorm of February, 1933.
[Copyright: Halifax Courier, Ltd.]

Sadly, the bright dawn of electric tramways which Mr. Holroyd Smith had helped to bring about, was now giving way to premature twilight. As the tramway between Stump Cross and Shelf was officially described as "done", i.e., worn out, the Department were preparing to replace the trams with J.O.C. "B" service buses. The intricacies of the Joint Committee arrangements unfortunately enabled the Hebble Bus Co. to claim that the section outside the Borough boundary at Northowram fell within Zone "C" and should therefore be handed over to them. Unable to resolve the impasse, the Department withdrew the regular tram service on August 16th, 1932, replacing it next day with a Corporation bus service as far as Northowram, leaving the outermost portion of the route to be served by a shuttle tram service. Thus, early every morning a solitary tramcar, usually single decker 103 or 105, made its way from the depot to Stump Cross to begin the ascent of Bradford Road and Back Clough, swinging round the long curves and sometimes gleefully passing a Hebble bus wearily labouring uphill on its way to Bradford or Leeds. Then, for the rest of the day, it patrolled between Northowram and Shelf, where the vibration generated as it clattered over the worn rail-joints sometimes caused ornaments to fall from domestic mantelpieces along the route.

The obvious inconvenience of a change of vehicle at Northowram displeased Shelf U.D.C., who initially contemplated supporting the J.O.C. in its efforts to provide a bus service to their village in co-ordination with Hebble's longer-distance services, but had second thoughts when it was pointed out that this might tie the J.O.C's hands should Shelf amalgamate with Halifax at a future date (their fears proved premature, as amalgamation was staved off until 1974). The wrangling therefore continued for the rest of the year, no doubt to the profound irritation of Coun. Gledhill, whom the press commend for giving "a very energetic lead" in transport matters. Similar negotiations in respect of the Hove Edge service also proved to be protracted.

Limited track repairs were carried out at Salterhebble, but the Warley Road and Spring Hall Lane installations received only the minimum attention, as the Department had plans for a bus service linking up with the Savile Park/Outer Circle buses at a future date. Conversely, the Highroad Well outward-bound track was to be relaid at a cost of £8,500 (the inward track still had seven years' life left), as the route was used not only by normal service cars but also by up to 30 "football specials" whenever matches were played at Thrum Hall. On the Causeway Foot section, £10,157 was voted for the renewal of the Bank Top – Nursery Lane section.

Tramway staff who operated skeleton services on Christmas Day, 1932, were paid double wages, with "time and a quarter" for work carried out on the two succeeding days, and the temporary wage reductions agreed upon a year earlier were terminated shortly afterwards.

The vulnerability of hilly Halifax and its neighbouring valleys to extreme weather conditions was spectacularly revealed in 1933 by the heaviest snowfall for 40 years, which began on the afternoon of February 23rd and did not abate for two days. Despite the most determined efforts of snowploughs and snow shovellers, the tram tracks and highways were soon impassable, and all tram and bus services had to be curtailed or abandoned for five days, with a consequential revenue loss of £1,668. The total bill for snow clearance in the Borough was £5,000, which included the wages of 100 men who had to dig a path to Mount Tabor when food supplies ran low. English weather being as unpredictable then as it is today, the snow was later followed by the warmest Whitsuntide since 1900, which helped to restore the tramways' finances.

The joint terminus of the Halifax (left) and Bradford (right) tramways at Shelf. Both services were numbered 12, but Halifax tram 77 (left) did not enjoy the luxury of an automatic trolley reverser like the Bradford model (top right). The two sets of wires were joined but insulated from each other midway between the two bracket arms in the foreground.

[Courtesy the late R.B. Parr]

Before Winter ended, however, climatic conditions brought about a sad sequel. Supervising snow-clearing operations in early March, the General Manager, Mr. Walter Young, contracted a chill which led to pneumonia and his death on April 5th at the early age of 53. During his seven years' tenure of office he had been involved in far-reaching changes designed to meet the challenges of unbridled competition, lost revenue, the Slump and co-ordination with the railways – a tremendous task and a source of much anxiety. Discerningly, he had taken great pride in his "De Luxe" cars, and being a friendly, genial gentleman, he had enjoyed much popularity.

The shocked Committee confirmed the high esteem in which Mr. Young had always been held, and sympathetically granted to his widow a gratuity equal to four months' salary. Pending the appointment of a successor, the day-to-day running of the Department was placed in the hands of the Chairman and Vice-Chairman, the Rolling-Stock Superintendent (Mr. Canning), Bus Works Manager (Mr. Burrows), Chief Commercial Assistant (Mr. Berry), Services Clerk (Mr. Dunstan) and Chief Inspector Binns (who was subsequently appointed Traffic Superintendent). Within days a rumour was circulating in the town that an offer of £600,000 for the Corporation transport undertaking had been made by "a national electricity company", i.e., the British Electric Traction Co., now owners of Hebble. While denying that any such offer had been received, the Council nevertheless debated for two hours on May 3rd as to "whether, if such an offer were to materialise, it would be entertained", to which the answer was a very satisfactory and emphatic refusal.

In the meantime, the rancorous dispute over the Shelf service had been resolved when the J.O.C. reluctantly surrendered its rights to Hebble, who were allowed to absorb the running rights beyond the boundary into their existing services. Accordingly, the last tramcar to perform the isolated shuttle service quietly departed from Shelf terminus on the evening of March 31st, 1933. Shortly afterwards the only physical link with Bradford's tramways was severed when Halifax's overhead linesmen dismantled the overhead wires, which were linked end-on with the Bradford installations at Shelf terminus; thenceforth the Bradford wires were anchored to a convenient tram standard until they, too, became redundant two years later. The discarded fixtures between Northowram and Shelf were removed by arrangement with the County Council, whereby Halifax salvaged the rails, setts and poles and reinstated the pavements, while the County Highways Dept. laid a new tarmac highway.

A curious postscript to the demise of the trams occurred on December 20th, 1933, when one of the Corporation's new AEC doubledeckers descending from Northowram to Stump Cross skidded on ice, plunged 30 feet down a hillside, overturned and lay perilously suspended above the roofs of nearby houses, injuring the crew and passengers. The service was halted until next day.

Brighouse Corporation, having decided that redundant tram poles did not necessarily constitute the most suitable form of lamp posts, requested Halifax to remove them, but the latter, believing themselves to have shed any liability two

A summer morning at Shelf in 1932, when the conductor of "De Luxe" car 126 was photographed swinging the trolley prior to departure for Hebden Bridge. In the centre of the photograph can be seen the 15 foot gap between the Halifax and Bradford tracks.

[Author's collection]

years earlier, stoutly resisted the claim until compelled by arbitrators to pay £171-17-9d to be rid of them at last.

Meanwhile, the surviving remnant of the former Brighouse tramway, to Hove Edge, had been under threat since December, 1932, but as a dispute with the Traffic Commissioners concerning bus fares to be charged by the J.O.C. and its competitors resulted in an appeal to the Ministry, it was not until the early evening of Friday, September 29th, 1933, that the last of the daytime-only cars to Hove Edge left the quiet outer terminus to climb up past Broad Oak and clatter over the three level crossings, being followed next evening by the final car from Hipperholme, which made the last-ever run down to Stump Cross and away to the depot.

A residual tram service as far as Stump Cross was retained for a while, but as the terminus and reversal point was at the nearest available stretch of single line in Leeds Road near its busy junction with Bradford Road, the process of swinging the trolley-boom proved somewhat risky, especially at night. The service was therefore discontinued on Tuesday, January 9th, 1934, after which an even shorter journey was substituted between Union Street and the crossover in Godley Lane at the entrance to Shibden Park, to which point tramcars operated on weekdays from 6p.m. to 7p.m. and after midday on Saturdays, these being now the only trams to ascend and descend New Bank.

A closer view of car 126 opposite the entrance to Shelf Hall Park.

[Author's collection]

CHAPTER 19

EVENING SHADOWS

The search for a successor to Mr. Young led in June, 1933, to interviews with three applicants:- Mr. F.H. Burrows (Halifax Tramways and Motors Works Manager), Mr. J. Atherton (General Manager Leigh Corporation Motor Omnibus Dept) and Mr. Frank Lythgoe (General Manager and Engineer, Rawtenstall Corporation Tramways and Motors). None of the candidates was considered suitable, although Mr Lythgoe subsequently proved his worth by transforming the Middlesbrough Corporation undertaking into a model of municipal excellence.

The post was therefore re-advertised at a salary of £1,000 per annum, with rent-free accommodation at Tramway House adjacent to the depot. This time a strong shortlist materialised:-

- Mr. James L. Gunn, General Manager, Aberdeen Corporation Transport;

- Mr. G. H. Napthine, in charge of Eastern National Omnibus Co. at Colchester and Clacton District;

- Mr. A. E. Scroggie, Chief Engineer, W. Alexander and Sons, Ltd;

- Mr. R. H. Tilling, Assistant to General Manager, Yorkshire Traction Co;

- Mr. A. F. Neal, Senior Assistant Engineer, Manchester Corporation Transport;

- Mr. G. F. Craven, Director and Commercial Manager, Park Royal Coachworks, Ltd., London; former manager, Reading Corporation Tramways;

- Mr. W. T. Cox, Chief Engineer, Pearson and Dorman Long, Ltd.;

- Mr. C. A. Hopkins, General Manager, Sunderland Corporation Tramways and Motors;

- Mr. H. J. Troughton, Acting Deputy Manager and Engineer, Bradford Corporation Tramways.

The list offered interesting possibilities. At Aberdeen Mr. Gunn managed trams as well as buses, but when subsequently appointed to Nottingham a few years later, he advocated the replacement of trolley-buses by diesel buses, a dismal prospect which was averted only by his early death. Messrs. Napthine, Scroggie and Tilling would undoubtedly have championed buses, and even though Mr. Neal in his later years as Manchester's manager purchased new trolleybuses, he too would probably have advocated buses. As chief engineer to the major supplier of Halifax's tram rails, Mr. Cox might have had an interest in retaining the trams, while Mr Hopkins, who was in the process of transforming Sunderland's tramways into an outstanding example of modernity and attractiveness, might conceivably have done the same for Halifax. Mr. Troughton, a gifted and imaginative electrical engineer, who had already introduced new ways and ideas to the Bradford tram and trolleybus undertaking, and subsequently created a completely new, ultra-modern trolleybus system in South Shields, would certainly have proved a staunch ally to electric traction if he had been appointed to Halifax.

However, it was on Mr. Craven that the choice fell, and his appointment doubtless owed as much to his commercial success with Park Royal Coachworks as to his previous managership at Reading, although his A.M.I.C.E, M.I.M.E., and M.I.E.E., qualifications obviously counted in his favour. An early indication of his probable preferences was revealed on October 19th, 1933, when the Committee agreed to seek licences to operate buses over all the tram routes at tram fares in case of breakdowns, as well as for journeys over the tram routes in connection with late-night excursions, dances and theatre performances.

Nevertheless, Mr Craven's electrical experience led him to investigate the merits of modern electric braking systems for the trams as a means of reducing the track wear on descending gradients caused by the large C.H. Spencer track-brake shoes (which, in his words, "tore up the track") and, to a lesser extent, the quick-acting compressed-air track brake system fitted to the "De Luxe" cars. In November, 1933, the Committee accepted a tender from Metropolitan Vickers Ltd, for the adaptation of one set of tramcar motors for regenerative braking. The cost, including new gear wheels and pinions, was to be £416-3-0d, and work began early in 1934.

During all the "changes and chances" of committee debates and future prospects, the workaday routines of tramcar operation continued as usual, with the familiar, dignified deep red and ivory cars proceeding on their stately way through the busy streets and conveying passengers young and old to their different destinations.

On the long, fairly level Hebden Bridge route, the "De Luxe" cars were able to maintain a good speed at all times, their gentle sideways sway adding to the smooth pleasure of the journey. The clockwork punctuality of the service ensured that each driver knew where he would encounter other trams travelling in the opposite direction, and on single-track sections not provided with colour- light signalling, the outward-bound cars always had precedence.

However, one day in 1938 the driver of an inward-bound car from Tuel Lane unwisely entered the single line between Trimmingham and King Cross without ensuring that it was clear, and not surprisingly found another tram travelling towards him. Observing these developments from the front balcony of the offending tramcar, 10 year old schoolboy Terence Cannon, quickly realised that neither driver intended to give way, and fled for shelter into the top-deck saloon.

Tram car 81 turns out of Gibbet Street into Spring Hall Lane on service no.1 – Stainland to West End via Old Station.

[J.A. Pitts collection, courtesy West Yorkshire Archives, Bradford

The force of the ensuing collision shook most of the windows out of their frames, whereupon both drivers furiously jumped off and squared up to each other on the King's Highway in the best traditions of Joe Louis and Tommy Farr, having to be dragged apart by a posse of

A handful of older open-top cars had to be retained to assist the modern ex-Exeter cars in the operation of the Sowerby Bridge and Triangle services. "Ben Hall" car no. 11 waits at the town terminus on July 14th, 1937, with two of Halifax's distinctive humped-roof AEC buses on the opposite side of Powell Street, with Fountain Street crossing from left to right.
[Photo: H.B. Priestley, courtesy National Tramway Museum]

amazed constables who emerged from the nearby police station. Unlucky Master Cannon received several whacks with a strap from his disbelieving headmaster when he arrived late at school!

When the Tramways Committee held their monthly meeting on November 22nd, 1933, they were confronted with a joint report by the Borough Treasurer and Engineer which summarised the outstanding loan debts on the tramways and an estimated cost of renewal of worn-out sections. The original loans dated from 1898, 1900,1905, and 1911, with repayment periods of between 30 and 48 years.

Having digested the statistics, the Committee made some drastic decisions, reaffirming their earlier decision to close certain routes when the track wore out. Thus, they voted to discontinue the Queensbury service beyond Boothtown, and resolved that when the Triangle route was cut back to Sowerby Bridge, the terminus should be in Wharf Street at the foot of Tuel Lane, between tram poles nos. 77 and 78, thereby allowing the service to be wholly provided by top-covered cars. Similarly, the King Cross via West End route was to be cut back to Pellon, subject to a census of passengers.

Much more ominously, however, the Committee decided not to spend the whole of the £22,880 which they had voted for the West Vale route in December, 1930, having been persuaded that the cost of relaying the King Cross – West Vale tracks would be greater than the outstanding loan on the relatively new West Vale – Stainland extension; also, the trams were being partly duplicated by the J.O.C. buses to Outlane, Barkisland, Norland and Hullen Edge.

Naturally, these significant decisions were not accepted without protest. Sowerby Bridge U.D.C. rejected the idea of tramcars reversing in narrow Wharf Street on a full-time

Safely returned from Queensbury, no. 65 and its crew rest for a few moments in Union Street. The ends of the canopy roof have been flattened to match the "Ben Hall" style platform vestibule. Note the parcels on the tram platform.

[Roy Brook collection]

Alderman Longbottom resolutely opposed all the above proposals, but was outvoted. Queensbury U.D.C. debated whether to request the retention of their trams or to thank the Corporation for the valuable service which they had received for over thirty years, but in view of Halifax's known ambition to absorb Queensbury into the Borough, decided not to say anything that might incriminate them!

For the tramways a black year lay ahead. The West End Circular ran for the last time on Sunday, February 4th, 1934, thus ending tramcar operation in Warley Road and cutting back the tram service to Pellon (Barracks), a few yards north of the right-angled crossing with the Highroad Well track. When the redundant overhead wires and the overhead curve from Gibbet Street into Spring Hall Lane were cut down, the remaining Pellon wires were anchored to a pole on the south side of the junction, crossing the Highroad Well wires at a higher level. Thus, although the Pellon and Highroad Well termini closely adjoined each other, they no longer had a usable physical connection.

Criticisms were soon voiced that the new Outer Circle buses were competing with the trams in King Cross Street and undermining their profitability even further. The fares between Town and King Cross were therefore altered to $1\frac{1}{2}$d (tram), 2d (Corporation bus) and 3d (J.O.C. bus)

basis, whereupon the Corporation reluctantly accepted that the traditional Station Road terminus would have to be retained, thus condemning the Sowerby Bridge passengers to the stark comforts of the older open-top trams for a few more years, and allowing the modern ex-Exeter cars a welcome reprieve from premature scrapping.

Next, it was the turn of the Queensbury and Shibden Park tram services, which were withdrawn simultaneously on March 31st. At Queensbury terminus the departure of the last tram was witnessed by a small crowd of onlookers, who may

When H.B. Priestley photographed "De Luxe" car 124 on a return journey from Highroad Well on July 14th, 1937, the Spring Hall Lane track (left to right) and the curve from Gibbet Street (centre right) had been abandoned, and the remaining Pellon wires (top left) crossed over the top of the Gibbet Street wires to be anchored to an unseen pole on the right. The section feeder cable (right) in front of the old Mile Cross depot fed not only the Highroad Well wires but also, as can be seen, the wires at Pellon terminus about 100 yards distant (left)

Queensbury terminus, surveyed from the Parish Church tower about 1929. In the foreground, Halifax tram no. 63 basks in the afternoon sunshine while in the distance, outside the "Granby Inn", Bradford tram no. 89 prepares to make the long descent to its native city. The Bradford anchor-pole can be seen to the right of car 63, and the Halifax anchor–pole is semi-visible outside the prominent house on the left. The joint waiting-room is on the ground floor of the three-storey building (right)

[Photo: Walter Scott, Bradford]

Eighteen surplus trams were then offered for sale, although in fact two dozen were taken out of stock, including the "Hall-Bostock" worm-driven single-decker, no. 106, which had languished disused since a minor collision with a brewery wagon at Northowram three years earlier; reputedly it had not been Mr. Young's favourite tram, as it was non-standard and much speedier than the trams with which it worked on its usual journeys to Queensbury, Shelf and Bailiffe Bridge. The other withdrawn cars were mostly old, open-platform top-covered cars but included also a "Ben Hall" car, no. 75 (theoretically only seven years old) as well as no. 100, which had been partly modernised with "bay-window" vestibules and red leather upholstered seats less than four years previously.

Minor improvements to the rolling-stock were still being carried out, however. The final closure of the South Lancashire Transport Company's tramways at Atherton led to the purchase for £40 of the curiously vague total of "about nine 50 h.p. box-type WT32 roller-bearing motors", which presumably were used to speed up modernised trams nos. 17, 77, 99 and 102, although as no. 17 was currently the subject of the regenerative braking experiment, it may be that nos. 97 or 101 received the motors instead.

also have included the driver and conductor of the Bradford Corporation tram standing a few yards away, and no doubt those present recalled past excitements of runaways and blown-over trams as well as the matchless scenic panoramas they had enjoyed so long on their steady journeys up and down the long hills. Queensbury U.D.C. agreed to purchase the tram standards in their area to which electric lights were attached (i.e., each alternate pole), so that as late as 1950 a continuous line of old tram poles flanked the whole of the 8 mile distance between Halifax and Bradford town centres. The simultaneous withdrawal of the evening and Saturday-only service to Shibden Park Gates attracted much less attention, even though it ended tramcar operation in New Bank.

Tramcar 100 encountered rocky track when it entered King Cross Street on a return journey from West Vale to Old Station about 1932.

[Courtesy Roy Brook]

As the withdrawal of the Queensbury service had greatly diminished the volume of trams passing through Boothtown, the Manager saw an opportunity of reducing maintenance costs by abandoning the outward track from Chester Road to Boothtown terminus and using the inward track as a single line, with a passing-loop at Grantham Place, to which the Ministry agreed.

Meanwhile, the agreed abandonment programme continued on its remorseless way. Negotiations in the Ryburn Valley having led to the purchase of the competing Ripponden and District buses by the J.O.C., the Triangle tram service was cut back to Station Road, Sowerby Bridge, on July 25th, thus depriving lovers of fresh air and beautiful woodland scenery of one of their most picturesque tram rides. The redundant tram standards were left in situ for street-lighting purposes: Sowerby Bridge U.D.C. attached

After the Triangle route closed, its tracks and wires were removed, but as shown above (centre), some of the redundant poles were retained for street-lighting purposes. Ex-Exeter car 129 is standing at Sowerby Bridge terminus, Station Road, with overhead wires now tied off to a new, heavy-duty pole (left).

(Courtesy Roy Brook]

gas lamps to them, but their more rural neighbour, Sowerby U.D.C. more adventurously bought about 35 of the standards for £2-10-0d each, "with the idea of installing electric lighting".

The Corporation's fast-dwindling interest in its tramways contrasted vividly with its bold ambitions for "the transport of the future" in the form of a Corporation aerodrome at Illingworth — a visionary scheme which met with the warm approval of the celebrated aviator Sir Alan Cobham, but the

The only known photograph of Halifax and Huddersfield trams together at West Vale was obtained in July, 1932, under severe difficulties – ladies hurrying to catch the Halifax tram, loiterers obscuring its fleet number (77) and a bus approaching from the right. Fully-enclosed Huddersfield tram no. 61 in Saddleworth Road is resting about twenty feet short of the end of its tracks, and the Huddersfield anchor-pole (to which the overhead wires were tied off) stands between the N and I in the sign for "Economic Stores", a familiar Halifax-area grocer's shop. The Halifax pole, left, bears a section feeder as well as a 10 - lamp overhead lantern fed from the tram wires to illuminate the busy crossroads.

[Photo: S.L. Smith]

idea never "took off". Neither did Mr. Craven's proposal for reducing tramway maintenance costs in Boothtown Road: within six weeks of receiving Ministry approval for the revised single track and loop arrangement, he changed his mind and persuaded the Committee to close the route altogether, ostensibly to save £8,197 on alterations and repairs. In vain councillors protested that the route was profitable, the track had five or six years' life left and that withdrawal of the trams would cost more than retention, i.e. £11,000 for new buses and highway reinstatement. The arguments were not disproved, but the trams ran for the last time on Sunday, August 5th, thus ending tramway operation on North Bridge, Northgate, Broad Street, Market Street and Union Street.

The premature demise of the Boothtown trams had a beneficial though indirect and unintended sequel. Local motorists had long been accustomed to relying on the gleaming tramlines to guide them on their way whenever Halifax was enveloped in dense fog, but when the rails in Haley Hill and Boothtown Road lost their sheen and disappeared into rusty obscurity, local businessman Mr. Percy Shaw devised a novel method of assisting fog-bound travellers in the new, tramless world. His invention, popularly known as "cats' eyes", has made an enormous contribution to the cause of road safety ever since.

On Tuesday, October 30th, 1934, the last Stainland tram slipped quietly away from the terminus at Crossfield at 10.55pm., un-noticed and unmourned. Stainlanders preferred to look forward rather than to mourn the past, even though it was barely thirteen years since they had eagerly cheered the arrival of the first tram. West Vale had lost its tram service also, as the formerly long route now operated no further than Jubilee Road, Salterhebble. Ironically, within two months the Stainlanders were complaining of petrol fumes and bus wheels mounting and destroying their pavements. But it was too late: the County Council had already agreed to lift the tracks and make good the highway for a payment of 5s 6d per yard.

These abandonments reduced the tramcar fleet considerably — by the end of the year only 56 cars remained in stock. Nevertheless, despite the cancellation of unexercised borrowing powers worth £42,422, the Committee decided to seek a loan for further track renewals:-

Hebden Bridge section:	
King Cross to Granny Hill	£1,121
Causeway Foot section:	
Club Lane to Pharaoh Lane	930
Broad Tree to Shroggs Lane	2,325
Sowerby Bridge section:	
Tuel Lane bottom to Station Road	625
Town Centre:	
Cow Green to Pheasant Hotel	1,100
Hall End layout	2,300
Crown Street	495
Crown St/Pellon Lane layout	1,250
	£10,146

The necessary points and crossings (including an additional crossover for Commercial Street and "double-connected big-head points for the Crown St/Pellon Lane junction") were ordered from Edgar Allen and Co. in Sheffield, where the Chief Engineering Assistant inspected them before delivery. The rails were bought from Dorman Long for £9-8-0d per ton plus £1-16-0d for Sandberg "Sorbitic" rail hardening treatment and £13-8-0d per ton for fishplates, and the work was carried out early in 1935.

In a renewed effort to persuade passengers to make more use of the Horton Street line which had just been re-laid, the Committee agreed that anyone who boarded a tram at Old Station instead of the town centre could do so at no additional cost. Similarly, transfer tickets were issued to Highroad Well tram users who wished to continue by bus to West End.

Trials with car no. 17 and its Metrovick regenerative braking system began on October 23rd , 1934, on the Causeway Foot route which contained many long descents on the inward journey as well as the steep downhill curves at Wrigley Corner, Illingworth. By December 11th it was calculated that there had been a 38% saving on current, equivalent to £147-13-2d per year, in addition to greatly reduced wear on the slipper brake shoes. The magnetic track brake shoes fitted to the "De Luxe" cars normally lasted 4,000 miles, whereas on no. 17 they would probably last up to 30,000 miles. Drivers appreciated the new device: with a slight backward motion of the controller handle they could in effect reverse the motors, creating a braking effect and

Tram no. 77 rumbles down Horton Street at the end of a journey from West Vale in 1932. The Picture House (domed) stands between Wards End and Fountain Street, and the Palace Music Hall has been in use since 1903.

[Photo: S.L. Smith]

feeding power back into the overhead line for use by other trams. In this way they eliminated the use of brake shoes except on the steepest gradients and for bringing the car to a standstill.

Six additional sets were ordered from Metropolitan-Vickers for a total of £1895-18-5d, and all had been fitted by December, 1935, to "De Luxe" cars 114,116, 118, 119,121 and 126, thereby providing them with an increased total of nine different braking systems.

Tramcar 17, the first of the "Ben Hall" cars in 1921, was subsequently modernised with a 3-window top deck and regenerative control, and was photographed at Pellon terminus in 1937, by the late W.A. Camwell.

Halifax Corporation Car ascending a Gradient of 1 in 9

The "De Luxe" cars did not need the "goodness of Bovril" to propel them up the 1 in 9.69 gradient of Salterhebble Hill: no.117, seen here about 1934, trusted in its powerful motors and eight different braking systems.

[Photo: "Tramway and Railway World" and J.A. Pitts collection, courtesy West Yorkshire Archives, Bradford]

Presumably these forward-looking conversions owed more to a desire to reduce running costs than to an interest in modern techniques, as the future of further tram routes was under investigation. The General Manager and Borough Engineer inspected the condition of the track in Pellon Lane and from Ward's End to Bull Green, although when the Committee were shown the Pellon findings, they took no action on them, and in December, 1935, they decreed that the heavily-used Gibbet Street/Thrum Hall Lane junction should be renewed at a cost of £650. During the Autumn the Waterhouse Street and Hall End tracks and the Crown Steet/Pellon Lane junction had been completed, the Bull Green curves re-laid, the disused curve at the foot of Horton Street into Church Street removed, and 81 redundant tram standards bought from Southend-on-Sea Corporation as replacements or where road-widening was taking place.

The sad remnant of the West Vale/Stainland route had not survived long, as it had lost money ever since it had been cut back to Salterhebble. When the Huddersfield Joint Omnibus Committee agreed to pay Halifax one quarter of all fares collected by them between Halifax and the Calder & Hebble Inn on journeys to and from Huddersfield, the last service tram departed on the night of Sunday, May 19th, 1935. The closure of this short section of tramway deprived the depot staff of their traditional Salterhebble Hill brake-testing

Alike but different: "Ben Hall" car 71 and "De Luxe" car 125 side by side in the depot on June 2nd, 1937. They shared one important feature – a prominent advertisement for the famous Halifax Building Society.

[Courtesy Roy Brook, copyright H.B. Priestley]

facility, though not immediately. During the evening, car 113 had been brought into the depot with faulty brakes, and having made the necessary adjustments, shedman Jack Naylor cautiously drove the tram out into Huddersfield Road next morning. Finding to his pleasure that the power had not yet been switched off, he drove no. 113 down the hill and back again before officialdom had bestirred itself, thereby fulfilling another chapter in his secret ambition to ride on every 'last tram'.

Ten further trams were then disposed of; open-top cars 12, 16, 19, 23 and 50 with Bradford-style vestibules, together with vestibuled canopy-top car 91 found their way either to the scrap yard or to gardens for use as summer-houses; "Ben Hall" canopy top tram 64 began a new, hectic life as a hen-house, while of the two remaining single-deckers, no. 103 became a bus shelter at Mixenden and no.105 a holiday bungalow at Flamborough Head. A more colourful interlude awaited several of the surviving trams which were decorated and illuminated for Safety Week (June 3rd-8th) and the Jubilee Shopping Festival (October 19th– November 2nd), thus demonstrating that the fast-dwindling tramcar fleet could still outshine its rubber tyred rivals.

But the year drew to an end on a sombre note. On September 18th the Committee agreed to seek licences for the replacement of the Sowerby Bridge trams by J.O.C. buses, and the meeting held on December 18th gave rise to a startling newspaper headline:-

"HALIFAX TO SCRAP TRAMS BEYOND TUEL LANE"
— Losing Sixpence a Mile Now"

Not surprisingly, the meeting had been stormy, and when its recommendations were reported to the Council on January 8th, 1936, the unpalatable prospect of cutting back the Hebden Bridge route to the Borough boundary at Tuel Lane top aroused determined attempts to refer the matter back or, if possible, to reject it. The abandonment of miles of sound track was condemned as unbelievably premature, having been laid at enormous expense and having a minimum of seven years' life left. Not only would the removal of the rails and reinstatement of the highway cost at least £8,500, but the Electricity Department would suffer a loss even greater than the £22,722 decrease in revenue it had already withstood. The trams used on the route were modern, and the sub-station at Brearley was of recent origin. Buses had only a short life and were wholly dependent on imported oil; bus fares would be higher than the existing tram fares, and half their receipts would have to be paid to the railway companies.

In defence of his recommendation, the Chairman (an Alderman once again) argued that the quarter-hourly tram service was now losing 6d per car mile, and as it was the last of the outlying unprofitable services, it was unreasonable to ask the Borough ratepayers to subsidise it any longer. While it was true that the bus fares would be higher, many people already preferred to pay more to ride on the competing buses, which were speedier, than to ride on the trams which were cheaper — an argument which blithely disregarded the many passengers who had remained loyal to the trams. In view of the unexpired life of the tram track, the railway companies

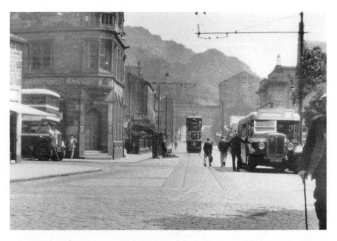

In later years the Hebden Bridge trams reversed about 50 yards short of their original terminus, in order to relieve traffic congestion. "De Luxe" car 116 has negotiated the trolley reverser in preparation for retuning to Halifax, while a Todmorden Joint Committee Leyland "Titan" lurks in Crown Street (left) and Halifax Joint Committee AEC "Regal" JX 1955 prepares to make the arduous ascent to Heptonstall. Photographed in 1932 by S.L. Smith.

had agreed to pay Halifax half the profits for a period of six years when the buses took over from the trams.

His proposal was agreed by the narrow margin of 25-22, and the closure date was set for March 31st. The County Council accepted a sum of £6,367-18-0d for reinstatement, and when Mytholmroyd bought the redundant poles in their area for 18s 9d each, the Corporation made a similar offer to Hebden Bridge.

Although the virtues of electrically-operated public transport had so far made little impression in Halifax, they achieved better appreciation elsewhere. Greetland U.D.C., now served exclusively from the Halifax direction by petrol and diesel buses, were pleased to learn that Huddersfield intended to replace their West Vale trams with modern trolley-buses of a type which existing users described as "spacious and swift". In view of a recent increase in fuel oil tax, Greetland pondered whether Halifax might consider using their redundant tram standards to support trolleybus wires. Halifax Corporation's Heating, Light and Power Committee were asking the same question, and in February, 1936, they conferred with their Tramways Committee colleagues in the knowledge that Bradford and Manchester were also planning trolleybus developments. From Portsmouth Mr Ben Hall offered one of his new trolleybuses for demonstration purposes, but his gesture was politely declined, as the Chairman and Manager were perfectly satisfied with their diesel buses. And so it was that the only sections of Halifax's tramway operating area ever to taste the delights of modern trolleybuses were in West Vale (Stainland Road) between Saddleworth Road and Rochdale Road, and Brighouse (between the "George" and the bottom of Bonegate Road), provided by Huddersfield.

At the Tramways Club annual dinner in February, 1936, the General Manager added unexpected harmony to the melodious strains of the newly-formed Tramways Band by revealing that his Department had at last achieved a small profit and was looking forward to an even larger one. "It is

Two views of tramcar 115 at Tuel Lane terminus. In the upper view, the modern tarmacadam road surface extended from the crossover (behind the tram) all the way to Hebden Bridge, but apart from the short stretch seen here, the tram tracks embedded in it had been discarded two years earlier. Photographed on July 2nd, 1938, the tram was about to negotiate the trolley reverser and cross to the inward track..

A survivor – old no. 74, modernised with "bay window" vestibules, extended fenders and a Halifax-designed Peckham truck, was photographed at Sowerby Bridge by Mr. H. B. Priestley on June 2nd, 1937.
[Courtesy National Tramway Museum]

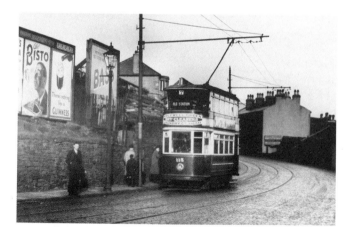

Probably photographed a year earlier (its paintwork is considerably smarter), no. 115 has crossed on to the inward track before returning to Halifax (Old Station).

very difficult to substitute an efficient tramway system with any other form of transport", he declared with dubious grammar and suspect sincerity. "You are all aware of the ability of the trams to deal with heavy loads, and they are particularly liked by the older people. So long as trams can be run profitably, I am sure the Tramways Committee will continue to run them". Probably not many people shared his apparent confidence.

Five weeks later, on the evening of Tuesday, March 31st, 1936, the good folk of Hebden Bridge foregathered to see the departure of their last tramcar. As the brilliantly-lit "De Luxe" car began its long, reluctant homeward journey, there were many who mourned its passing. Even the local "Times and Gazette" paused momentarily to pen a few cool words of tribute. "Although it has often been criticised, it has been a most useful means of transport," the editor wrote. And so, with all its accustomed vigour and resonance the last tram rolled steadily along the winding valley through Mytholmroyd, Brearley and Luddenden Foot, where small knots of onlookers waved and bade their farewells to thirty-four years of trusty tramcar transport

Next morning the replacing J.O.C. bus service was supplemented by a new, all-day tram service from Old Station to the Borough boundary at Tuel Lane, on which normal tram fares operated. Surprisingly, no trams were scrapped, although "Ben Hall" open-top tram no. 9 was converted into a snowplough tram, and "De Luxe" cars, displaced from the route for which they had originally been designed, now appeared on all the town routes. The Sowerby Bridge route was now the only line which operated outside the Borough and which needed open-top trams, although some of the latter continued to enjoy popularity on summer-weather outings to Causeway Foot.

The remaining routes still needed a reasonable amount of upkeep, and in May, 1936, approval was given for track renewal in Commercial Street and from Pellon terminus to Queen's Road (inward track only). A month later a revision of the Causeway Foot schedules led to the inauguration of a peak-hour service to Beechwood Road as well as the laying of a new crossover at Raw Lane, Illingworth, to which

Photographed on the summer afternoon of July 14th, 1937, in Commercial Street, tramcar 123 is being boarded by an elderly lady dressed in 1920's style, at the Pellon loading-point at the bottom of George Square. On the "De Luxe" cars the destination names were often comprehensively expressed, e.g., "Pellon (Barracks)" in place of the more customary "Pellon". On the left, car 111 returning from Highroad Well is about to pass under the town centre feeder-point and section breaker.

[Photo: the late W.A. Camwell, courtesy the National Tramway Museum]

additional shortworking cars operated at peak hours with the aid of a new trolley reverser supplied by Brecknell, Willis. On June 17th 50 tons of tram rail were ordered form Dorman Long @ £9-13-0d per ton, this being the last such purchase made by the Department.

Pleasingly, the trams were still in demand for special events. In September, one was decorated and illuminated for another Shopping Festival; then on December 16th the Committee voted £100 for a tram to be prepared for festivities marking the forthcoming Coronation, having learned a few days earlier that the new sovereigns were to be King George VI and Queen Elizabeth, rather than King Edward VIII and his transatlantic inamorata. When the great day arrived, on May 12th, 1937, colourful, brilliantly-illuminated tram 108 gave pleasure to all who beheld it as it passed to and fro — and then the fittings were removed, in the almost certain knowledge that they would not be used again.

As if to confirm this, on October 17th, 1937, the Tramways Committee renamed itself the Halifax Passenger Transport Committee in acknowledgement that the trams were now only junior partners in the Corporation's public enterprise. New, improved electric street lighting was attached to the tram poles in King Cross Street, Orange Street, Lee Bridge and Lee Bank as far as the new Park Lodge housing estate, but it seemed unlikely that the poles would be shared with the trams for much longer.

For the Coronation of King George VI and Queen Elizabeth in May, 1937, "De Luxe" tramcar 108, suitably decorated and illuminated, visited all the remaining routes, and is seen here in Pellon Lane, passing the "Queen's Road Hotel".

[Copyright: Halifax Courier, Ltd.]

"All Inward Cars Stop Here" by order of the Board of Trade, and *"De Luxe"* car 127 on a return trip from Tuel Lane duly halts to allow a smart, bowler–hatted businessman and a cloth capped workman to board. The tram-stop post, surmounted by a stylish finial, is painted in the usual red-oxide colours but with a white band to denote a stopping place and red bands to illustrate that the stop was compulsory. New, high-level electric street lamps have been mounted on the tram poles, and the Halifax Building Society has made home buying easy – or so the advert claims!

[Photographed on July 14th, 1936, by H.B. Priestley, courtesy the Tramway Museum Society]

CHAPTER 20

FAREWELL

In June, 1937, the Municipal Tramways and Transport Association accorded Ald. Gledhill the distinction of electing him as their President in recognition of his work on behalf of the industry.

International events in Europe were now beginning to arouse deep fears and forebodings, and farsighted people were questioning how the United Kingdom would fare if a second World War were to break out. In September, the Halifax press predicted that although the trams were being ''killed off'' by the buses, the buses themselves might have to be superseded by trolleybuses if the duty on fuel oil were to continue increasing, "or if a war emergency makes these commodities prohibitive" either in price or availability. This forecast was echoed by the Minister of Transport, Mr Burgin, who stated that,

> "Just as I am desirous that the tram should be removed and its place taken by a bus, so I think that the bus should be a trolley-bus using an equivalent output of electricity generated by coal"

— the inference being that in wartime conditions, petrol and diesel buses would be wholly dependent on Middle East oil supplies which would be vulnerable to enemy attack and disruption.

It must be assumed that Halifax Passenger Transport Committee did not read these warnings, as only two months later they applied to the Traffic Commissioners for permission to conduct an eight weeks' "experiment" with buses on the long outer section of the Causeway Foot tramway, i.e. beyond Mason's Green. Permission having been granted, the last trams to round "Illingworth Corner" and climb up to Bradshaw and the quiet moorland terminus made their final journeys on Tuesday, January 18th, 1938, over tracks which had been relaid and resited not many years previously — indeed, the crossover at Raw Lane had seen only eighteen months' use. The press rightly doubted the temporary nature of the "experiment", commenting that,

> "In all probability this means the end of the trams to the Ogden Moor area. If this is the case, there will be quite a number of regrets, especially among Halifax families, for in the Summer time particularly a ride on the tram to Ogden Moor and back has been a frequent and enjoyable treat. The trams, with their stately progress, allowed for full appreciation of the journey, and enabled parents to give the children a good rest."
> Wistfully they added, "We have heard the same opinions expressed concerning the now –lost Hebden Bridge tram ride".

Next morning (January 19th) a revised and greatly truncated tram service to Mason's Green and Ovenden (Club Lane) was commenced, and not surprisingly the Causeway Foot bus experiment was judged a great success, as three buses were able to achieve a 20 minute journey time previously performed by four trams in 30 minutes — but perhaps no one realised that the buses with their protective minimum 3d fare made far fewer stops than the trams.

The operational tram fleet was now reduced to 40 vehicles:-

nos. 39, 74, 128 –131 – vestibuled "open-toppers" reserved for the Sowerby Bridge route, nos. 17, 63, 71, 73, 76, 77, 82, 99, 102 – vestibuled canopy-top cars used on the Pellon and Highroad Well routes, "De Luxe" cars 107-127 and four vestibuled "open-toppers", 9, 10, 11, 34, retained for snowplough duties.

On April 4th a driver on the surviving Mason's Green trams was injured when he alighted in Keighley Road and was struck by a motor-car as he crossed the road to "punch" the time-recording clock on the wall below Providence Chapel.

Fate in the form of the Corporation Drainage Department intervened next. On the day that the Causeway Foot "experiment" began, Mr Craven informed the Committee that the impending renewal of a sewer in Gibbet Street would shortly necessitate a temporary suspension of the Highroad Well tram service. However, before any action became necessary, he also drew attention to the nearby Pellon route, reminding the councillors of their 1932 decision to keep the tracks in order but not to renew them. Brandishing estimates of expenditure which might be needed within the next four years and emphasising how housing development had spread far beyond the tram terminus, he persuaded the Committee to close the route on March 31st. The haste was almost indecent; not only good track and recently-laid points and crossings but also sound, serviceable tramcars would have to be prematurely scrapped. A five-day stay of execution pending the arrival of new buses was granted, but the busy and well-patronised Pellon trams made their way up and down their narrow, workaday route for the last time on April 5th.

Their Highroad Well stablemates were not far behind: as soon as temporary bus licences had been obtained, the tram service ceased on the night of April 19th, leaving Gibbet Street to the buses and the sewer excavators.

By mid-1938 the international situation had become distinctly threatening; this was the year of Munich, of worthless promises and unprovoked invasions, and Halifax Corporation had already set up an Air Raid Precaution (ARP) Committee to plan the safety of residents should war break out. Nevertheless, the Borough's increasing dependence on imported oil was not considered serious enough to win a reprieve for the trams, and on July 12th Mr. Craven confronted the Committee with seemingly irrefutable statistics. Reviewing the option of retaining the trams for a few more years or replacing them by trolleybuses or motor-buses, he advised that the time for final abandonment had arrived. To persevere with the trams until 1942 would, he claimed, entail expenditure of £48,777 on the permanent way, whereas early closure could be achieved for a lesser cost. Impressed by the size and thoroughness of his report,

Shortly before the "experimental" introduction of a bus service to Causeway Foot on January 19th, 1938, several evocative views were taken by the late W.A. Camwell and H.B. Priestley.
[Courtesy The National Tramway Museum]

Sleet and wintry conditions awaited tramcar 126 on its arrival at Causeway Foot terminus. The Causeway Foot Inn (not shown on the photograph) stands close by on the left, and Syke Lane (to the right of the gas lamp) leads to Bradshaw village and Mountain.

Having just negotiated the overhead trolley reverser (centre left), car 122 on a short-working to Club Lane, Ovenden, awaits the signal to return to Halifax. The photographer is standing at the entrance to Club Lane itself, and the overhead equipment in the foreground is typical of the modern span-wire installations which had replaced much of the older bracket-arm equipment when road-widening took place.

Another trolley reverser, this time at the Bradshaw short-working terminus, where car 121 is about to depart for town. Pavement Lane (behind the tram) leads to the little village of Bradshaw.

the Committee recommended the Council to agree that: -

(1) the Highroad Well route should not re-open;

(2) the Tuel Lane and Mason's Green services should be merged with existing bus services in the area, and

(3 the J.O.C. should be approached to take over the Sowerby Bridge route.

The press reported the fateful debate in banner headlines:

"BUSES TO REPLACE ALL HALIFAX TRAMS AS SOON AS POSSIBLE"
Financial Gain of £10,950 a Year.
"Outstanding Debt to be cleared by 1945 from Bus Profits"

— which was not an unreasonable arrangement, as it was the buses which had deprived the trams of their ability to earn profits.

Seen at Highroad Well terminus shortly before the tram service ceased, car 109 was displaying the late Walter Young's advice to "Travel by Tram" in the half-light of the second saloon window, but his successor, "G.F.Craven, General Manager" (see the rocker panel, bottom right-hand corner) preferred his passengers to use the bus.
[Copyright: the late W.A. Camwell]

By the time that this photograph was taken by the late W.A. Camwell on April 3rd, 1938, smartly-painted open-topped car 39 had been relegated to works duties.

Surprisingly the Highroad Well tram service was reinstated only a few days later when the sewerage project reached completion; perhaps there was a temporary shortage of buses, but the reprieve was too good to last, and on the night of Thursday, August 23rd, the last trams left their upland terminus rumbling sonorously over the long-disused Spring Hall Lane crossing, past the old Mile Cross depot and down the gloomy confines of Gibbet Street to join the growing

queue of redundant trams in the scrapyard alongside Skircoat Road depot. These included five of the Highroad Well and Pellon "regulars" – no. 63 which had served many times as the illuminated tram; 77, fitted with new Halifax-style vestibules only three years previously; 99 with its "De Luxe" vestibules, 102 which had recently been repainted in the mostly-red livery; and even no. 17 with its modern regenerative braking and roller bearings. All were well-maintained vehicles, and all but one were comfortably upholstered. The permanent licence for the Highroad Well buses was granted on October 25th, after which the overhead wires were dismantled.

Negotiations with the J.O.C. were amicably concluded in September, and the ever-willing motor-bus manufacturing workshops continued to disgorge a steady stream of gleaming new vehicles contrasting favourably with the trams, which had ceased their visits to the paintshops and were beginning to appear shabby and unwanted. The Manager decided to wait until he had accumulated sufficient new vehicles to replace all the trams which still journeyed to King Cross and beyond, and so, on Tuesday, November 29th, a night of sweeping changes and nostalgic farewells, the Tuel Lane and Sowerby Bridge routes closed simultaneously.

Gliding serenely along the still-sound tracks, the last "De Luxe" car from Tuel Lane hummed its stately way along Burnley Road, up the wide sweep of Cote Hill and away down King Cross Street to Bull Green and the depot, while at Sowerby Bridge the last of the open-top cars – immaculate ex-

A truly atmospheric view of Halifax in the tramway era: taken in 1938 (either April 3rd or July 2nd) with Tuel Lane car 111 at its departure point in Horton Street, seemingly dwarfed by a stately gas street-lamp. The overhead lines continue round the corner into Church Street, the original loading point, although the track had been removed a few years earlier. Behind the tram is Old Station, whose forecourt the trams had never been allowed to enter. The dramatic background of mill chimneys, multi-storied houses and Beacon Hill once provided the scenery for the "Tramcar in the Sky" – the Southowram tram which formerly ascended Beacon Hill Road.

[Photo: the late W.A. Camwell, courtesy the National Tramway Museum]

Long stretches of expensively-laid permanent way now lapsed into disuse – King Cross Street, Bull Green, Cow Green, Barum Top, Horton Street, St. James' Road, the Ward's End curves and Fountain Street with its sidings in Powell Street and Harrison Road. The complex Ward's End junction now saw trams only on depot journeys, as Halifax's surviving route, to Mason's Green, route no.11, with its Ovenden (Club Lane) and Beechwood Road shortworkings operated from and to the Post Office in Commercial Street.

Now composed entirely of "De Luxe" cars, the fleet had been reduced to fifteen trams – 107, 109-113, 115-118, 120, 122-124 and 127, of which only half were needed for the basic service. When cars 115 and 118 developed minor faults in January, 1939, they too were despatched to the scrap yard, reducing the numbers to a final, unlucky total of thirteen.

Exeter no. 129 – began its final departure from Station Road, its powerful motors making light work of the once-feared ascent of Bolton Brow and Pye Nest. Crossing the Borough boundary for the last time, it joined its redundant fellows in the depot yard where the sidings were well-filled now that home-built "open-topper" no. 39, snowplough 11 and the works cars had had to quit the now-closed Stannary yard.

Farewell to the Sowerby Bridge trams: gleaming ex-Exeter car 129 at the Station Road terminus was about to begin its last homeward journey. On arrival at Skircoat Road depot in the first moments of November 30th, 1938, it was driven into the scrapyard together with all the remaining open-topped cars.
[Copyright: the Halifax Courier Ltd.]

Car no.11 was hopefully displaying the destination name, "Thrum Hall", when photographed in the depot yard, but was probably due for dismantling.
[Copyright: the late M.J. O'Connor]

For a few more weeks the familiar, homely tramcars continued to roll majestically along Commercial Street and Waterhouse Street and ascend the long, sinuous curves of Lee Bank and Ovenden Road to reach the quaint, tree-shaded terminus at Mason's Green, where disused tracks still stretched away into the distance towards the moors where the air was fresh and invigorating. But it was winter now, and those who travelled on the Mason's Green trams were warmly clad to keep the chilly Pennine winds at bay.

Passengers dismount from well-laden car 119 as it pauses at Lee Bank Top before resuming its journey to Club Lane. At peak hours, the combined tramcar journeys to Causeway Foot, Bradshaw, Raw Lane, Beechwood Road and Club Lane provided a three-minute service to the last-mentioned stage – the most intensive tram service in Halifax. In this 1938 view, modern electric street lighting has superseded the old gas lamps, and a Corporation bus (right) is making its way back to town. All the buildings in this photograph vanished years ago, and today the modern Ovenden Way branches away to the right.
[Photo: the late M.J. O'Connor, courtesy the National Tramway Museum]

Winter. Although this stark view of tramcar 111 at Mason's Green was taken on April 3rd, 1938, it was winter once more when the last trams departed from the terminus in February, 1939. Standing outside White Hill Lodge, the car was being inspected by a young Ovenden gentleman who today will be about 69 years of age.
[Photo: the late W.A. Camwell, courtesy the National Tramway Museum, Crich

The remaining weeks dwindled to days, during which the Borough Electrical Engineer, Mr. G. A. Vowles, took the opportunity of securing what the press called " a similar post" at Ipswich. Similar but better: Mr. Vowles had been appointed Manager of the Electricity and Passenger Transport Departments, as Ipswich's municipal services were provided exclusively by trolleybuses.

On February 10th one of the new buses was driven to the terminus to be photographed alongside tram no. 124 and its crew. Then it was the last day of all – Tuesday, February 14th, 1939 – when from early morning until tea-time it was still "business as usual" for the trams carrying the millworkers, shop assistants, bank clerks, housewives and schoolchildren from home to workplace and back again. Next, it was the turn of cinemagoers and theatre-lovers, and as the evening wore on, there was a growing sense of nostalgia as passengers savoured what they knew would be their last experience of the familiar, trustworthy trams which had served them, their parents and their children for four decades.

All too soon it was time for the last scheduled departures. Dashing along Commercial Street shortly after 10.30pm, an Ovenden man managed to leap on board the penultimate tram, to be greeted by its conductor with the words, "Come on, lad, tha'd better get on. There'll noan be sa monny more!" One by one the eight trams — 107, 109, 110-113, 122 and 124 — made their way up to Mason's Green, so that by 11p.m they were lined up awaiting the final procession. The Passenger Transport Committee, officials and guests

arrived by special bus, presumably to ensure that late-night locals were not deprived of their last homeward trip by tram. All the way from Ovenden Cross to the terminus, crowds had gathered on the causeways, and when the dignitaries reached their destination they found "a thousand or two people crowded around, as it was a dark, cold night".

The time for the parting of the ways was approaching now, and the cheerful crowds clambered aboard the waiting vehicles as they stood in a dignified line, casting a pool of bright light on the dark road and gleaming tramlines. Within a few minutes all the cars were filled to capacity, with standing passengers on both decks of each car, including no. 109, the last in line, which was reserved for the Mayor and the official party.

Reluctantly, slowly, the stately procession began to move off at intervals, with no. 109 bringing up the rear at 11.32 p.m. in the hands of Mr. Whiteley Lumb (driver of the last Bailiffe Bridge tram ten years earlier) and Mr. John Nicholl, the oldest tram conductor. "Not even a Cup Tie tram has borne more people or a more boisterous company", the surprised press noted. "The Chairman of the Passenger Transport Committee got to know what it feels like to stand on a crowded upper deck."

Ald. Gledhill's fellow passengers included ex- Alderman Hey, now retired, Mr. C. H. Greenwood, the Mayor's secretary, who had ridden on the first tram in 1898, Mr. B.M. Bagott, chief clerk at the transport offices in Powell Street, who had begun his career at the old Mile Cross Depot, and

The last day, Tuesday, February 14th 1939. Flags adorned the entrance to Skircoat Road depot as tramcar 109 stood in the yard alongside motor-bus 80 and a group of admiring staff.

[Copyright: Yorkshire Post, Ltd.]

Only four more days to run: tramcar 124 with a new AEC/Park Royal bus in the orange, cream and green livery adopted for the motor-bus fleet several years earlier, posed with their crews and two inspectors outside the "Queen's Head Inn" at Mason's Green terminus on February 10th, 1939. Websters' Ales were brewed in Halifax.

[Copyright: the Halifax Courier Ltd.]

Mr. H. Binns, traffic superintendent, who was selling special commemorative tickets. While bystanders in Ovenden Road were lustily singing "Ilkla Moor baht 'at," tramcar 109's passengers were joining in the more appropriate refrains of "Auld Lang Syne" and "Roll along, Covered Wagon, roll along", and dropping donations for the Transport Benevolent Fund into one of the long-obsolete fareboxes. At Lee Bank Top another large assembly cheered the trams as they descended the gentle gradient, while others leaned sleepily out of bedroom windows.

Soon the historic cortege was passing along a deserted Commercial Street and rumbling over the Wards End

junction before arriving at Skircoat Road and turning left into the depot precincts. The first seven cars were driven straight into the waiting scrapyard, but tramcar 109 passed beneath a decorated arch to enter the depot on the stroke of midnight.

When it had rolled to a halt and disgorged its complement of distinguished guests, Ald. Gledhill spoke briefly and unemotionally. "The electric tram has passed into history without dishonour," he declared, adding significantly that, "If the £85,000 taken for the relief of rates had been placed into a reserve fund at a 3% interest, all liabilities could have been discharged." In the prevailing atmosphere of goodwill and appreciation of "a job well done" by the tramways, no one ventured to enquire why the Chairman had not made that particular suggestion ten years earlier, when it might have secured the future of the trams. Neither did anyone see fit to comment on the Vice-Chairman's recent appointment to the new Regional Committee which was to advise on the problems of public transport in wartime, even though earlier that very day an ominous mass testing of air-raid sirens had taken place.

Instead, Driver Lumb was invited to recite the poem he had composed for the last Bailiffe Bridge tram; the Chairman was presented with the clock taken from car no. 109, and following entertainment provided by the Fletcher Singers and Mr. A. Hodgson, humorist, the gathering slowly dispersed, surreptitiously concealing pocketfuls of light bulbs and any small souvenirs which could be removed by screwdrivers. Then the night shift went about their duties, leaving the solitary tramcar silent and unattended.

Tramcar 109 was a lone figure in the depot, which had been given over to the buses which were to replace the last trams next day.

[J.A. Pitts collection, courtesy West Yorkshire Archives, Bradford]

The LAST TRAM- HOME.

After to-morrow, there will be no trams running in Halifax. The last route, Mason Green, will be replaced by a bus service on Wednesday.

MONDAY FEBRUARY 13th 1939

The Halifax Daily Courier and Guardian

The Last Tram Home

TERMINUS

The slow descent from the wind-swept hills
The last sad journey is begun.
Passing the moors, the streets, the mills,
Passing away, her day is done

Like an ancient schooner she lifts and dips,
Nodding, it seems, to the wayside throng:
Like an elderly dowager, now deposed
By something newer, if far less strong.

For her strength was shown through the weary years
When taking the gradients in her stride,
Grinding and groaning with secret fears,
With top deck loaded and 'full inside'.

She comes to rest in the echoing sheds:
But no one waits to make her glow
With grooming for the next long day:
The curtain falls: she's history now."

J.J.M.

Next day, after one or two final photographs, no. 109 was unobtrusively driven out of the depot to join its colleagues in the yard, while simultaneously the Transport Committee were resolving,

> "That certificates engrossed on vellum be presented to Whiteley Lumb and John Nicholl, driver and conductor respectively on thelast tram of the Halifax Municipal Service being taken from Mason's Green to the Skircoat Depot on 14th February, 1939, and that the Corporate Common Seal of the Borough be affixed thereto."

The certificates were duly presented on May 22nd, prior to which on April 8th the "Halifax Courier" published a photograph of the more senior of the newly-retired tramway men:-

> J. C. Collier (23 years' service), W. Buckley (15), R. Pickering (24), T. Hartley (19), D. Berry (15),
>
> W. Frankland (19), G.H. Lightowler (29), J.E. Hargreaves (19),
>
> T.Nash (22), W. Naylor (26), T. Whinnary (38), T. Anderson (30),
>
> G. Albon (34), G.W. Whitehead (40) and M.W. Mason (40).

The task of disposing of the now-redundant installations was carried out with varying degrees of reluctance by the Transport, Electricity and Borough Engineer's Departments. Tram poles to which Borough Police telephone wires were attached became the responsibility of the Watch Committee, whilst most of the others within the borough were transferred to the Street Lighting Department who were still using a few of them sixty years later. In June, 1939, the Council were recommended to pay £1,374-16-ld to the West Riding County Highways for reinstatement within Sowerby Bridge U.D., making due allowance for the removal and sale of the poles, overhead equipment, rails and copper bonds, as well as the granite setts which were to be retained by Halifax.

Conscious that the "De Luxe" tramcars now quietly accumulating grime in their exposed outdoor resting-place were capable of many more years of public service, the Transport Committee offered them to other 3'6" gauge operators such as Llandudno and Birmingham, but Llandudno did not use "four wheelers" or top-covered vehicles, and Birmingham were gradually abandoning their network. After all avenues seemed to have been explored, the process of selling the bodies and metal or burning them was begun. Last to go were tramcars 111 and 113 which succumbed to the flames on August 16th.

But the shadows of war were lengthening alarmingly. Only twelve days after the charred remains of the last trams had been cleared away, the deepening European crisis impelled the Corporation to man its first-aid and air-raid wardens' posts; with the invasion of Poland on September 1st, local troops were mobilized, and a blackout was imposed as a safeguard against air attacks. War was then declared on September 3rd, bringing with it a strict petrol and oil rationing scheme and a consequential reduction of bus services; Mr Craven, the General Manager of Halifax Transport Department and the J.O.C, was appointed as Fuel Controller.

Earlier in the Summer, Coventry Corporation had replaced one or two of their tram services with buses, but in view of the deteriorating situation had cautiously kept the installations intact and were thus able to re-open the routes when hostilities began. Anxious to augment their fleet with modern vehicles, they enquired whether Halifax had retained any of their trams either for re-use or disposal. Alas............! Bradford, too, re-started two tram services, and like neighbouring Huddersfield was well placed to escape the worst rigours of fuel shortages.

The physical traces of Halifax's tramways lingered for many years. Even after the war ended, the positions of former passing-loops and single-line sections were visible in the stone and tarmacadam paving at Priestley Hill and elsewhere; in Powell Street one pole proudly retained its bracket arm and overhead line "hanger" and "ear", and immaculate tarmac-paved tram tracks continued to grace King Cross Street until 1953. Tramcar lower decks serving a variety of purposes — bus shelters, cafes, summerhouses, seaside caravans and the like — were dispersed far and wide. Throughout the Second World War no. 34 played a stirring role as a Home Guard outpost on the Albert Promenade, accompanied by no. 103 as an air-raid warden's post on Beacon Hill, while no. 126 was to be seen at Flamborough Head as late as 1980, almost certainly the last survivor. Even in the early years of the 21st century, tracks can still be seen in Skircoat Road depot, as well as glimpses of street track whenever the tarmac wears thin at Hipperholme. At Bradshaw the long-forgotten tracks across the fields from Keighley Road to the old stone-depot were carefully lifted in 1986 for possible use at the nascent West Yorkshire Transport Museum — only to be stolen by sharp-eyed scrap merchants.

Tramway connoisseurs of the present day have reason to be grateful to Messrs. Eric Thornton, Lyndon Reeve and the late Arthur Brooke for their wonderful scale models which continue to delight the eye and conjure up fascinating glimpses of the richly-varied trams which served Halifax and its neighbours more than sixty years ago.

Let the last word lie with Mr. Jack Naylor, the long retired depot foreman, who commented on October 5th, 1964 that:-

> "It is a far cry from the waggonette ambling through the snow on its way to Tuel Lane to the no. 30 bus rushing down the hill from Southowram. Who can tell what the passenger transport of 1998 will be? If similar progress is maintained, the by-ways and sky-ways will be full of jet propelled vehicles hurling themselves through space!"

Long may the skies above Beacon Hill be free from all such unwelcome visitations.

Unwanted: tramcar 113 in Skircoat Road depot yard sidings four days after operations ceased.
[Photo: H.B. Priestley, courtesy the National Tramway Museum]

Retirement: the lower deck of car 126 photographed at Bridlington by the author in March, 1960. Inside the saloon the fleet number, gilt ceiling transfers, clock and polished woodwork were well preserved.

ROLLING STOCK

APPENDIX 1

Cars 1 – 58

Type:	Milnes
Body:	G.F. Milnes short-canopy open-top double-deck, four side window lower saloon with semi-elliptical curved windows tops; open platforms; 90° direct stairs; Dickenson side-mounted trolley mast. Nos. 1-10 had, briefly, detachable brass oil headlamps, quickly replaced by electric (fixed). Unladen weight of complete tramcar: 8 tons.
Seating:	24 outside, 22 longitudinal inside, total 46
Truck:	Peckham type 8A cantilever, wheelbase 5'6", wheels 30" diameter (originally chilled iron, later steel)
Motors:	Nos 1—10 two Electric Construction Co., 25 h.p Nos 11—18 two General Electric GE 1000 25 h.p. Nos 19—28 two General Electric GE 1000 25 h.p.
Controllers:	Nos 29—58 two Westinghouse 25 h.p. Nos 1—12 B.T.H. type K10 Nos 13—18 G.E. type K10 Nos 19—58 Westinghouse
Brakes:	Mechanical (hand/wheel) and rheostatic
Lighting:	2 circuits of 7 lamps in series, only 5 lamps per circuit being in use at any time as 5x110v lamps = 550 volts, i.e., the overhead line voltage
Known dimensions:	Length – body 16'0", platforms 5'3" each. fenders 6" each , overall 27'6". Width – over sills 5'6"; over window posts 6'0" ; over top deck floor 6'3¼".
Major Modifications:	Milnes mechanical track ("slipper") brake fitted before entered service; replaced by C.H. Spencer 3'3" track brake by Feb. 1910, Cars 1-10 re-equipped 1900 with Westinghouse 25 h.p. motors (type 46?). Two cars of the 11-14 batch received Westinghouse controllers while 19-28 received GE K2 and two GE K3 controllers. In Jan. 1906 two cars (possibly including no. 33) fitted with GE 58 6T 35 h.p. motors. In May 1908 eight sets of Westinghouse type 200 30 h.p. motors and TLD controllers were bought. After 1912 balconies (extended canopies over the platforms) were fitted to many cars to increase seating capacity by 8, and nos. 41-58 received not only balconies but also Brush 3–window canopy tops with offset sliding doors and enclosed sections which were shorter than the lower saloon. The weight of the top covers necessitated the reconstruction of several lower saloons with new pillars and oblong windows, and some sported flush side panels. In March 1920 car 50 was the first double-decker to be fitted with platform vestibules, of the Bradford style with angular wooden panels, and was reconverted to open-top after being blown over 9 months later. Nos 9,11 and 34 survived as snowploughs until 1938. Cars 1, 2, 13, 14, 22, 27, 29, 30, 31, 32 and 35 were never altered.

Fleet No	Entered Service	Withdrawn		Disposal and Notes
1	June, 1898	1930		Ran away at Ovenden, 25/6/1921. Sold to Peel of Greetland, 7/1930
2	" "	1929		Sold to Peel 9/1929
3	" "	1931	Balconies 1912,	Sold 7/1931 as a café at Elland
4	" "	1929	Balconies 1912,	Sold to Peel 9/1929
5	" "	1931	Balconies 1912,	Converted to bus shelter, Northowram 7/1931
6	" "	1930	Balconies 1912,	Sold to Peel 7/1930
7	" "	1929	Balconies 1912,	Sold to Peel 9/1929
8	" "	1929	Balconies 1912,	Sold to Peel 9/1929
9	" "	c 1921		Converted to snowplough 1922
10 (see car 76)	" "	1925	Balconies 1912	Sold 1925 for a cricket pavilion at Armitage Bridge, Huddersfield.
11	Nov 1898	1922		Converted to snowplough 1922
12	" "	1935	Balconies 1912.	June 1911 decorated for Coronation Bradford-style vestibules 1920. Ran away in Bull Green Nov.23rd, 1920. Scrapped July, 1935
13	" "	1929		Sold to Peel, Sept. 1929
14	" "	1929		Sold to Peel, Sept. 1929
15	Jan 1899	1930	Balconies 1912.	Sold to Peel, July, 1930
16	" "	1935	Balconies 1912.	Bradford-style vestibules 1920 Scrapped July, 1935
17	" "	1921		Scrapped 1921
18	" "	1930	Balconies 1912	Sold to Peel, July 1930
19	" "	1935	Balconies 1912	Bradford-style vestibules 1920
20	" "	1935	Balconies 1912	Scrapped July, 1935
21	" "	1930	Balconies 1912	Sold to Peel, July 1930
22	" "	c. 1925		Scrapped c. 1925
23	" "	1935	Balconies 1912	Bradford-style vestibules 1920 Scrapped July, 1935
24	" "	1930	Balconies 1912	Bay window vestibules c. 1925 Sold to Peel, July 1930
25	" "	1931	Balconies 1912	Scrapped July, 1931
26	" "	1931	Balconies 1912	July 1931 to bus shelter, Mixenden
27	" "	1931		July 1931 to bus shelter, Wheatley
28	" "	1930	Balconies 1912	Aug.1902 decorated for Coronation Sold to Peel, July 1930
29	" "	1931	Balconies 1912	Sold to Peel, July 1931
30	" "	1929		Sold to Peel, Sept. 1929
31	" "	1929		Sold to Peel, Sept. 1929
32	" "	1929		Sold to Peel, Sept. 1929
33	Nov. 1899	1930	Balconies 1912	Sold to Peel, July, 1930
34	" "	1930	Balconies 1912	"Bay Window" partial vestibules c. 1925. Snowplough c.1934 to July 1938; in Stannary permanent-way yard 1938; Home Guard post on Albert Promenade 1940

Fleet No	Entered Service	Withdrawn	Disposal and Notes	
35	Nov. 1899	1929		Sold to Peel, Sept. 1929
36	" "	1931	Balconies 1912	Scrapped July, 1931
37	" "	1931	Balconies 1912	Scrapped July,1931
38	" "	1931	Balconies 1912	Sold July 1931 as summerhouse in Leeds Rd, Huddersfield
39	" "	1938		Experimental 40hp motors 1905: balconies 1912: "bay window" vestibules c.1927 Metrovick 40hp motors and DK DB1 K3 controllers c.1927: roller bearings (ex car 106?) 1934; in Stannary permanent –way yard 1938: Home Guard post at Fly Flatts 1940; seen in 1960
40	Nov. 1899	1931	Balconies 1912, canopy top 1912.	Scrapped July 1931
41	" "	1931	Balconies 1912, canopy top 1912.	Scrapped Feb. 1932
42	" "	1931	Balconies 1912, canopy top 1912. bay window vestibules c.1926.	Scrapped Feb. 1932
43	" "	1931	Balconies 1912, canopy top 1912.	Sold for hen-hut at Cragg Vale Feb. 1932; burnt 1937.
44	Nov. 1899	1931	Balconies 1912; canopy top 1912.	Briefly renumbered 91 about 1910. Scrapped Feb. 1932
45	Jan 1900	1931	Balconies 1912; canopy top 1912.	Seen at Lodstone House, Norland, Feb. 1932.
46	" "	1931	Balconies 1912; canopy top 1912.	Scrapped Feb. 1932
47	" "	1931	Balconies 1912; canopy top 1912.	Scrapped Feb. 1932
48	" "	1931	Balconies 1912; canopy top 1912.	Seen at Lodstone House, Norland, Feb 1932.
49	" "	1931	Balconies 1912; canopy top 1912.	Scrapped Feb. 1932
50	" "	1935	Balconies and canopy top 1912;	First car to be fitted with Bradford-style angular wooden vestibules 1920; blown over Dec 3, 1920; rebuilt July 1921 as open-top. Seen at Lodstone House, Norland, July 1935
51	Jan 1900	1931	Balconies and 3 window canopy top 1912.	Scrapped Feb 1932
52	" "	1931	Balconies and 3 window canopy top 1912.	Scrapped Feb 1932
53	" "	1931	Balconies and 3 window canopy top 1912.	Scrapped Feb 1932
54	" "	1931	Balconies and 3 window canopy top 1912.	Scrapped Feb 1932
55	" "	1931	Balconies and 3 window canopy top 1912.	Scrapped Feb 1932
56	" "	1931	Balconies and 3 window canopy top 1912.	Scrapped Feb 1932
57	" "	1931	Balconies and 3 window canopy top 1912.	Scrapped Feb 1932
58	" "	1931	Balconies and 3 window canopy top 1912.	Experimental 45 h.p motors later. Scrapped Feb 1932

Cars 59 – 82

Type:	Brush
Body:	Brush short-canopy open top double-deck, four side-window saloon; open platforms; 90° direct stairs; side mounted trolley mast. Flat polished maple saloon ceilings with ventilator windows.
Seating:	26 outside and 22 inside, total 48
Truck:	Brush "A", 5' 6" wheelbase, 30" diameter wheels
Motors:	General Electric GE58 2 x 35hp
Controllers:	Westinghouse.
Conductor's bell:	Electrically operated
Brakes:	Mechanical (hand/ wheel, hand/track) and rheostatic. (C.J. Spencer track brake)
Known dimensions:	as nos 1 – 58. Unladen weight $7^{1}/_{2}$ tons

Known modifications: In 1903 car 71 fitted with experimental "Kennington roll-top" cover by Mr. R. Turner of Queen's Road; subsequently no. 66 received a Milnes-Voss flat-roof top cover, and both cars served the Savile Park route. In March 1904 no. 78 received Mozley patent wind-guards comprising upper deck windows without a roof, but a conventional top cover replaced it later. In Oct. 1907 Mr. Turner built twelve Milnes-Voss type top covers, all without balconies, plus a replacement in 1908 for car 71's "roll-top" cover. Brush 3-window short saloon canopy tops were fitted to numerous cars in 1912, in which year most open-top cars were rebuilt with balconies. Similar balconies were provided for the Turner-top trams about 1921, increasing their seating by 10 to 13 per car, but restricting the enclosed portion of the top cover to the area above the lower saloon. Bradford-style angular wood vestibules fitted to four cars c. 1920—21. In February, 1925, no. 63 was rebuilt as a top-covered vestibuled-platform car, dimensions per E. Thornton drawing HI/3, 30/1/1944, length of saloon 16'0", platforms 5'6" each, fenders 6" each, total 28'0";

Width:	5'9" over sills, 6'0" over window-posts, 6'4$^{1}/_{2}$" over top deck floor, 6'5" over roof. Truck 6'3" over journals.
Height:	Rail to underframe 2'3$^{1}/_{2}$", lower saloon 7'3", upper deck 5'9", rail to trolley-plank 15'8".
Seating:	Lower saloon 10 on double transverse seats, 5 on single transverse seats and 4 on single corner seats; upper saloon 12 on double transverse seats and 12 on longitudinal benches; balcony fixed seats – 6 each balcony and 3 on trapdoor seat over staircase = total 58. Truck wheel base 6'6"; Dick Kerr DB1 Form K3 (anti-runback) controllers, 30" diameter wheels, Dick Kerr 50hp motors (presumably type 30); Cars 65, 72-77, 79, 81, 82 and probably others received DK DB1 form K3 (anti-runback) controllers about 1920. Electric bells all replaced by strap-pull version.

Fleet No	Entered Service	Withdrawn	Known Details
59	Aug. 1901	1937	First car to West Vale, 1905. Balcony and canopy top, 1912. Metrovick MV 307 VB 45hp motors c. 1925. Halifax-style vestibules Feb 1927. Scrapped 1937.
60	" "	1934	Balcony and canopy top, 1912. Sold to Grahamsleys May, 1934.
61	" "	1934	Balcony and canopy top, 1912. Sold to Grahamsleys May, 1934.
62	" "	"	Balcony and Canopy top, 1912. Sold to Grahamsleys May, 1934.
63	Aug 1901	1938	Turner top-cover 1907/8. Balcony c.1912 Bradford-style angular wood vestibules February, 1920. Rebuilt as canopy-top car with Halifax-style vestibules, February 1925 (see above). Decorated for special occasions in October, 1931, May, 1935 (the Silver Jubilee), June, 1935 and June, 1936. Fitted with bus seats in lower saloon, 1934. Sold April, 1938, as a hut at Mount Tabor.
64	Aug 1901	1938	Dismantled after the Pye Nest accident on October 15th, 1907.
65	Spring 1902	1937	Turner top c.1908; rebuilt with sloping sides for proposed dual-gauge running (date unknown); top cover converted to 4-window canopy c.1920; Halifax-style vestibules about 1927 (incorporating destination indicator), second-hand 3-window canopy c.1931. DK DB1 Form K3 (anti-runback) controllers c.1923. Scrapped 1937.
66	Spring 1902	1934	Milnes-Voss top cover about 1906: Brush 3-window canopy top 1912; Halifax-style vestibules about 1927. Bus shelter at Wainstalls from June, 1934.
67	" "	1934	Balconies and Brush 3-window canopy top, 1913. Sold to Grahamsleys, 1934.
68	" "	1934	Balconies and Brush 3-window canopy top, 1913. Sold to Grahamsleys, 1934.
69	" "	1934	Balconies and Brush 3-window canopy top, 1913. Sold to Grahamsleys, 1934.
70	" "	1938	Balconies and Brush 3-window canopy top, 1913. Sold to Grahamsleys, 1934.
71	July 1902	1922	Experimental "roll-top" cover fitted February, 1903, considered to "resemble a Dumont airship". The cover was destroyed by fire June, 1904. Turner top fitted c.1908.
72	July 1902	1937	Turner top c.1908; balconies 1912; rebuilt with sloping sides for proposed dual-gauge running (date unknown); "bay window" vestibules c.1925, also Turner top converted to 4-window canopy top, with quarter-lights. Bus shelter at Withens Inn, Wainstalls from 1937.
73	July 1902	1922	Turner top cover, c. 1908. Scrapped 1922.
74	" "	1938	Turner top cover, c. 1908. Turner top converted to canopy top c.1920: in 1925 given "bay-window" partial vestibules, converted to open-top. In 1928 Halifax-style Peckham cantilever truck and longitudinal red leather upholstered saloon seats. Withdrawn July, 1938 and used as a hut at Causeway Foot until 1961.
75	July 1902	1925	Turner top cover c. 1908; presumably converted into a 4-window canopy top c.1920
76	July 1902	1925	First service car to Bailiffe Bridge, Oct. 18, 1904. Turner top cover c.1908, slightly lengthened over newly-fitted balconies, 1912. Turner top converted into 4 window canopy top c.1920. rebuilt with a new lower deck as a vestibuled open-top car about 1925 and numbered 10. (Sold to Autowrecks Dec,, 1938)

Fleet No	Entered Service	Withdrawn	Known Details
77	July 1902	1938	Turner top cover 1908, converted into 4 window canopy top c. 1921, when Bradford-style angular wooden vestibules were fitted. Bus seats fitted 1934 and a Halifax-style vestibule about 1935. Sold for a hut at Mount Tabor, April 1938. Burnt 1979
78	July 1902	1934	Mozley patent upper deck wind guards March, 1904. Balconies about 1907; Brush 3-window canopy top 1912, "bay window" vestibules c.1925. Sold to Grahamsleys, May 1934.
79	July 1902	1937	Turner top cover 1908: balconies 1912; top cover converted into 4 window canopy top cover c. 1920; "bay window" vestibules c. 1927
80	" "	1926	Balconies and canopy top c. 1913 Scrapped 1926.
81	" "	1923	Turner top cover 1908, converted into 4-window canopy top c. 1920; scrapped 1923.
82	" "	1937	Turner top cover 1908; converted into 4-window canopy top c. 1920; Halifax-style vestibules 1929; bus seats 1934. Bus shelter at Causeway Foot from late 1937.

A fine model built by the late Mr. Arthur Brooke of Elland. Car 58 is shown in circa 1921 condition, with H.C.T – monogrammed Prussian blue, ivory and cream livery, red-lined corner posts, grey roof, red-oxide painted truck and a "pillar-box red" postbox hung on the dashplate.

[Photo: Mr. Ray Wilkinson, Greetland]

Cars 83 – 94

Type: Brush

Body: Brush double-deck open top balcony cars with four side window saloons, 180° direct stairs and open platforms

Seating: Saloon – 22 longitudinal; upper deck – 28 on locally made transverse and bench seats; total 50.

Truck: Brush "A"

Motors: Two Westinghouse 35h.p

Controllers: Westinghouse

Brakes: Mechanical (hand/wheel and hand/track) and rheostatic.

Dimensions: as cars 59 — 82

Known Modifications: By February 1910, all had been re-fitted with C.H. Spencer track brakes. One car decorated for the 1911 Coronation and two for the Royal Visit in July 1912. Car 86 lower saloon rebuilt with flat tapered sides for proposed dual-gauge working. Brush 3-window canopy tops fitted 1913. No. 86 (and probably the others) received English Electric Dick Kerr DB1 Form K3 (anti-runback) controllers 1923.

Fleet No	Entered Service	Withdrawn	Known Details	
83	June 1903	1934	Halifax-style vestibules 1925.	Sold to Grahamsleys, May 1934.
84	June 1903	1934		Sold to Grahamsleys, May 1934.
85	June 1903	1934		Sold to Grahamsleys, May 1934.
86	June 1903	1934		Sold to Grahamsleys, May 1934 – pigeon loft at Queensbury.
87	Aug 1903	1934		Sold to Grahamsleys, May 1934.
88	Aug 1903	1934		Sold to Grahamsleys, May 1934.
89	Aug 1903	1934		Overturned at Lee Bridge, May 1915. Sold to Grahamsleys, May 1934.
90	Aug 1903	1934		Sold to Grahamsleys, May 1934.
91	Aug 1903	1934	Briefly renumbered 44 in 1910 (truck exchange?): "Bay-window" vestibule c.1925.	Sold to Lodstone House, Norland, July 1935.
92	Aug 1903	1934	Lower deck re-built with "Ben Hall" vestibules c.1924. Bus shelter at Norland Church, 1934.	
93	Aug 1903	1934		Sold to Grahamsleys, May 1934.
94	Aug 1903	1934		Overturned on Northbridge, June 1st, 1906. Recruiting car 1914. Sold to Grahamsleys, May 1934.

Cars 95 /96

Type: Demi Car

Body: Brush with clerestory roof, vestibules and front exits. Cost £520 each

Seating: 24 Longitudinal

Truck: Brush-built Du Pont, 5'6" wheelbase (Peckham 9A?)

Motors: Raworth regenerative type, Brush-built, 2 x 27hp?

Controllers: Raworth

Brakes: Regenerative, hand/wheel and hand/track

Dimensions: per E. Thornton drawing H1/12, 15/4/1955 (Courtesy Roy Brook).

Length: Saloon 10'6", platforms 4'7" each, fenders 7½" each, overall 20'11".

Width; Body 5'8", over sills, 6'0" over window posts, 6'2" over roof.

Height: Rail to underframe 2'2½", rail to floor 2'8½", rail to trolley plank 10/10¼".

Truck: Width 5'3¾" between truck side centres, 6'6½" over journals.

Known Modifications: Following the Horton Street runaway and collision they were repaired, refitted with BTH K10 controllers and mechanical braking for holiday services to Hebden Bridge etc. Early in 1910 they were rebuilt as cross-bench cars for the Salterhebble (Exley Zoo) service but stored about 1911. No. 95 again rebuilt as an enclosed demi-car with oblong side windows and ventilator windows above, while in May, 1918, no. 96 was converted into a mobile soup-kitchen. After the war, it served as a unpowered salt and sand trailer. Car 95 served for several years as a paying-in car, usually stationed in Union Street or George Square; latterly it was used as a welding car until withdrawal about 1928.

Fleet No	Entered Service	Withdrawn	Disposal and Notes
95	Aug 1904	c. 1928	c.1920 to paying-in car, later welding car.
96	Aug 1904	c. 1927	c.1920 converted to permanent way trailer..

Cars 97-102

Type:	Brush Double Deck
Body:	Canopy-top cars, four side window saloon; short three-side window upper deck saloon; high balcony decency panels
Seating:	Upper deck 31, lower saloon, 22: Total 53.
Truck:	Halifax-style Peckham cantilever, 6'0" wheelbase; $31^{13}/4$" diameter wheels
Motors:	Two Siemens 40 h.p.
Controllers:	Westinghouse type 90 (probably all changed to Dick Kerr DB1 Form K3 in 1920, when 60 sets — i.e. 30 pairs – were bought from English Electric)
Brakes:	Mechanical (hand/wheel, hand/track) and rheostatic
Dimensions:	As cars 59-82
Service:	Until 1934 used regularly on the steep Queensbury route on account of their more powerful motors

Fleet No	Entered Service	Withdrawn	Disposal and Notes
97	1913	1937	"Bay window" vestibules c. 1930 Sold for bungalow at High Sunderland, Boothtown, 1937.
98	1913	1934	Blown over at Stocks Gate Dec. 3rd, 1920, and rebuilt as open-top car with Bradford-style angular wooden vestibules, 1920. Sold for shelter at Bradshaw, June, 1934.
99	1913	1938	Overturned at Ambler Thorn, July 15th, 1917. Modernised in 1929 with 2-and-1 upholstered lower saloon sera, "De-Luxe" style platform vesitubles, full-width sprung fenders and the mostly-red livery. Lower saloon re-fitted with bus seats, 1934, Scrapped April, 1938.
100	1913	1934	Modernised in 1930 with "bay-window" vestibules, longitudinal red leather upholstered lower saloon seat. Sold for bus shelter at Stocks Lane, Luddenden, June 1934.
101	1913	1937	Modernised in 1930 with "bay window" vestibules and 2-and 1 upholstered lower salon seats. Sold for bungalow at High Sunderland, Boothtown, 1937.
102	1913	1938	Rebuilt 1930 with "bay-windows" vestibules, lower saloon upholstered seats (2-and1?). Bus seats in lower saloon 1934. Mostly-red livery 1937. Scrapped April, 1938

"BEN HALL CARS"

Bodies built by Halifax Corporation to Mr. Hall's design, with vestibuled platforms reminiscent of Wigan trams. Trucks (except where otherwise stated) Halifax-style Peckham cantilever, 6'6" wheelbase, 30" diameter wheels.

Motors: Metrovick type 307 40h.p. (open top cars) and Metrovick type 307B 45h.p. (top-covered cars).

Controllers: English Electric DB1 Form K3, anti-runback.
Numerous small design differences are detectable. The three-window canopy tops fitted to some of the "Ben Hall" cars seem to be about a foot longer than those fitted to older cars; the red rear light occupied different positions at different periods of development – on nos. 9, 11, 71 and 76 it was always above the windscreen, whereas when no. 17 received its top cover, the rear light was removed to the vestibule corner window.

Car 17 Vestibuled open-top; seats 41 (upper deck) and 22 (lower saloon) – total 63, truck (as above), with roller bearings .
Dimensions: saloon 16'0"; overall length 28'0", overall width 6'6"; height to top of trolley mast 14'9".
In 1932/4 received a 3-window canopy top taken from another car; Metrovick regenerative braking and bus seats in the lower saloon fitted 1934, altering the seating to 39 (upper deck) and 19 (lower saloon) – total 58.
Entered service 1921; withdrawn 1938 (April?). Disposal: to summerhouse at Shay Lane, Ovenden, July 1938.

Car 64 Vestibuled open-top, cost £890-12-0d; details as no. 17. Received a second-hand top cover c.1930.
Entered service 1921; withdrawn 1935. Disposal: to hen-hut at Shay Lane, Ovenden, July 1935. Last seen 1960.

Car 9 Vestibuled open-top car.
Retained original unmodified Peckham truck. Repainted in mostly- red livery c 1931. Used as snowplough car from 1936.
Entered service 1922; withdrawn 1938. Disposal: sold to Norland Holiday Home, July, 1938.

Car 11 Open-top car with Halifax-style vestibule. Retained original unmodified Peckham truck.
Used as snowplough car from 1937.
Entered service 1922: withdrawn 1938. Disposal: sold to Norland Holiday Home, July 1938.

Car 71 Canopy top car with Bradford-style angular vestibules. Entered service 1922: withdrawn 1937. Disposal: sold 1937 to Norland Holiday Home,.

Car 73 Vestibuled canopy-top car.
Entered service 1922; withdrawn 1937. Disposal: sold 1937 to Norland Holiday Home.

Car 81 Vestibuled car; a four-window canopy top without quarter lights.
Entered service 1923, withdrawn 1937. Sold 1937 to Pye Nest allotments.

(Cars 103 –105) see separate entries.

Car 76 Canopy-top car with Halifax-style vestibules, lightweight top deck and domed roof as car 104, the frame of the roof having been rebuilt from the roof salvaged from car 50 after it had been blown over. One-piece lower deck side panels. Similar to no.17, but lower deck 6" higher and overall height 15'3".
Entered service 1925; withdrawn 1937.

Car 80 Vestibuled open-top car. 3-window canopy top from a scrapped car fitted in 1932, and new longitudinal red leather upholstered seats installed in lower saloon.
Entered service 1926/7; withdrawn 1934. Disposal: bus shelter in Turbary Lane, Greetland, June, 1934.

(Car 106 – see separate entry)

Car 75   Canopy-top car with vestibules; quarter-lights above the upper deck side windows.
Entered service 1927, withdrawn 1934. Disposal: bus shelter at Wheatley, June 1934.

These completed the ten lower deck bodies which Mr. Hall had been authorised to construct as replacements for scrapped bodies, but in addition Mr. Jack Naylor listed a new vestibuled lower deck rebuilt from the remains of open-top car 22 dismantled in 1925, and in 1927 a top-covered double-decked car with platform vestibules built from spare parts and given the vacant number 96.   Both were shortlived, and disposal details are unknown.   The phrase "bus seats" used by contemporary observers almost certainly refers to upholstered 2 and 1 seating with fixed corner seats.

Car 103

Type: Single-deck three-compartment enclosed car.

Body: Halifax Corporation. The central saloon seated 24 passengers on longitudinal seats while the two end compartments both seated 3 at the nearside front ends (total seats 30), with luggage space at the offside ends which had no doors. Folding jack-knife doors at the nearside front. Six side windows; clerestory roof; folding platform steps. Resemblance to Wigan single-deckers. Introduced new red and yellow livery, later Indian Red and ivory.

Truck: Halifax-style Peckham cantilever 8'6" wheelbase; 33" diameter wheels.

Motors: 2 x 45 h.p. Vickers type 307 VB

Controllers: English Electric type DB1 Form K3B anti-runback

Brakes: Mechanical — hand/wheel, hand/track, rheostatic.

Dimensions: Length 35' (E. Thornton) or 35'4" (J.C. Gilham)
Width 6'2" (E. Thornton) or 6'6" (J. C. Gilham)
Saloon Length 26'
Height 11'3"

Entered Service: June, 1924

Modification: Saloon seating later reduced to 22, but luggage spaces replaced by 3 seats each – new total 34.

Withdrawn: 1935

Disposal: Retired people's shelter on Beacon Hill, then (1940-1945) air raid wardens' look-out post during Second World War.

Car 104

Type: Halifax Corporation.
Double-deck. Four side-window lower saloon with platform vestibules; lightweight top deck with four drop-framed windows on each side (no half-lights), single-piece side panels; single skin domed roof; low balcony tins. Painted red and yellow as car 103.

Seats: Lower saloon 22 passengers on longitudinal seats; top deck 41, total 63.

Truck: Halifax-style Peckham cantilever 6'6" wheelbase; 33" diameter wheels.

Motors: 2 x 40 h.p. Metropolitan Vickers type 307 VB

Controllers: Originally Westinghouse 90 (presumably from a scrapped car) and probably DK type DB1 Form K3 anti-runback later.

Brakes: Mechanical — hand/wheel, hand/track, rheostatic.

Dimensions: Length 28'; Width 6'6"; Saloon Length 16' ; Height 15'3"

Entered Service: July, 1924

Withdrawn: 1937 (Last car to Bailiffe Bridge 1929).

Disposal: Bus shelter at Clough Lane, Mixenden.

Car 105

Type: Single-deck two-compartment enclosed car.

Body: Halifax Corporation. The two compartments were separated by a central bulkhead with double sliding doors; the driver's section was integral with the compartments, and the entrance/exits were fitted with folding jack-knife doors. Cantilevered dropped platforms for easy access.

Seating: 18 in each compartments, total 36.

Truck: As no. 103

Motors: As no. 103

Controllers: As no. 103

Brakes: As no 103

Dimensions: As no. 103

Entered Service: 1924 or early 1925

Regular use: Queensbury, Bailiffe Bridge, Brighouse and Hove Edge services; Triangle occasionally; Northowram to Shelf shuttle service 1932 –3.

Withdrawn: 1935

Disposal: July 1935 to holiday bungalow at Flamborough Head.

Car 106

Type: Single–deck two-compartment enclosed car.

Body: Halifax Corporation. The internal arrangements were as for no. 105, but as the wheels were of smaller diameter, the platforms were not dropped to the same extent, thus allowing a shallower step from the platform into the saloon. Folding platform doors interlocked with the raising and lowering of the platform step. The first Halifax-built tram with an electric bell-push. The roof was a plain, low arch without the clerestory ("monitor") roof as used on cars 103 and 105, and the consequential overall height reduction (to 10'0") did not allow the trolley to exert sufficient upward pressure, and after numerous trolley de-wirements, a small steel platform was mounted on the roof plank to raise the trolley-base to the same height as that of nos. 103/105.

Seating: 18 in each compartment; total 36.

Truck: Halifax-style Peckham cantilever 8'6" wheelbase; wheels 26" (or 27") diameter; roller bearings. Extremely silent in operation.

Motors: (ordered from EE 11/9/1925): 2 x 42 h.p. (also quoted as 40 or 45) DK85C box-frame lightweight motors, 1050 rpm., each mounted lengthwise and driving via a Bostock worm-drive/cardan shaft to an axle, gear ratio $5^{1}/_{4}$ to 1 (similar design to Hull Corporation tram 101 in service 1923). Gave reduced power consumption and higher speeds.

Controllers: English Electric DB1 Form K3B, anti-runback

Brakes: as nos. 103/105

Dimensions: Length 35'4"; Saloon Length 26'; Width 6'6"
                    Height 11'0" reduced to 10'11".

Weight: unladen $7^{1}/_{2}$ tons; fully laden 13 tons.

Entered Service: January, 1926

Withdrawn: 1934, but disused after collision with a brewery wagon at Northowram in November 1931.

Disposal: To bus shelter at Holmfield, June 1934

Inside Skircoat Depot c. 1927 - cars 34, 71 open top 10, a bay window vestibule car and single decker 103, with depot staff

[J.A. Pitts Collection courtesy West Yorkshire Archives , Bradford]

Cars 107-127

Type:	Double-deck "De Luxe", designed by Walter Young
Body:	Nos.107-113, 124-127 Halifax Corporation

Nos .114-123 English Electric Co., Preston.
The design incorporated some characteristics, e.g., the platform vestibules, of the Ben Hall cars. Four side- window teak-framed lower saloon; lightweight top deck with four plate-glass side windows and ventilator windows above; a single-skin domed roof. The balconies had wing windows on each side to provide the maximum permissible protection. Full-width sprung collision fenders. Top-deck livery details reminiscent of Mr Young's Dundee trams, but of course in the standard Halifax Indian Red and ivory colours.

Seating: In saloon, Siddall & Hilton red and black diamond– pattern cut moquette fully-sprung upholstery, seating 19 on 2-and-1 seats and four fixed corner seats which concealed the sand-hoppers; upper deck saloon 20 passengers on 2-and-1 Siddall & Hilton red leather upholstered seats, and 6 seats on each balcony – total 51. No standing passengers allowed on these cars. Two bulkhead-mounted clocks in lower saloon.

Truck: Halifax-style Peckham cantilever 7'6" wheelbase, 33" diameter wheels. Trucks for nos. 114-123 built by Brush to E.E. order; remainder presumably assembled by Halifax.

Motors: English Electric DK 30/1L 2 x 50 h.p., box frame

Controllers: English Electric DB1 Form K33C anti-runback (107-110). English Electric DB1 Form K33E anti-runback (111-127)

Resistance: E.M.B.

Brakes:
1) Hand/wheel, operated by conventional brake staff;
2) Hand/track operated by horizontal spoked wheel concentric with the hand-brake staff;
3) Air/wheel (Maley & Taunton) operated by a valve handle situated between the controller and the hand-brake staff:
4) Air-operated magnetic track brake (Maley & Taunton) actuated by a valve on top of the controller;
5) Air/wheel and air/track combined (Maley & Taunton) actuated by the above valve on top of the controller;
6) Rheostatic emergency brake actuated by a reverse movement of the controller handle;
7) Automatic runback prevention via controller;
8) Last resort: reverse the controller key and use as a rheostatic brake.

Dimensions: Saloon 16'0"; platforms 6'0" each. fenders 6" each; overall length 29'0" (also quoted as 29'4").

Width: 6'4" over side-pillars. Height 15'5".

Known Modifications: As delivered, the first seven E.E. cars were allocated the vacant fleet numbers 1, 6, 15, 20, 28, 33 and 95, but were soon renumbered 114 to 120, apparently consecutively.
Nos. 107-110 did not receive air-braking until late 1929.
No. 121 fitted with roller-bearing journals in 1931.
Nos. 114, 116, 118. 119, 121 and 126 received regenerative braking between Jan and Dec., 1935, thus providing them with a total of nine forms of braking, although the regenerative brakes were for deceleration on downward gradients, and needed additional air/wheel braking to halt them completely.

Disposals: Cars still remaining intact in February, 1939, were offered to Birmingham and Llandudno. Nos. 108, 121 to mill yard at West Vale; no. 114 to Illingworth, near Fire Station; no. 115 to Ripon; no. 119 as bus shelter at Rishworth (Commons) bus terminus; no. 125 to Highroad Well; no 126 to holiday bungalow at Flamborough (last seen May, 1980), nos. 107, 109/110, 112, 116, 117, 122, 123/124 and 127 burnt in depot yard between February and July, 1939; nos, 111 and 113 the last to be burnt, on August 16th, 1939.

Highroad Well terminus, July 14th, 1937, with "De Luxe" car 116 ready to use the Bracknell Willis patent trolley reverser erected a few years earlier.
[Photo: H.B. Priestley]

Fleet No	Entered Service	Withdrawn
107	May 1928	Feb. 14, 1939
108	Dec 1928	Sept. 1938
109	Early 1929	Feb. 14, 1939
110	Sept 1929	Feb. 14, 1939
111	Late 1929	Feb. 14, 1939
112	" "	Feb. 14, 1939
113	" "	Feb. 14, 1939
114 (ex 1?)	" "	Sept 1938
115 (ex 6?)	" "	Jan 1939
116 (ex 15?)	" "	Feb. 14, 1939
117 (ex 20?)	" "	Feb. 14, 1939
118 (ex 28?)	" "	Jan. 1938
119 (ex 33?)	" "	Sept. 1938
120 (ex 95?)	" "	Feb. 14, 1939
121	Feb 1931	Sept. 1938
122	March 1931	Feb. 14, 1939
123	March 1931	Feb. 14, 1939
124	Jan 1931	Feb. 14, 1939
125	" "	Sept. 1938
126	" "	Sept. 1938
127	" "	Feb. 14, 1939

(Payments made to E.E. Company: Nos.114-120 by
August 1929, 121- 123 by May 21, 1931.)

A Triangle-bound vestibuled open top car about to pass Jerry Lane at the boundary between Sowerby Bridge and Sowerby, abut 1929.

[Lilywhite Ltd]

Cars 128-131

Type:	Ex-Exeter Nos. 1 to 4. Ordered by Exeter Corporation in March, 1929, for use on a route extension from Pinhoe Road to Whipton which because of a change of policy was never built. Sold to Halifax in 1931 for £200 each, and used exclusively on the Triangle /Sowerby Bridge route.
Body:	Brush open-top with vestibuled platforms. The side window arrangement was unusual in that 3 half-width windows were interspersed with 2 full-width. Sheet metal rocker panels.
Seating:	Saloon – 25 on 2 and 1 transverse upholstered seats; Top Deck – 28 on 2 and 1 transverse wooden seats. Total seating: 53
Truck:	Brush/Peckham P35 flexible-axle, 7'6" wheelbase, 30" diameter wheels.
Motors:	General Electric Co. WT28S, 2 x 50 h.p.
Controllers:	English Electric DB1 Form K4
Brakes:	Hand/wheel; hand/track operated by handwheel concentric with handbrake staff; magnetic track brake.
Dimensions:	Length of body 17' 4", platforms 5'9" each, fenders 6" each; overall 29'10". Width 6'4".
Disposals:	All sold December, 1938. Three (numbers not known) later noted at Deanhead (farmyard), Queensbury (rear of Co-op) and Pasture Lane, Bradford

Fleet No	Entered Service	Withdrawn	Note	Entered Service in Exeter
128	Aug 1931	Nov. 29th, 1938		1929
129	Aug 1931	Nov. 29th, 1938	Last car to Sowerby Bridge	1929
130	Aug 1931	Nov. 29th, 1938		1930
131	Aug 1931	Nov. 29th, 1938		1931

Tramcar 131 at King Cross 1938
(Photo: W.A. Camwell.
courtesy National Tramway Museum, Crich)

(Or, colloquially "Th' Muck Trams")

Constructed between August 1900 and April 1901, by Mr John Hird joiner, of Boothtown.

Nos 1 and 2 classed as "setts wagons", were used to convey permanent-way materials to locations where track construction and renewals were taking place. Probably stationed at the Stannary Yard originally.

No 3 was a motorised flat-bed wagon with very short platforms, a trolley mast located towards one end of the car, with a wooden tower at the other end for overhead line maintenance and the repainting of bracket arms. Its earliest known truck was a Brush "A" type, which was replaced in later years by a Peckham cantilever truck salvaged from a scrapped tramcar. The type of motors fitted to the trucks is unknown, but possibilities are:- two 30 h.p. Type T52-3 units manufactured by the Societe l' Electrique et l' Hydraulique of Charleroi, Belgium, and sold to Halifax in 1900 by Witting, Eborall, agents, or even some GE800 17 h.p. motors bought at a later date.

The works fleet was later augmented by:-
i) one of the ex-Dundee railless cars (no. 104), which, with the aid of one trolley boom placed on the overhead wire and a cast-iron "skate" placed in the groove of the tram rail to complete the electrical circuit, was used from 1924 to about 1930 as a welding-unit during the Hebden Bridge relaying project.
ii) Demi-car 95 which served from about 1920 as a paying-in car for the convenience of conductors, being stationed in the town centre (e.g. George Square), then as a second welding unit.
iii) Demi-car 96 which was used from 1921 as an un-motorised sand and salt car for wintry conditions.

TOWER – WAGONS

In the early years, all the tower-wagons were horse drawn, but by 1906 the length of the routes was preventing the Department from complying with the Board of Trade requirements for the whole of the overhead installations to be tested every six weeks. Tenders for a petrol-driven wagon were therefore sought, and within the Borough 38 departmental telephone boxes were mounted on tram standards at strategic points for direct communication with the Tramways, Police and Fire Departments in case of emergency.

(Destination names shown in Capitals)	Opened	Closed
KING CROSS	O June 9th 1898 B June 29th 1898 P June 29th 1898	Nov 29th 1938
HIGHROAD WELL	T May 17th1898 O June 9th 1898 B June 29th 1898 P June 29th 1898	Aug 23rd 1938
OLD STATION (Horton Street)	B June 29th 1898 P July 26th 1898	Nov 29th 1938
SALTERHEBBLE (Heath Road)	T Jan 16th 1899 B/P Jan 20th 1899	May 18th 1935
SKIRCOAT GREEN (New Inn)	B Jan 20th 1899 T March 13th 1899 P March 14th 1899	Jan 31st 1932
BOOTHTOWN (Claremount Road) " (Punch Bowl Inn)	B/P March 29th,1899 B March 29th,1899 P Dec 22nd, 1900	Aug 5th 1934 Mar 31st 1934
King Cross via SAVILE PARK (Free School Lane via Pellon)	B/P June 6th, 1899 Feb 1st 1932	July 28th 1931 March 31st 1932
PELLON	T July 28th 1899 P Aug 5th 1899	April 5th 1938
MASON'S GREEN	T July 28th 1899 P Aug 5th 1899	Feb 14th 1939
ILLINGWORTH (Post Office)	T July 28th 1899 P Aug 5th 1899	Jan 18th 1938
Ratten Clough (from Illingworth)	T Aug 29th 1900 P Aug 30th 1900	Jan 18th 1938
Cote Hill (Burnley Road)	T Aug 29th 1900 P Aug 30th 1900	Nov 29th 1938
WEST END (Warley Road)	B Aug 29th 1900 P Jan 12th 1901	Feb 4th 1934
CAUSEWAY FOOT (from Ratten Clough)	P Sept 21st 1900	Jan 18th 1938
St James' Road (Stannary)	In use 1901 B Sept 1902	May 1936 (Official) Nov. 1938 (Probable) *(see asterisk)
TUEL LANE (from Cote Hill)	B Dec 17th 1900 P Dec 18th 1900	Nov 29th 1938

(Destination names shown in Capitals)	Opened	Closed
Stocks Gate (from Boothtown)	B Dec 17th 1900 P Dec 22nd 1900	March 31st 1934
Cavendish Inn (from Stocks Gate)	approx Jan 25th 1901	March 31st 1934
STUMP CROSS (Staups Lane)	P June 5th 1900 O June 27th 1900	Jan 9th 1934
STUMP CROSS (Shibden Park)	P June 5th 1900 O June 27th 1900	March 31st 1934
STUMP CROSS (Stump Cross Inn)	O Jan 27th 1901 P Jan 28th 1901	Jan 9th 1934
LUDDENDEN FOOT (from Tuel Lane)	B/P Apl 25th 1901	March 31st 1936
NORTHOWRAM (Stocks' Arms)	B/P Apl 25th 1901	Aug 16th 1932
QUEENSBURY (from Cavendish Inn)	B/P Apl 25th 1901	March 31st 1934
SHELF (from Northowram)	B/P July 1st 1901	March 31st 1933
Pismire Canal Bridge, Brearley (from Luddenden Foot)	B July 1st 1901 P July 2nd 1901	March 31st 1936
MYTHOLMROYD (New Road) (From Pismire Canal Bridge)	Sept 7th 1901	March 31st 1936
SOUTHOWRAM	O/P Sept 19th 1901	July 21st 1931
Fallingroyd Bridge (from New Road, Mytholmroyd)	P Dec 2nd 1901	March 31st 1936
HEBDEN BRIDGE (from Fallingroyd Bridge)	T March 13th 1902 B March 20th 1902 P March 21st 1902	March 31st 1936
SOWERBY BRIDGE (Wharf St)	T Sept 12th 1902 B Sept 13th 1902 P Oct 17th 1902	Nov 29th 1938
SOWERBY BRIDGE (Jerry Lane, from Wharf Street) Station Road, from Wharf St	P May 21st 1903 P May 21st 1903	July 25th 1934 Nov 29th 1938
TRIANGLE (from Jerry Lane)	B Feb 5th 1905 P Feb 10th 1905	July 25th 1934
HIPPERHOLME (from Stump Cross)	B Nov 7th 1902 P Nov 10th 1902	Sept 30th 1933
HOVE EDGE (from Hipperholme)	B June 29th 1903 P June 30th 1903	Sept 29th 1933

(Destination names shown in Capitals)	Opened	Closed
BRIGHOUSE (from Hove Edge)	T Feb 5th 1904 B Feb 24th 1904 P Feb 26th 1904	May 6th 1931
BAILIFFE BRIDGE (from Brighouse)	B Oct 13th 1904 P Oct 18th 1904	March 30th 1929
THRUM HALL Lane (from Gibbet Street)	B Dec 21st 1905	Aug 23rd 1938
SALTERHEBBLE (Jubilee Road)	B Aug 2nd 1905 P Aug 3rd 1905	May 18th 1935
WEST VALE (from Salterhebble)	B Aug 2nd 1905 P Aug 3rd 1905	Oct 30th 1934
Holywell Green (from West Vale)	T Mar 14th 1921 B Mar 16th 1921 P Mar 24th 1921	Oct 30th 1934
STAINLAND (from Holywell Green)	P May 14th 1921	Oct 30th 1934
SKIRCOAT GREEN (Dudwell Lane Top, from New Inn)	P June 12th 1925	Jan 31st 1932
Powell Street siding Harrison Street siding (first track) Harrison Street siding (second track)	Dec 15th 1926 March 1926 Dec 15th 1926	Nov 29th 1938 1927? 1927?

B – Board of Trade Inspection
O – Official Opening
P -   Public Service Commenced
T – Trial car

* St James' Road overhead wires brought down on 12/3/1936 when a lorry skidded on snow and demolished a pole. In May the manager recommended the abandonment of the line, and a £731 loan for its removal was sought and approved, but apparently not used until the closure of the Cow Green track in 1938.

Skircoat Road Depot in 1938 with (left to right) five cheerful traffic staff (drivers and conductors), 'De Luxe' cars 112 and 120 (labelled 'Hebden Bridge, 7' and 'Bradshaw 10' respectively) and open top car bearing the destination name 'Mytholmroyd' but revealing its true allegiance to its usual Sowerby Bridge run by its route number , 6.
[Courtesy Roy Brook]

ROUTE LENGTHS			Miles	Yards
Post Office to Pellon (Barracks)			1	1,188
Post Office to Skircoat Green (Dudwell Lane)			1	940
Post Office to Savile Park (via Free School Lane)			1	1,082
Post Office to Old Station				616
Post Office to Post Office (Circular via Gibbet Street, West End and King Cross Street)			3	432
Post Office to Nursery Lane	1ml	1,233yds		
Post Office to Raw Lane	2ml	1,068yds		
Post Office to Bradshaw	3ml	639yds		
Post Office to Ratten Clough	3ml	1,453yds		
Post Office to Causeway Foot			4	551
Post Office to Parkinson Lane		1,147yds		
Post Office to King Cross	1ml	253yds		
Post Office to Cote Hill	2ml	102yds		
Post Office to Tuel Lane	2ml	1,282yds		
Post Office to Luddenden Foot	4ml	560yds		
Post Office to Brearley	5ml	450yds		
Post Office to Mytholmroyd	6ml	494yds		
Post Office to Hebden Bridge*			7	1,132
Post Office to Sowerby Bridge (Wharf Street)	2ml	517yds		
Post Office to Jerry Lane	2ml	1,749yds		
Post Office to Triangle			3	1,375
Post Office to Highroad Well			1	902
Post Office to Salterhebble (Jubilee Rd)	1ml	1,100yds		
Post Office to West Vale	2ml	1,254yds		
Post Office to Stainland			4	132
Union Street to Stump Cross	1ml	930yds		
Union Street to Northowram	2ml	930yds		
Union Street to Shelf			3	879
Union Street to Boothtown	1ml	484yds		
Union Street to Stocks Gate	2ml	933yds		
Union Street to Queensbury			3	1,307
Union Street to Hipperholme	2ml	1,209yds		
Union Street to Hove Edge	3ml	1,165yds		
Union Street to Brighouse			5	294
Brighouse to Bailiffe Bridge			1	726
Thrum Hall Lane				187
*Hebden Bridge route —				
In County Borough of Halifax	2ml	1,282yds		
In West Riding Administrative Area	4ml	1,610yds		
	7ml	1,132yds		

KNOWN DESTINATION NAMES

HALIFAX	SAVILE PARK	SKIRCOAT GREEN
OLD STATION	OUTER CIRCLE (Via Savile Park)	SHELF
STAINLAND		NORTHOWRAM
WEST VALE	THRUM HALL	CAUSEWAY FOOT
SALTERHEBBLE	TRIANGLE	BRADSHAW (Also Bradshaw Lane Only)
BAILIFFE BRIDGE	SOWERBY BRIDGE	
BRIGHOUSE	SOUTHOWRAM	RAW LANE
HOVE EDGE	HEBDEN BRIDGE	MASONS GREEN
HIPPERHOLME	MYTHOLMROYD	(or MASON GREEN on some cars)
STUMP CROSS	LUDDENDEN FOOT	OVENDEN (CLUB LANE)
SHIBDEN PARK	TUEL LANE	OVENDEN (NURSERY LANE)
HIGHROAD WELL	KING CROSS	DEPOT
PELLON	QUEENSBURY	COW GREEN (used in early years only)
PELLON (Barracks)	BOOTHTOWN	POST OFFICE ((used in early years only)
WEST END		PRIVATE CAR (or PRIVATE on some cars)

FAREWELL

APPENDIX 3

SOME LOCAL PURCHASES

One of the incidental benefits of municipally-owned transport was that supplies were usually bought from local sources whenever it was practical to do so. A few examples given below.

Drivers' Overcoats	A.E. Rawbon, Crown St and George Sq
Conductors' Overcoats	H.H. Stocks, Woolshops
Uniform Trousers	Sam Stocks, 34, Crown St.
Coach Paint	Lancs & Yorks. Varnish & Colour Co., 9, Broad St (Indian Red or Vegetable Black) W. Aske, Ovenden (Also gold leaf) T.H.Williams & Co, Ripon. Robert Kearsley & Co., Ripon
Metal Polish for Brasswork	J.R.Granger, Halifax
Lubricants, Undercoat Paint	Arthur Lumb, Halifax
Transfer gold, Size, Lacquer	G. Wadsworth, Portland St
Steel Wheels and pinions	R.E. Hattersley, Keighley
Steel axles	Elkanah Hoyle & Sons, Halifax
Iron Brake Blocks	W Horsfall and E Hargreaves, Halifax
Iron Slipper Brake Shoes	J Charnock, Halifax, C.H. Spencer, Gargrave.
Wire netting for 1898 type lifeguards, Tramcar Bells and footgongs	Gabriel and Co.
Ticket Clippers	Nicholson and Co.
Waybills (for recording tickets issued)	Pearson Bros, Halifax
Trolley Heads (the phosphor-bronze fitting attached to the end of the trolley-boom which housed the trolley wheel)	Gawkrodger, Sykes and Roberts, Halifax and Helliwell, Whitaker and Co., Halifax
Trolley Cords (the ropes with which the conductor manhandled the trolleys)	Charles Shaw, Halifax
Bamboo Trolley Sticks (which replaced the cords from 1908)	W Nutting, Halifax
Cast-iron pole bases and finials	E Hargreaves and Co., Water Lane.

The most unusual tramways Dept payment (Aug 1900) – "Paid £2-7-8d to Parks Committee for taking down and replacing Ivy at Allangate."

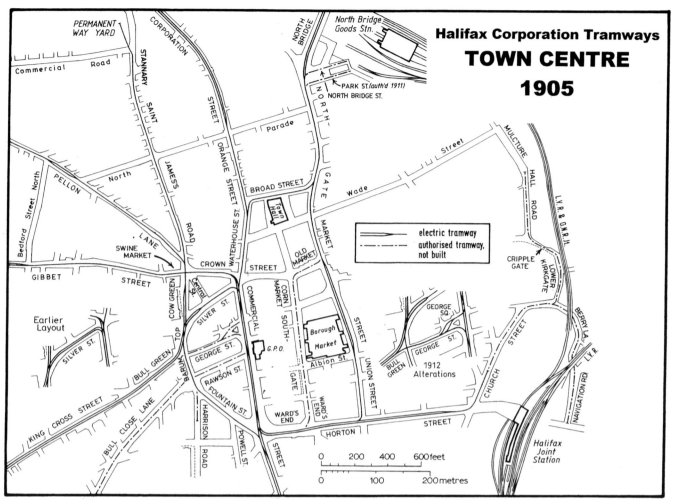

Halifax Corporation Tramways
TOWN CENTRE
1905

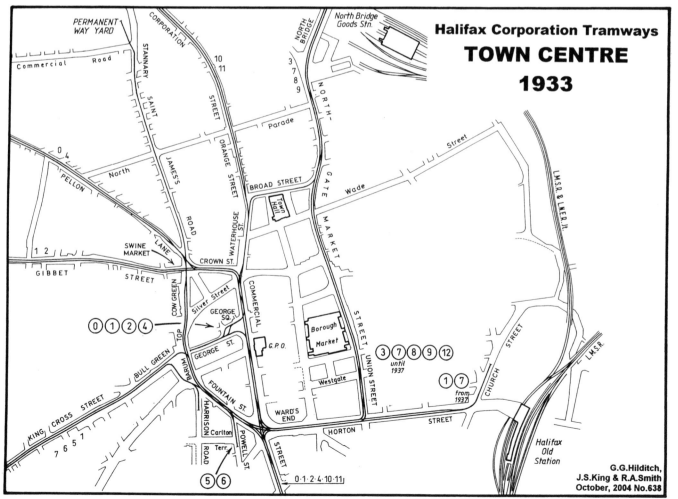

Halifax Corporation Tramways
TOWN CENTRE
1933

G.G.Hilditch,
J.S.King & R.A.Smith
October, 2004 No.638

Halifax Corporation Tramways SKIRCOAT ROAD DEPOT

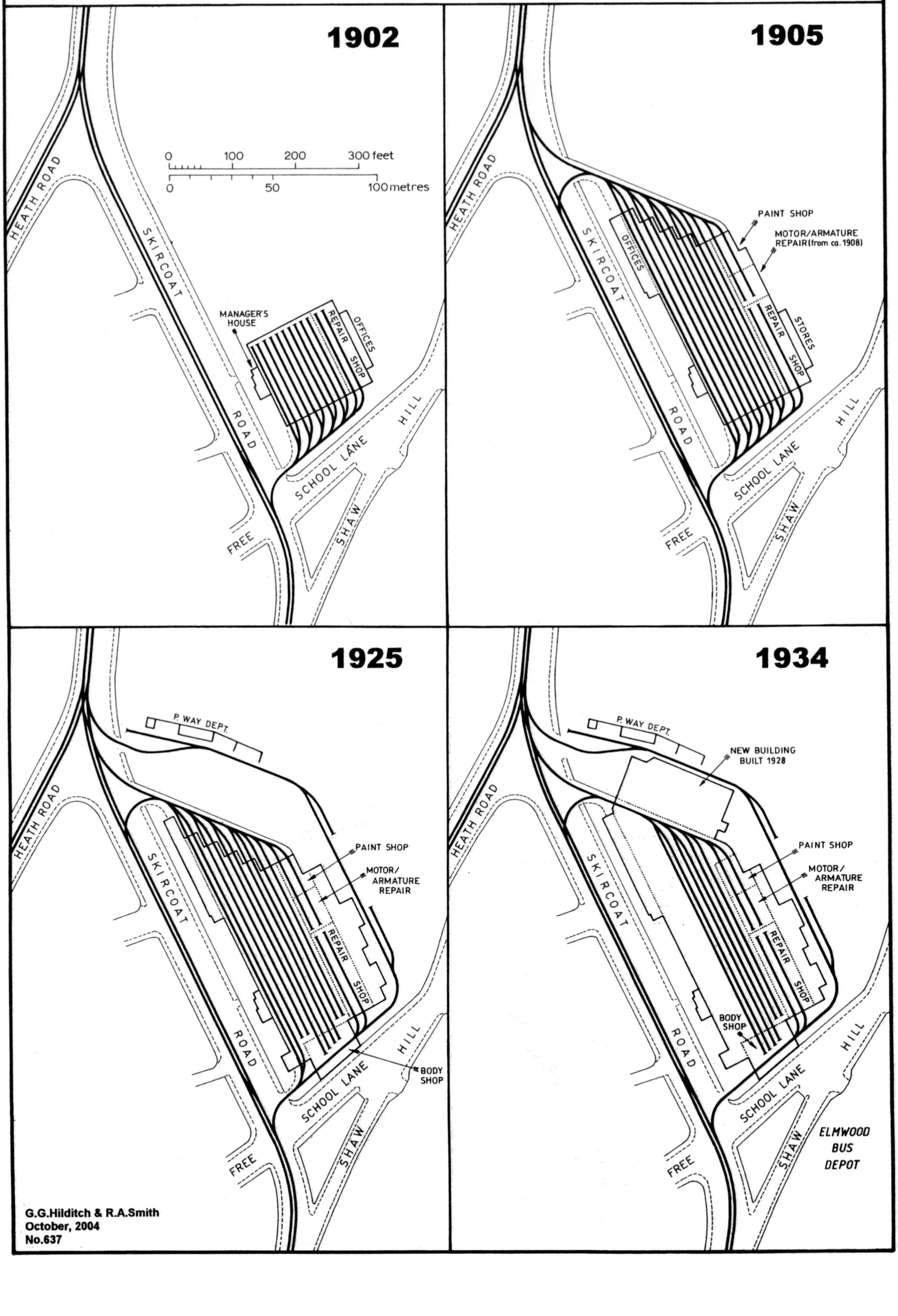

1902

HEATH ROAD

SKIRCOAT ROAD

0   100   200   300 feet
0   50   100 metres

MANAGER'S HOUSE

REPAIR SHOP

OFFICES

SCHOOL LANE

HILL

SHAW

FREE

1905

HEATH ROAD

SKIRCOAT ROAD

OFFICES

PAINT SHOP

MOTOR/ARMATURE REPAIR (from ca. 1908)

REPAIR SHOP

STORES

SCHOOL LANE

HILL

SHAW

FREE

1925

HEATH ROAD

P. WAY DEPT.

SKIRCOAT ROAD

PAINT SHOP

MOTOR/ARMATURE REPAIR

REPAIR SHOP

BODY SHOP

SCHOOL LANE

HILL

SHAW

FREE

G.G.Hilditch & R.A.Smith
October, 2004
No.637

1934

HEATH ROAD

P. WAY DEPT.

NEW BUILDING BUILT 1928

SKIRCOAT ROAD

PAINT SHOP

MOTOR/ARMATURE REPAIR

REPAIR SHOP

BODY SHOP

SCHOOL LANE

HILL

SHAW

FREE

ELMWOOD BUS DEPOT

HALIFAX CORPORATION TRAMWAYS *Opening Dates -1*

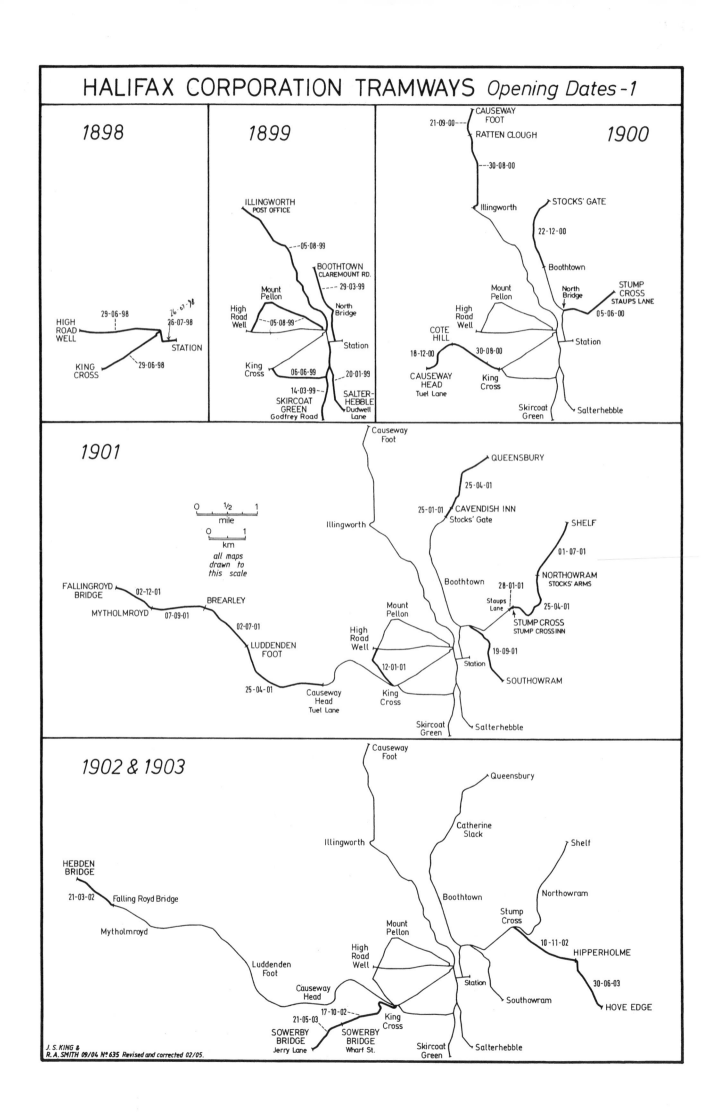

1898

HIGH ROAD WELL — 29-06-98
STATION — 26-07-98
KING CROSS — 29-06-98

1899

ILLINGWORTH POST OFFICE
05-08-99
BOOTHTOWN CLAREMOUNT RD.
29-03-99
Mount Pellon
High Road Well — 05-08-99
North Bridge
Station
King Cross — 06-06-99
SALTER-HEBBLE Dudwell Lane — 20-01-99
SKIRCOAT GREEN Godfrey Road — 14-03-99

1900

CAUSEWAY FOOT — 21-09-00
RATTEN CLOUGH
30-08-00
Illingworth
STOCKS' GATE — 22-12-00
Boothtown
Mount Pellon
North Bridge
STUMP CROSS STAUPS LANE — 05-06-00
High Road Well
COTE HILL — 18-12-00
Station
CAUSEWAY HEAD Tuel Lane
King Cross — 30-08-00
Skircoat Green
Salterhebble

1901

O   ½   1
mile
O   1
km
all maps drawn to this scale

FALLINGROYD BRIDGE — 02-12-01
MYTHOLMROYD — 07-09-01
BREARLEY
02-07-01
LUDDENDEN FOOT
25-04-01
Causeway Head Tuel Lane
Causeway Foot
QUEENSBURY — 25-04-01
CAVENDISH INN Stocks' Gate — 25-01-01
Illingworth
SHELF
01-07-01
NORTHOWRAM STOCKS' ARMS
Boothtown
28-01-01
Staups Lane
STUMP CROSS STUMP CROSS INN — 25-04-01
Mount Pellon
High Road Well
12-01-01
Station
19-09-01
SOUTHOWRAM
King Cross
Skircoat Green
Salterhebble

1902 & 1903

HEBDEN BRIDGE
21-03-02
Falling Royd Bridge
Mytholmroyd
Luddenden Foot
Causeway Head
21-05-03
SOWERBY BRIDGE Jerry Lane
17-10-02
SOWERBY BRIDGE Wharf St.
King Cross
Skircoat Green
Salterhebble
Causeway Foot
Queensbury
Catherine Slack
Illingworth
Shelf
Boothtown
Northowram
Stump Cross
10-11-02
HIPPERHOLME
30-06-03
HOVE EDGE
Mount Pellon
High Road Well
Station
Southowram

J. S. KING & R. A. SMITH 09/04 N° 635 Revised and corrected 02/05.